with love

THE
SECRET TOUR CADDY

THE
SECRET
TOUR
CADDY

**A Year in the Life
of a Professional Caddy
on the European and
PGA Golf Tours**

First published by Pitch Publishing, 2024

Pitch Publishing
9 Donnington Park,
85 Birdham Road,
Chichester,
West Sussex,
PO20 7AJ
www.pitchpublishing.co.uk
info@pitchpublishing.co.uk

A CIP catalogue record is available for this book
from the British Library.

ISBN 978 1 80150 674 8

Typesetting and origination by Pitch Publishing
Printed and bound in Great Britain by TJ Books Limited, Padstow

Contents

Acknowledgements

During my career as a tour caddy there have been a few occasions when I've been lucky enough to have been sat to one side, tucked away out of sight, listening in case the winner of that week's tournament remembers to say something nice about me. And on those occasions when they did, some of the time I've been pretty sure they meant it; other times, less so.

But for the people who are about to get a mention here, rest assured that I do mean it. I really do. Starting with my favourite literary agent for all that initial wisdom, advice and encouragement, not to mention the introduction to Pitch Publishing. To Pitch Publishing themselves whose immediate belief in this project, and support throughout the year it's taken to write this book, is the only reason it's now in your hands. And finally to my amazing editor, Andrea, who then ensured that what's now in your hands hangs together in a fashion that belies it's been written by someone who usually only writes numbers in yardage books.

But fairly obviously the most thanks, and my heartfelt gratitude, goes to my tour caddy colleagues who have inadvertently provided a lot of the anecdotes, stories, experiences, material and even some of the opinions you're about to read. Without them this book would have been way harder (if not impossible) to have written, and immeasurably less interesting to read. And while I am The Secret Tour Caddy, in reality we could all be The Secret Tour Caddy.

TSTC
December 2023

Introduction

I am The Secret Tour Caddy

'And how do you identify yourself?' is a question I'm thankfully never likely to be asked. But if I was, I'd undoubtedly reply, 'As a professional tour caddy.'

Because I am one. It's what I do. And what I've always done. It defines who I am, and the life I lead. Being able to call myself one makes me incredibly proud. Even after all these years.

And yet it's not something I, or any other tour caddy, ever tend to advertise.

Well, not until now. Or rather not until, in the dark recesses of a bar somewhere towards the end of my 20-something season on tour, someone suggested that I write the story of my 20-something-plus-one season down, and 'throw in some stuff about what you guys actually do because golf fans will lap that up'. I laughed. Basically because the only writing I ever do is numbers in a yardage book.

But it was late. And because when it's late, you sometimes say yes to stuff you wouldn't usually say yes to, I said yes. And then promptly forgot all about it. Until he reminded me as I emerged from the scorer's tent the following Friday afternoon – he was waiting to interview the guy in our group who'd just shot 65 by the way, not me.

And so here I am: the Secret Tour Caddy. But before you hear the story of my 2023 season on the DP World Tour (which was indeed my 20-something-plus-one one), here's a few things that will hopefully make the next however many pages make a bit more sense.

First off, I am a professional tour caddy. I have been virtually ever since I left school. I currently work for a guy who plays on the DP World Tour. He's bloody good at golf. I make my living on the back of this talent. I travel the world carrying his golf bag and offering (what I think is) sage advice when he needs it. We celebrate together when things go well; I get it in the neck when they don't. I am self-employed. If my player has a good year, I can earn a lot of money. If my player has a bad year, I do not. I pay tax. If my player has a good year, I pay a lot of it. If my player has a bad year, I still pay tax, just not as much. If my player has a week off, I have a week off. And don't get paid. Because I do not work for anyone else but him. He plays around 30 tournaments a year. Which means I am away from home living out of a suitcase for 30 weeks of the year. I have precious few of the workplace rights you have in your workplace. Like I could be fired tomorrow without being told why.

But I wouldn't swap my job for yours. Which is equally true of the other 150 or so full-time professional tour caddies I work alongside each week. Together we are a unique, exclusive, close-knit band of brothers, and sisters. And even after all these years, I'm genuinely still in awe of most of them, even the ones I don't really get on with. Because every single one of us is bloody good at what we do. In fact, we are the best golf caddies in Europe as of now. If we weren't, we wouldn't be working on tour. And yes, that includes the guys who don't necessarily work for the household names and stars of European and world golf. And if we're honest, the story of my 2023 could equally be their story too: one that took us to three of the four corners of the earth. And back again.

But if you've picked this up expecting to hear tales of excess and scandal from them, then you're going to be disappointed: that's not what this book is about. If, however, you've picked this up because you're interested in what life inside the ropes on the DP World Tour is actually like for a regular tour caddy, while learning all about what it is we all actually do, then you're in the right place. And right now, that right place is actually at home in my living room watching the final round of the final tournament of the 2022 DP World Tour season. One that by the looks of things Jon Rahm is about to win.

Here We Go Again …

And that's exactly what happens. Because at around 12.15pm UK time on Sunday, 20 November, Jon Rahm rolls in the final putt on the final green of the final tournament of the 2022 DP World Tour season – which means only one thing.

No, not that he just won €2,891,271. Nor is it that every single tour caddy who is there this week is breathing a sigh of relief that they don't have to walk around that course until the same time next year because no matter what you might hear on Sky Sports or think looking at it on TV, it is, to use the tour caddy vernacular, a '**** of a walk'. Nor is it that everyone there can pile on the last bus back to Al Barsha, dig out some clean clobber and head down for an end-of-season party at Barasti. And it's not even my own feeling of utter indifference about Rahm winning the tournament or Rory winning the Race to Dubai because, if truth be told, unless it's a mate on the bag, most tour caddies don't really care who actually wins. Anything.

No. It's none of these things. Instead, what it actually means is that my 22nd season of caddying on the European Tour (I still struggle to call it the DP World Tour) is officially over, and all that's between me and the start of my 23rd is a last afternoon at home and the overnight flight down to Johannesburg.

Although, if we're being picky, my 22nd season actually finished a few weeks ago when my current player had made enough to keep his card, but not enough to make the end-of-season Final Series that culminated in the Race to Dubai Final Rahm just won – which actually is just as well as, if he had, then all that would have been between me and the start of my 23rd might have been a taxi ride up Sheikh Zayed Road to DXB and Emirates EK761 down to Johannesburg. Either way, it shows you that for tour caddies there is sometimes literally no off-season: no sooner has one season finished, than the next begins.

So, anyway, here I am at the start of my 2023 season before 2022 has even ended. And that start comprises three weeks down in South Africa before Christmas culminating with the Alfred Dunhill Championship at everyone's favourite stop of the year, Leopard Creek. I'll then fly home for Christmas itself, reacquainting myself with the wife and kids in the process, before disacquainting myself with them again in mid-January via Abu Dhabi and the latest reinvention of the old Seve Trophy should my man get a pick.

More likely, though, is that my 2023 will actually properly start in the third week in January with the two tournaments in the Middle East that remain from the old Desert Swing – Abu Dhabi and Dubai (which thankfully now have prize funds that their prestige in world golf have long merited) – before heading up to the tournament in Ras Al Khaimah.

Now at this point in the season, if you're caddying for someone who's in the top 50 in the world or who is exempt over there anyway, it's Foxtrot Oscar to the PGA Tour to play for more money against better fields on better golf courses (which counts as 'supporting the Tour' obviously), while everyone else (including me most likely) slinks off for a lap of Singapore, Thailand and India. Although no one in their right mind – or right size of earnings – will want to go to India to play the golf course that Gary Player, to quote one of my more frank colleagues, 'butchered'.

My man has already said he's not playing the events in South Africa that month, so March looks like an entire month of house husbandry for me while watching the favoured few play for millions on the PGA Tour, and the LIV Golf guys playing for even more, while April offers up the prospect of playing the new Jet Lag Swing round Japan and Korea, although not until later in the month.

After that, Europe beckons in May, starting with a pre-Ryder Cup visit to Marco Simone, followed by the tour de Belgium, Holland, Germany, Sweden and Germany (again). HimmeLland is then the nice filling between the stale bread of The Belfry and Renaissance, before The Open Championship at Hoylake.

A second spell of house husbandry, or maybe even a family holiday, beckons after The Open as for once there's a decent break in the schedule late July into August, before the second half of the European season starts in Northern Ireland in mid-August. From there it's on to Prague, Crans Montana (which I absolutely detest), before heading back westwards for the Irish Open, Wentworth and Paris National (which I absolutely love).

Sadly the smart money is on us then mourning another mauling when we reconvene the week after the Ryder Cup, in St Andrews for the Dunhill Links, before heading back to sunshine in Spain to close out the regular season.[1]

By which point, hopefully my player will have kept his card for another year (the minimum we're after), qualified for the Nedbank in Sun City and the Race to Dubai Final (the expectation), added to his total of wins on tour (the hope), and given me plenty to write about along the way. Which is kind of what this book is all about.

---

1 In the end Qatar was added to the 2023 schedule and that became the last event of the regular season.

So follow us as we travel to three of the four corners of the earth. Get a unique insight into what it's really like being a tour caddy. Discover what we actually do, what it's like to walk alongside some of the best players on the planet, what we talk about, what it's like to be in contention down the stretch on Sunday and what happens when things go wrong – like getting the sack, or your player looking like he will lose his card, what we think of LIV Golf, what professional golf's most tumultuous season ever was really like from inside the ropes, why tour caddies have zero job security but wouldn't swap their job for yours for all the tea in China. And why you should absolutely not even think about swapping yours for ours.

Welcome to the world of The Secret Tour Caddy.

Chapter 1

Africa Awaits

The Story of the Week of the Joburg Open 24–27 November 2022

This season the players had a choice as to where to play the first week back out: Joburg or Queensland. If it had been up to me, I'd have forgone the lure of £15 for a glass of wine and steak the size of a doormat in The Butcher's Shop restaurant in Joburg and instead opted for the 22-hour wallet-draining trip down to Australia, mainly on the basis that the two courses down there are just way better. Especially Kingston Heath, which is in my top three favourite courses in the world.

But my preferences count for jack shit, and even if they had, he chose Joburg anyway. Basically because we get to play three weeks in a row without any real travelling in between, and the third week is at Leopard Creek which is everyone's favourite stop on tour. That, and, I now find out, because he's bringing the family and current girlfriend down for that week as none of them have been there, and he's keen to show them what he keeps harping on about when he comes back from there every year.

So as usual at this time of year I'm back at Heathrow for the overnight flight down to Joburg to begin my love–hate relationship with South Africa for the 25th-odd time. I love it because it's a stunningly beautiful country, it's the cheapest place in the world to get Falke socks which are THE best for caddying in, and the steak is out of this world.

And I hate it because, like it or not, you do need to be a wee bit careful down here. And after a few days, that can become slightly grating to say the least. For example, this week you definitely don't want to be staying anywhere more than a few hundred yards from Nelson Mandela Square in Sandton, which is where the players are staying and the transport to the golf course, complete with police escort, goes from. And even then it's best to be in a hotel that has a minibus service to and from it. One thing you don't do is take a leisurely walk back to the hotel after dinner: that is out of the question. Even though it's probably only a long par four away. And again, like it or not, there's crime because (at least) one generation was deprived of education and other basic human decencies, so poverty is rife. Witness the townships that we pass in our convoy up to the golf course each day.

Anyway, BA55 gets us into Joburg on time at 7am and we leg it off the plane to ensure we get past the Hong Kong flight that lands about the same time, as we know from experience that if we don't, then the queue at immigration could take hours. Which we do, so by 9ish we're through and already at the Houghton having a second breakfast. And as I've not been here before, this gives me a chance to walk the course before he gets there later on today, ready for a practice round tomorrow and the pro-am on Wednesday. Which I duly do, and discover it's decent, it's got tight grasses and fast slopey greens, making it pretty much like every other of the courses we play on in this neck of the woods. Scoring will therefore be low low low.

There are plenty of other guys doing the same as me, and as we can't check into the hotel until after 3pm, we take our time doing it. And we're joined along the way by guys we know who caddy predominantly on the Sunshine Tour. This is a big, important week for them if their normal player is in the field (it's a co-sanctioned event with the DP World Tour) or if he's not, then it's important to get the bag of a DP World Tour player who's come down without their usual caddy. We, of course, tip off the guys we know as to who might be looking for a caddy so they can get work.

It's the least we can do. That and making sure we give them all the old balls this week, which is more than matched by the generosity of a lot of the players who bring down their old shirts and hats to give to these guys too. And never publicise it. It doesn't even matter that these guys are half the size of the guys giving them clothes. One local caddy famously asked his player if he could have some clothes at the end of the week, and his response to the question, 'What size are you?' or 'Your size, Sir,' is still trotted out every time we come down here.

It's super-hot by mid-morning Monday, especially for those of us who've come from the start of the English winter, which means that a thunderstorm isn't too far away. And looking at the forecast, that's going to be the pattern for the rest of the week too. And sure enough, a really meaty one heaves into view just as we've finished walking the course and also happens on the tournament days. Only, in that case, we were all still on the course, and had to leg it with bolts of lightning lighting up the sky just to the north, with play being abandoned for the day shortly afterwards leading to the first – but I'm guessing certainly not the last – rain delay of the season.

Rain delays can be a right pain if you're on the wrong side of the draw. Thankfully we weren't. And equally as thankfully, he makes the cut easy enough despite being a bit rusty, having not played a tournament since Mallorca at the back end of last season.

Someone who also hadn't played much was Dan Bradbury, basically because he hadn't even got a card. Not that that seemed to be much of an issue as rounds of 67, 66, 67, 67 saw him hold off Valimaki and a host of South Africans for a three-shot win. A win that also sees him into The Open at Hoylake in July and an exemption to the end of 2024. And a good few quid.

Valimaki's consolation for finishing second was that it gets him straight into The Open as well. His local South African caddy didn't need any consolation whatsoever. Because not only had he picked up the bag solely after we'd tipped him off it was going, but the healthy bonus he picked up from Valimaki paid for his wedding a few weeks later. On the back of him not being on the ill-fated Ethiopian Airlines Flight ET302[2] in March 2019 when he was supposed to be makes him still the most appropriately named human on earth: Lucky.

The silver lining of the threat of thunder never being too far away was that Sunday's U-draw meant everyone was finished by early afternoon, and so we made it across to Lanseria a good few hours earlier than we might have otherwise done. This left more time to eat more steak, as if we'd not eaten enough already in what is only week one of the trip down here.

Incidentally, a U-draw is where, usually due to the weather forecast being so poor that it threatens an on-time finish, the field is effectively split in half, with the top half of the field teeing off the 1st tee so the leaders go off last as they would normally, while the bottom half of the field tee off the 10th tee with the guys with the worst scores going off last. That way (for example) four hours of tee times magically become two hours, which gives wiggle room should any bad weather come early.

And with week two being the South African Open, one of the oldest golf championships in the world, on a course I've

---

2 ET302 crashed six minutes after take-off, killing all 157 people on board. Had Lucky been on the phone, it would have been 158.

never seen before, once steak time was over I was off to bed, earlier than some, because Monday of week two is now a work day with an early start. Or if you want to look at it another way: my eighth day in a row without a day off.

And that's not about to change anytime soon.

The Story of the Week of the Investec South African Open Championship 1–4 December 2022

At the end of the round on Sunday our routine is always the same. He exits the scoring tent (where the players sign their cards), I hand him his watch, wallet, phone and any clothes he might have had in the bag (e.g. the jumper that he wore because it was cold when we teed off); he heads for the Players' Lounge to feed and shower; I head to the locker room, empty his locker, pack the tour bag away in his travel bag, leave it somewhere where he can find it and then head for my own food and shower. After which it's time to either jump in a car with him or whatever transport is laid on to get us from the golf course to the airport.

The only thing that varies is the speed at which we do this. Some weeks you have literally minutes to get everything done before the car/bus that will get you to the airport just in time for the flight to wherever we're going next; whereas other weeks there's plenty of time so everything can be done at leisure. Last week at Houghton we were very firmly in this latter category given that there was a U-draw on Sunday.

So when we finished at Houghton there was definitely no rush to do anything; in fact, had we been in any way so inclined we could have done everything we needed to do and still had time to watch the conclusion of the tournament. Now I have no idea what he did, but not having a caddy mate 'up there' I jumped in the hire car with a couple of similarly minded colleagues and headed across to the other side of Joburg while it was (a) still dry; and (b) still daylight.

But every silver lining has its cloud. And this week's was that instead of Monday being effectively a day off where we could have travelled in the morning, found the hotel and then found somewhere to do some laundry, it ended up being a work day. Mainly because I suspect he had fuck all else to do. That and his roommate MCd (missed the cut) last week and wanted to play a couple of practice rounds this week: something which he'd already told me on Sunday afternoon.

So that meant my (increasingly tired) arse had to be dragged out of bed at another godforsaken hour, and plonked in an Uber down to the golf club (the other guys were going up to the course much later on so bagged the hire car) to try and get the course walked before his lazy arse was dragged out of its bed at a rather more sensible hour and plonked in a nice BMW courtesy car to meet me.

But on the bright side, at least it's always light and reasonably warm even at silly o'clock in a South African summer so getting up so early actually isn't too much of a chore. And, anyway, having a leisurely walk round is pretty much zero stress, plus the fact that I don't have to haul the clubs round, or listen to him bleating on about stuff from the previous week that he hasn't let go of yet while doing it. And that is, when you think about it, the silver lining to the cloud of the previous silver lining.

And added to that is also the prospect, assuming he sticks to Sunday's plan of a wee bit of Monday practice followed by nine holes, I could yet be back at the hotel in time for an afternoon snooze or, better still, an afternoon sleep, which, amazingly, I am, proving my theory that he was only up there because he couldn't think of anything better to do. And in that respect he's no different from 80 per cent of tour pros I've worked for.

But back to walking the course. We ventured out around 7am having first had to find where the yardage book guy was hiding. And the walk round was pretty useful given that I've never been here before, and there are certainly a few holes where, because Joburg sits at 1,753m, or nearly 6,000ft, above sea level, the ball travels a lot further than it ordinarily does, so you do really have to factor this in when looking where, for example, you want tee shots to finish. It was a pretty long walk too, as at 8,300 yards the course is a monster, and that's without the bloody hills. There's a fair amount of water lurking too and lightning-fast greens, especially if you get above the hole on some of the holes coming in. Now granted it does play a lot shorter with the altitude and the heat, but by 11am Monday when we troop off the 18th, I can already confidently predict that it won't be a short hitter who wins round here this week.

Nor is it likely to be the week for anyone who doesn't like a good rain delay, and all the disruption that can cause. Because, as is always the case in Joburg, the threat of a thunderstorm is never far away, especially, as it turns out, this week with a particularly heavy one washing out most of one of the practice days (no complaints from any tour caddy on that one obviously), and several more across the tournament days, meaning it's pretty tight getting finished even with a U-draw and a two-tee start in three-balls on both Saturday and Sunday.

But even with the length of the course and it playing even longer due to the wet fairways, eight under leads after the first round, with the cut (which came on Saturday morning due to the adverse weather) falling at three under – which frankly shows how good these guys are. And remember that, despite being the oldest national golf championship in the world, the field isn't exactly the best the event has ever seen, which, not for the last time this season, shows how good anyone who calls themselves a tour pro actually is.

Not that that bothers Thriston Lawrence one little bit. It's his eight under that leads at the end of the first round. He's still leading at the end of Round 2. And at the end of Round 3. And despite surviving a five over on the last seven mini-meltdown on Sunday afternoon, his name is still on top of the leaderboard after 72 holes for his third win in a year.

My man has another half-decent week given that we both know his game isn't quite where it needs to be to contend and, frankly, both our eyes have been on next week since making the cut. And that's because we know tomorrow morning we'll be jumping straight in the hire car and heading up to everyone's favourite destination: Leopard Creek Country Club.

Where no one minds working on a Monday.

The Story of the Week of the Alfred Dunhill Championship 8–11 December 2022

There's nowhere on this earth where you can theoretically see all of the Big Five[3] on your way to work. Except when work is at Leopard Creek. And there's also nowhere on this earth where you can definitely bribe a policeman on your way to work, and still get there. Except when work is at Leopard Creek. Or to give it its proper name, Leopard Creek Country Club: a piece of golfing heaven on the edge of the piece of safari and wildlife heaven that is the Kruger National Park.

And while we're actually here for the Alfred Dunhill Championship, a lot of guys come here as much for the opportunity to go on safari in the park every day as for the opportunity to play in the tournament itself. Indeed, there's a healthy majority who see way more of the Kruger Park than they do of the practice facilities, even though they are out of this world, and sat alongside is a par-three course where every hole is a replica of a great par three from somewhere in the world. This is in itself a joy to play, never mind the main course. They even used to televise the two par-three tournaments that everyone playing in the tournament plays

---

3 The Big Five being lions, leopards, rhinos, elephants and buffalo.

in on either the Tuesday or the Wednesday before things get properly underway on the Thursday morning.

Before any of that, though, we jump in a hire car early Monday morning for the five-hour drive up to Malelane from Joburg, or more precisely from the Emperors Palace casino just round from the airport where virtually every tour caddy who ever comes down here stays on a Sunday night: a ridiculously opulent place for a ridiculously small price. Albeit before you factor in the rest of the night eating steak, going to Hooters and gambling in the casino.

Amazingly we manage to get to Malelane without getting stopped by the police, which in all the years I've been coming down here is something of a rarity. Not that we've ever been doing anything wrong when we've been stopped by the police in previous years, apart from being a foreigner driving a hire car below the speed limit the week before Christmas which, although not strictly a crime in itself, is an opportunity for the local cops to stop you, fine you for some made-up traffic offence and then pocket the money. They know they're doing it and so do we.

One colleague even said, 'Look, Officer, will 500 rand make this problem go away?' when he got stopped this year – admittedly for the second time in 15km and frustrations were running high. Only in South Africa could the answer be 'Yes.' So money changed hands, he got a big smile off the crooked cop and within two minutes was on his way again, safe in the knowledge that he'd have got the same 'Yes' in Europe only because it would have been replaced by a rather more serious one of trying to bribe a policeman.

Every time we come this way we know to hide any cash, apart from say 1,000 rand (about €50) somewhere the police won't find it (underpants were always my favourite), and ask to pay at the police station at Malelane because 'we've just come from the airport and have no cash on us'. To this day none of us have ever been there, and somewhere there's a landfill with about 2,000 tour caddy traffic offence tickets in it, around 15 of them mine. After all, this is Africa.

In fact the only place we really go in Malelane is the Duck and Dive pub off the main crossroads; well, there and the B&B we're booked into overlooking the Crocodile River. The former allows us to (oddly enough) eat steak for not very much money, proper game steaks like kudu or wildebeest for not very much more, and play darts against the locals every night; while the latter allows us to watch elephants wandering up and down the river each evening literally a soft wedge away from the observation deck.

You also get to see these magnificent beasts from the 13th green on the golf course itself, located high above the same Crocodile River, affording you views right across the Kruger Park itself. And it's here that everyone takes a million photos every year, and uses the laser to see if they can spot anything else of note lurking in the shade of the trees once the sun gets up.

And get up it does, because this can be the hottest place we caddy on tour all year. In fact it's not unheard of for the temperature to nudge well into the 40s in the afternoon. And with often very little wind, just carrying the bag is physically very demanding even with soaking-wet cold towels round your neck to try and keep cool, and guzzling litre after litre of water on the way round. Without needing to pee.

Not that it's particularly wise to pop into the bush off the fairways for a pee anyway: after all, we are on the edge of a game reserve the size of Wales, and you never know what's out there. But at least the two giraffes who wandered out of the bush, walked up to the ropes, took a good look left and right, before deciding golf wasn't their thing and wandering back again the other year probably won't eat you. You might not be so lucky with some of their fellow bush dwellers.

What you are getting, though, at Leopard Creek is lots of birdie opportunities, especially on the back nine. Case in point being South African Merrick Bremner, who had seven threes on the back nine on Friday to be home in six under 30 to make the cut on the number.

And with players taking the back nine to pieces over the weekend as well, it was ultimately Ockie Strydom taking his first tour win come Sunday afternoon, winning by two from Otaegui with Laurie Canter one shot further back. Whether they'll ever play here again depends on what happens with the ongoing LIV v DP World Tour shenanigans, although it's very, very hard to see Mr Rupert (who bankrolls the tournament and owns the entire place) not being able to invite the likes of Louis Oosthuizen and Charl Schwartzel next year. But time will tell on that one.

Anyway, by the time Strydom was holing the winning putt, we were all three hours deep into a safari in the Kruger, meaning by the time we got out of the park and on the road back to Joburg for another cultural evening in the Emperors Palace, all the crooked cops had gone home, so we made it a round trip without needing to bribe a single policeman.

Christmas had indeed come early.

Happy Mondays

Three tournaments into my year and I'm definitely straight back in the tour caddy work routine of walk round, practice round(s), pro-am round, followed by the tournament rounds. Just in time to get out of it over Christmas.

This makes now a good time to look at this routine, specifically the bit where we leave one venue on a Sunday afternoon and get to the next one on a Monday. No prizes for guessing that first up it's travelling. Some weeks, like between weeks one and two on this trip, it's really easy; some weeks it involves a slightly longer journey, like last week's drive from Joburg to Malelane; and some weeks it involves planes and time changes. Some weeks you have plenty of time; some weeks it's a mad dash to make the flight to make the other flight to make the other flight to next week's venue two continents away. Some weeks everything goes smoothly; other weeks it manifestly does not. And from my experience it's best to expect the latter, and be pleasantly surprised when it's the former. That, and not being dumb as a stump because, if you are, travelling can become a nightmare and something you might end up doing on your own, as your colleagues conclude you're a jinx and avoid you like the plague.

But whether that week's travel has gone well or catastrophically badly, eventually we all end up getting to where we need to be. Along, hopefully, with our luggage. But not always. Either way the first thing everyone asks on arrival at the golf course is 'Where's Dion?'

Dion is Dion Stevens, owner of Dion Stevens International (DSI), who makes the yardage books we use out here. And has been doing so for over 15 years now. He might be an Aussie; he might be permanently harassed; and he might be occasionally 'grumpy', but his yardage books are the finest anywhere in the world.

And his yardage book is THE tool of our trade. In fact, while it might be heresy to even say it, there is definitely an argument that while you could have a professional golf tournament without caddies, you couldn't have one without yardage books. So once you do find him, you just pick up whatever combination of his yardage books you've ordered that week, and your week can properly start. My yardage book goes straight in my back pocket the minute I pick it up, and from that point on it's rarely out of my sight all week. My player's yardage book (most players carry their own in the modern era) then goes into his locker in the locker room, and therefore becomes his responsibility, not mine.

Then it's time to go 'walk the course': ideally before your player arrives. If you've been there before, you'll remember every hole (tour caddies have this innate ability to tell you about every hole on every course they've caddied on) and are really just checking for any obvious changes. But if you've not been there before, walking the course will take a wee while longer.

We start on every hole by looking at the line we'll take off the tee. This is based on the carry over any hazards, how far any run-outs are on that hole and the target landing area (which might mean you re-evaluate your initial thoughts). And then it's on to the green to look, fairly obviously, at where the main slopes are, how severe they are, whether or not there are potential back-stops to certain pin positions, where the likely pin positions will be, and where the best and worst misses are to these.

Ideally it's not raining when you 'walk the course'. If it is, your 'Happy Monday' might just become an 'I don't like Mondays' Monday. Very few things in life are worse. Because done properly, walking the course can take a good few hours. Especially if you're one of those caddies who likes to have every single possible number that could ever conceivably be required.

But at some stage you're done. And it's off to the Caddy Lounge to see what's in store food-wise this week. Some weeks it's exceptional, restaurant-class in fact; some weeks it's decent, and some weeks not so decent. Thankfully there's not many of the latter weeks these days. And there's also not many jobs in the world where you get a free breakfast and lunch every day.

By this time in Europe, the 'bag run' should have arrived from the previous week's venue. This is the truck that transports the players' travel bags containing their clubs from one venue to another, so sparing them from the ball-ache of having to manhandle these things through airports and pay handsomely for the privilege of putting them on a plane. And typically it's your job as a tour caddy to locate this bag, unpack its contents, stick the bag in the bag store at the golf club (tour players rarely take their clubs 'home' with them at night) and sort out his locker.

Next stop: the truck. The various giant tour trucks are where you go to pick up your player's balls and gloves for the week: generally three-dozen balls and four new gloves. And while you're there you'll pick up any new shoes, clothes, etc. that they might have ordered, as well as dropping off any clubs that need 'tweaking' or checking after the previous week (each truck has a workshop fitted out with every tool imaginable as well as hundreds of thousands of €s worth of shafts, iron and driver heads, apparel and so on).

If your player isn't arriving until that night or Tuesday morning first thing … and it's not been raining … you'll have had a stress-free Happy Monday and nothing else to do, and so it's time to go back to the hotel and unwind. Making Monday nights the best nights to unwind. If unwinding is your thing.

Otherwise it's time to meet up with your player for some range time followed, sometimes, by nine holes. The thing that stops this meaning that Monday is an 'I don't like Mondays' Monday is that this MAY mean that tomorrow you'll only do the other nine holes rather than 18 stuck behind those guys who are playing a match and taking forever like the guys who've just had a Happy Mondays Monday.

Every cloud.

Chapter 2

The Sand Pit

The Story of the Week of the Abu Dhabi HSBC Championship 19–22 January 2023

This week always feels like the first week back at school. And for the second year running, school is Yas Links on Yas Island with a $9,000,000 prize fund as it's a Rolex Series event. So let's hope everyone has been doing their homework over the winter.

Whether Yas is as good as the Abu Dhabi Golf Club where we used to play, and Kaymer used to dominate (or collapse: one of the two), is still a matter of some debate. But what's not up for debate is that Yas Links is a lot easier. Unless of course the wind decides to blow, in which case the threat of running up a big number at every hole becomes a real threat, like it is at the Abu Dhabi Golf Club – only that's with or without the wind.

Another thing that's not up for debate is how much more convenient this venue is for us caddies. Mainly because we stay on Yas itself, meaning we can walk to and from the course instead of sitting in Abu Dhabi's infernal traffic for 50 minutes to and from the hotel like we used to have to.

Time that you can now better spend going cycling on the Abu Dhabi F1 track next door to the hotels, visiting Ferrari World and the world's fastest roller coaster, or simply going for a wander round the mall to escape the monotony of happy-hour excesses in the Stars n Bars Sports Bar.

On the downside, though, we don't all get to go to that amazing curry house opposite the hotel we all used to stay in downtown; nor does everyone hang out in the bar below the old Sands Hotel, which basically became a Northern England-type social club for a week. It's the only place I've ever been where the first song on the karaoke was 'Anarchy in the UK' or where a notoriously quiet caddy was unceremoniously told by one of his colleagues that 'you're up next on the karaoke son: I've put you down for an instrumental'. Proving that there is no humour like caddy humour.

Aside from all this, it's nice to see a lot of faces that I haven't seen since before the Final Series last year, which was when my 2022 season prematurely ended. It's like a belated New Year's Eve, shaking hands with people from all four corners of the caddying earth every two minutes. Although out of the corner of my eye I do spy one of the very few people out here I really don't get on with – which is a shame because I had half hoped never to see them again after hearing about their very obvious and acrimonious split with their player at the end of last season. But incredibly someone has employed them again at the start of this year. Although looking at who the player is, that's one partnership that won't last long. And when they do go their separate ways, the player's life will be better for it. As will ours.

Meanwhile, back at the tournament, Yas Links can get really tricky when it brings along its only defence: the wind, which it kind of did on Thursday when only 44 of the 132 players broke par, but after it went home that night, all Yas had was its half-brother, light winds, to protect it, so the course was pretty much there for the taking. So much so that the cut ended up dropping to two under: five lower than in 2022 when that wind popped up on day one and stayed the whole week. All of which meant that there were a fair few notable names heading off to Dubai a few days early in search of their games for next week.

In the end, though, it was all pretty tight into the back nine on Sunday, and remained that way until Perez spun a bunker shot back into the hole at the 17th for birdie, opening a two-shot lead over the guys in the second-last group out. And even with a bit of a chop show up the last he still clung on to win by a shot, and a $1.4m cheque to start the year with.

For other caddies and players, however, their MC here might just be a foretaste of things to come. Anyone with their ear to the ground next to us in the Stars n Bars this week might well have heard the names of a few players who we think will struggle this year, and also those caddy/player partnerships that are just not going to work. Time will tell: but tour caddies, as you'll no doubt hear me say a few more times this year, well, we just 'know': so they will and they won't.

Interestingly, though, and again this might well become a recurring theme this year, there are the first signs of differing views on LIV Golf. And some tension around it. Now for me, it's basically 'good on you' if you happen, or happened, to be working for someone who has 'jumped ship' to LIV and are basically making more money for doing the same job less days a week and less weeks a year; but for others, these guys and their caddies shouldn't be here. Along, presumably, with the green-eyed monster that is jealousy.

Maybe it's just me, but I simply fail to see the difference between a European Tour player going to play a LIV Golf event and a European Tour player going to play a PGA Tour event. Basically it's brand protection turned ugly. And childish.

Opinion is also split on whether the DP World Tour will win their arbitration against the LIV Golf guys: the hearing about which is scheduled for February – which might explain why, if rumours are to be believed, the CEO of the DP World Tour, Keith Pelley, isn't here this week when he usually would be. And because I'm a bit of a cynic, I'd also say the DP World Tour is actually half hoping to lose, as then the likes of Cam Smith, who are 'barred' from the PGA Tour, will be able to play all the DP World Tour events. And that – especially for sponsors – is a way bigger silver lining to the current legal cloud hanging over the Tour.

One thing that opinion is definitely not split on, though, is that next week is the best week of the Desert Swing: the Dubai Desert Classic at the iconic Emirates Golf Club.

And that is where our Uber is headed in about ten minutes' time.

Carry on Carbon Footprint

I could claim that our journey up to Dubai from Abu Dhabi was designed to reduce our carbon footprint. Only it wasn't. It was solely based on getting there as fast as possible so we could get to Barasti at a half-sensible time. So we hopped in an Uber and urged Ismahil to get his foot down on the race track that is the highway between Abu Dhabi and Dubai. He did, so we did.

I mention this only because the DP World Tour's carbon footprint seems to be a hot topic this year already. Now I totally get that the right thing to do in this day and age is to be responsible about these things, and in creating new roles around sustainability and carbon reduction the DP World Tour are doing just that; but I'm not entirely sure that, if the rumours are to be believed, doing some form of tracking of all players' and caddies' travel to and from venues with the aim of calculating, and presumably then reducing, the Tour's overall carbon footprint is particularly useful.

Because, as astounding as it might seem, a global golf tour that has tournaments across five different continents is actually going to have one, and probably a fairly substantial one at that. We're all part of that. And unless the Tour pulls back its boundaries, that's not changing anytime soon, making anything like this 'can't be arsed' territory in my book.

And I have to say the opinion of virtually everyone I speak to as well: many of whom weren't shy in saying they'll be taking a 'Get Tae Fuck will I tell you' stance on this one should it get past the drawing board. And I for one am with them.

But what might change my stance, mind and opinion would be the DP World Tour being radical and putting on a single, cheap, not-for-profit and convenient travel option or options from one venue to the next each week. Now that would be radical, and possibly make some radical reductions in our messy footprint. But with the vested for-profit interests of the Tour's Travel Service I'm afraid that's highly unlikely.

Anything less in my book, though, smacks of playing round the edges, and ends up being simply small-fry transparent virtue signalling. Something I am not a fan of. These things should just be done as a matter of course, without the need to shout from the rooftops. Because, if nothing else, your audience really doesn't care.

And anyhow, put your own house in order first. Like last week, when despite 90 per cent of us choosing to stay within walking distance of the course, some of the 'old guard' wanted to stay in Abu Dhabi city where everyone used to stay for the Abu Dhabi Golf Club, because 'we've always stayed there'. But instead of a polite refusal from the Tour to put buses on, suddenly there they were: a few petrol-guzzling rickety old buses that ran half empty for 40–50 minutes each way four times a day. Bet no one was tracking the carbon that spewed into the air.

This 'it's always been this way' is a real blocker to change in our world as caddies, as well as across the Tour itself. But change does come from the young, and that's exactly what's happening out here. I really do like how the younger guys just shake their heads at some of these ludicrous 'traditions', before going and doing their own things, and creating the new, and rather better 'It's always been this way.'

Anyway, we're now here in Dubai where the Dubai Metro is the preferred mode of transport. And whether that is carbon neutral, positive or whatever is someone else's concern. Not mine. Ironically, though, my guy wants a nine holes at dawn's crack in the morning, and as the Dubai Metro won't be running at that time, I'll be burning carbon in an Uber.

Hey hum.

The Story of the Week of the Hero Dubai Desert Classic 26–29 January 2023

Back when the European Tour first came here in 1989, the Emirates Golf Club sat on its own in the middle of the desert miles away from anywhere, which, if you have somehow managed to miss the annual rehash of 'that photo', takes some getting your head round when you see where it sits today surrounded by the massive skyscrapers around Dubai Marina.

Back then everyone had to stay 20km or so up the road in what is now referred to as 'old Dubai'. Or, the nice part, as I prefer to call it. And to a degree everything was way simpler back then, although way less convenient: you certainly never had to do battle with the traffic and road layout around the golf course, which seems to get harder to navigate every year.

For example, one of my more simple colleagues was in the wrong lane literally 200 yards from the course, but didn't get back to where he'd just been for another 25 minutes due to the ridiculous detour that lay in wait for anyone making the same mistake. Oh, and there's no signposts either. Just as well he wasn't looking for sympathy, though, as it served him right for trying to save a few quid by staying in a hotel miles away and having to hire a car to get to work. And for not caring about his carbon footprint. All of which made him late for work, and could yet bring forward his next change of player.

And he didn't really need a car this week anyway. Well, certainly not if he'd been staying in Al Barsha just down from the Emirates Mall where everyone has 'traditionally' stayed for this week, on the basis that it's only a couple of stops up from the golf course on the Dubai Metro, the Emirates Mall is a short walk away, the hotels around here are decent, and their bars don't rip your eyeballs out should you want to drink alcohol or anything else for that matter.

And back in the day, in fact way back in the day, the hotel bar of choice for not having your eyeballs ripped out was at the bottom of Al Barsha. And that's where everyone went on account of their extended happy hours, cheap prices and large quantity of scantily clad Asian ladies. None of whom were shy. And flitted around anyone Western, presumably in search of someone who would say yes to the dress. Although there was never too much of it to say yes to in the first place. Even if you were so inclined.

But these days things are altogether a lot more genteel, and a lot more guys are choosing to stay on Dubai Marina for pretty much the same reasons as we all used to choose Al Barsha: there's a huge range of accommodation, plenty of bars and restaurants, a decent-sized mall, and it's only a couple of stops the other way on the metro from the golf club.

And anyway, the metro is way safer than the roads. Especially after it's been raining, which it does here, and a lot more often than you would think. Like this week for example, when the incessant rain on Wednesday basically flooded the course, leading to a pretty significant delay before play could actually get underway on Thursday morning: so much so that only half the field actually got to play.

But if that was carnage, judging by the constant squeal of brakes and clanging of metal, it was nothing to that which appeared to be occurring on the Sheikh Zayed Road next to the course. Proving once again that while they might do an awful lot of things well in Dubai, teaching the locals how to drive in the rain isn't one of them. Thank God we were all going home on the metro.

By Friday night, everyone had played at least 18 holes, Blandy and Poulter were leading on eight under, and the more contrary of us were daring to dream of a 'LIV player' winning on Sunday, if only for the sport of seeing how sulky the DP World Tour would be congratulating a winner they didn't really want to congratulate.

Except that no one was going to be winning on Sunday as, after yet more heavy rain overnight Thursday, resulting in another two-hour delay to play on Friday morning, the sensible decision was taken to go to a Monday finish rather than trying to cram everything in. And quite right too: after all this is a Rolex Series event and, if we're honest, the most important event in the Desert Swing, so it deserves a proper finish.

My man makes the cut easily enough on Saturday, but we've long since finished our third round on Sunday before watching Rory hit probably the worst shot he'll hit all year straight into the water at 18 so reducing his lead to three going into the last round, and reviving hope of a LIV player winning.

Our wait goes on though, as Rory again proves that great players do what they have to when they have to do it: which in this case was to birdie 17 on Monday, have their drive stop 3ft short of the water at the 18th, lay it up in the fairway to a good wedge distance, and then roll it in from 14ft for birdie to win. All of which proves what we all know: that when he's on his game, no one gets near him.

Oh, and in case you missed it and haven't heard, apparently earlier in the week one of the big boys in the playground threw a tee at one of the other big boys because he wasn't being very nice and didn't say hello to them; they told on him, and so everyone else inside and outside the playground got to hear about it. All of which was very childish.

But for the grown-ups, it's off up to Ras Al Khaimah for the second edition of the Ras Al Khaimah Championship tournament and the final event in this year's Desert Swing.

Albeit a day late.

Oh No, It's a Monday Finish

Any time we go to a Monday finish – like last week in Dubai – it's a logistical nightmare for us caddies. Flights have to be changed. Hotel bookings altered. By us. Because unlike the Tour staff and players, we don't have someone to do it for us. And to do either costs money.

And that money comes out of our pockets. Because we pay. Not the Tour. Not our player. And definitely not our insurance. So now is probably a good time to look at how tour caddies get paid. Because it's a question we often get asked. Or to be precise: 'How much do you get paid?' Usually asked in a pro-am, or when someone we don't know finds out what we do for a living.

Now aside from it being a pretty rude question to ask someone who you might have only just met, it leaves you open to a well-rehearsed reply that you didn't want to hear or, at very least, weren't expecting. Like in pro-am once when a very funny colleague was asked by one of the amateurs, 'Do you mind if I ask you how much you get paid?' Quick as a flash he said, without the hint of even a smile, 'No. Not at all. But I'm not fucking telling you.'

What we can tell you, though, is that, apart from a tiny minority who are salaried, a professional tour caddy gets a weekly wage and a percentage of whatever prize money their player happens to win that week. That percentage is agreed between player and caddy when they first start working together. Legend has it that it's five per cent of anything, seven per cent for a top ten, and ten per cent for a win; but that is kind of old hat these days because – while none of us really know what our colleagues agree – we're all on a flat rate (of more than five per cent) for any earnings and ten per cent for a win. Mind you, it doesn't matter what percentage you've agreed because if your player misses the cut it's a percentage of €0, which is zero. And it's also zero if they happen not to be playing that week.

So, in case you haven't guessed, a tour caddy makes their REAL money from these bonuses, not the weekly wage. So it's best to be working for a guy who is either a decent player, or someone who is having a decent year. Or better still, someone who is a decent player having a decent year in which he's been saving his best golf for the Rolex Series events.

Either that or be lucky enough to be caddying for one of the guys who's decided to play their golf on LIV Golf. Because with last place every week worth around $130,000, then that's a decent bonus each week in anyone's book. Especially when you then multiply that by the number of tournaments on their 2023 schedule. In fact, it can turn you from a caddy who has basically struggled all their caddying career into someone suddenly around $300,000 better off just a few months later: which is what happened to a colleague who just happened to be on the bag of a guy who went over to LIV when it first launched. And on top of that, at least the first season, it was LIV who picked up the bill for every caddy's expenses, including their hotels and return flights from wherever in the world they lived. And that is why he buys dinner whenever we happen to meet up.

No such luck for those of us who work on the DP World Tour (or the PGA Tour for that matter), because we pay for our own flights and travel, our own hotels, our own yardage books, our own food at night, etc. So suddenly that €1,300 weekly wage (at least that's the unofficial/rumoured average wage out here) magically becomes around €400: which is actually not a lot for someone who is basically one of the best at what they do in the whole of Europe. And why it can be quite important to be working for a player who is actually earning decent money. Something that was summed up years ago by another veteran caddy who had told his player he was leaving for another bag and was asked whether it was 'for health reasons'. 'No,' he replied, 'I'm leaving you for wealth reasons.'

All of which is worth remembering the next time you're tempted to ask a tour caddy how much they earn, because then you won't have to. And instead you can talk to them about why, if one tour can pay all their players' and caddies' expenses, then how come the world's other major golf tours can't.

Because that'll be a much more fun conversation.

The Story of the Week of the Ras Al Khaimah Championship 2–5 February 2023

Albeit a day later than envisaged, everyone gets to Ras Al Khaimah safely and promptly ditches their hire cars as everyone is staying on or around the golf course this week.

I say 'on or around' as the 'around' option was the apartments lots of guys stayed in last year, which had an in-house boat service across the water to the course and electric scooters that you could also use to get to work. Only this year the boat was undergoing maintenance and the scooters had disappeared, so 'around' suddenly became a long walk to the course and a source of much grumbling from the guys who'd chosen to stay there.

The 'on' option was, however, as the name suggests, basically on the golf course and a five-minute walk to work, which made the 'on' option substantially better than the 'around' option. This made those guys who had booked this, which was actually the 'official' caddy hotel for the week, feel quite smug and take the piss mercilessly all week. Which proves two things: that some weeks you win even before the tournament starts, and when you don't, it's a week when you'd better have a fairly thick skin. Or at least be able to take a joke. Every day. For a week.

Mind you, not having a car meant we definitely didn't need to worry about the Tour moving the caddy car park with zero notice like they did last week. Not without reason, though, as it has to be said that ours was well and truly flooded after the storm that ultimately meant we went to a Monday finish; but sadly also without any prior notice. So that anyone who was driving that week turned up at 5am only to be refused entry, and told to go and park in the American University car park situated at the other side of Sheikh Zayed Road. And while this might actually only be a short walk to the course, the detour to get there through the Dubai road system was anything but short. Meaning that a few guys ended up effectively being late for work. If you work in an office, that might not be too much of an issue, but when your office is a golf course and your boss is a stroppy golfer who is already five over after the first round after a missed cut last week, then it can quickly become a very big issue, resulting in you getting fired. And while apologies were subsequently offered and accepted, I just think that this was one of the times when we weren't the last to be thought about (which is kind of fine), we just weren't thought about at all. And in 2023 that's pretty disappointing. Cue more enviable glances in the direction of LIV.

But this week it was a different story, and praise where it's due, we were looked after royally by the Tour and the promoter – principally in a Caddy Lounge that will struggle to be bettered all year in terms of location (right next to the 18th green, the locker room, and the scoring area with a tremendous view right across the lake on 18), in terms of food (restaurant-class just like last year) and in terms of extras (like the tournament putting on drinks for the first weekend of the Six Nations Rugby on the Saturday afternoon).

Although my personal highlight of the week wasn't that. It was hearing about one of the young lads who'd just got on a really good bag facing down a nasty little wannabe bully who, green to the gills with envy and free alcohol, tried to give him the full 'I've been out here for years' bullshit. Because like all little cowards, this pint-size carry-bag-toting piece of poison had soon pulled up his ridiculous long socks, turned on his size sixes and run away, having been firmly put back in his schoolboy-esque place. Reminding me once again why I really like the young lads who are coming out to caddy on tour these days: they come with no attitude, no sense of entitlement and take no shit.

Meanwhile, back at the golf, this week is the first week the guys who got their cards through Challenge Tour and Q School get the chance to play, mainly due to the prize fund being 25 per cent of last week's and Phoenix coming up on the PGA Tour.

Cue a fair amount of tour caddy 'much to learn, grasshopper' headshaking when we overhear a few of these guys saying how the course is tight and the rough is long, because it might be compared to the average Challenge Tour course, but it's nothing compared to the set-up from the last two weeks, or what you'll have to get used to out here. Some will adapt and thrive; others won't and will be back where they came from come the end of the year. That's the harsh reality out here.

And something that it's hard to appreciate from your golf club lounge, because unless you're standing on the range watching these guys every week, it's impossible to gauge just how good they are. Every single player with a DP World Tour category would reasonably expect to beat the course record at most golf clubs. Every time they went out. But pitch up at a DP World Tour event with a DP World Tour set-up and it's a different matter: believe me, the average club golfer couldn't actually shift it once the ball settles to the bottom of the Kikuyu rough, which you'll have to if you miss the 15-yard-wide fairways.

And although the fairways here might be slightly wider than that, it's still a decent test of golf, and, for the Middle East, a very picturesque one if you open up Google Earth and take a look. That said, from what I saw walking round early Tuesday morning, it will be another low-scoring week round here.

And it doesn't take long for Ryo Hisatsune to prove me correct, starting Round 1 with six birdies in a row en route to a 64. But he ultimately fades to finish T28. Too many putts sees my man resigned to a weekend's practice in the sunshine, but you can tell his game is trending in the right direction, so for once two days divot-watching is more than bearable. Especially looking at the weather at home.

Looking in the opposite direction at the scores though, a 63 from Zander Lombard on Saturday raises hopes of his and his caddy's first win on tour, but level par on Sunday means Daniel Gavins can enjoy the luxury of being able to make two visits to the water at the 72nd and still record his second win in the last couple of years.

Oh, and by the way, only two players from Categories 17 (Tour School) and 14 (Challenge Tour) finished inside the top 20, which kind of suggests us tour caddies weren't shaking our heads for nothing earlier in the week.

And that, if nothing else, proves we know our shit.

LIV or Die

I'm writing this before the LIV and the DP World Tour go to binding arbitration next week over whether the latter has the right to ban players from the former from their tour, even though they have an earned status on that tour.

So what follows may or may not end up being a case of caddy clairvoyance. In short, I reckon the DP World Tour can't actually lose here. Because on the one – and the smart money says likely – hand they win, a fair percentage of their members will be pretty damn happy and think they're wonderful, while their virtual lords and masters at the PGA Tour will give the Tour's belly a bit of a stroking, pat them on the head, tell them they're wonderful as well, and mumble some bollocks about the continuing benefits of the supposed strategic alliance. All good.

But on the other – and we all reckon unlikely – hand they lose, they don't actually lose at all, because that will mean all the LIV players currently banned from the PGA Tour will likely come play DP World Tour events, especially as they carry World Ranking points, which will be nectar to the current sponsors, and likely attract others. Yes, the DP World Tour hierarchy will make some statements about being disappointed, but behind the scenes they may well be punching the air. Cynics would suggest it's actually their preferred outcome, especially as it would potentially also allow them to back out of the to-date singly one-sided strategic alliance with the PGA Tour with some of their face saved. But we'll see when the judgement comes through.

What we've seen so far, though, is a vision of what could or can be done on a golf tour, and the difference that makes to caddies.

Because, if nothing else, LIV turns on its head the best summation of caddying I've ever heard, and that is that caddying on Tour is 'a lifestyle, not a job'. And that's because if you caddy on the LIV Tour, you are guaranteed a minimum bonus of $6,500 every week: which is what you'll get even if your man finishes DFL (Dead Fucking Last as we caddies call it) every week, which he likely won't obviously. So the least bonus you can possibly earn across their 14-tournament schedule for 2023 is $92,400. And that's on top of whatever wage you'll get paid by your player.

And it gets better, because LIV pay for caddies' and players' accommodation and travel, so there's a saving of around (let's say) $8,000 on what you'd have had to pay to get to the events and stay there. And the right as a caddy to question why the world's main golf tours don't choose to do the same.

So whatever you think of LIV, the people involved, the people backing it, the people playing on it, from a financial perspective, as a caddy, it's not a bad place to be. In other words it's a proper well-paid job. And not a lifestyle. So no wonder caddy ears are close to the ground for any LIV players looking for a new caddy. Mine included.

But don't tell my current boss.

Chapter 3

Free Jet Lag Anyone?

The Story of the Week of the Singapore Classic 9–12 February 2023

First time back in Singapore since about 2010. And it's still hot and steamy. On and off the course. Believe me, it's no fun stepping out into 35-degree heat with 110 per cent humidity no matter what time of day you play. And actually it's worse in the early morning where the moisture rises out of the ground before your eyes, whose lids are dripping with sweat before you get to the 1st tee shot.

This being exactly the issue we faced on Wednesday morning. Inexplicably my player and I had allowed a drink over dinner on Tuesday night to become more than one; in fact quite a few more than one. Even though we knew we were in the pro-am. Looking back, I really have no idea what possessed us: not even the naivest of rookies make such a rookie mistake. But on Wednesday morning my head seemed to have been possessed by the devil along with a deep sense of foreboding at having to carry the bag around for five hours at 7.30am. Only then I remembered that this is Asia, and the pro-ams are all in carts so there would be no walking involved – which was enough to make me believe in God; if only for that instant of realisation.

Because even though Laguna National is flat, tour bags do not carry themselves. And I reckon being violently sick by the 4th hole would have been a real possibility. Although actually it's usually pretty much okay for me as my body seems to adjust well over here. Mainly because I'm not five stone overweight. And don't use beer as a means of hydration on an evening. Or not usually anyway.

Others struggle. Some to the point where many a 'local' ends up carrying the bag in the practice rounds and pro-am; and in some cases all week as the odd fat lad ends up in hospital on a drip for half the week.

One guy a few years ago had had a cataclysmic amount of post-practice-round beer followed by a massage, hadn't had time for a shower before coming to the course the next morning, and basically got basted like a Christmas turkey before his player dispatched him to the medical tent after nine holes. Unlike the previous evening, that was not a happy ending.

Pre-tournament, though, the busiest place has been the chipping green. Well, the busiest place if you're European, because the vast majority of European-based players aren't used to the tight grainy grasses that proliferate here in Asia, especially when that grass sits on soft ground like it does here. Chipping suddenly becomes something you almost need to relearn how to do, as anything less than perfect contact and the ball is finishing three feet in front of you every time. The strike has to be absolutely perfect and boy does it take some getting used to. A fair few Europeans may as well just fake a back injury and pull out now while the flight prices to London or Bangkok are still reasonable.

This alone, even before you take into account the weather, makes it a fair bet that an Asian-based player or someone used to this type of grass (e.g. guys who've wintered in Florida not Frimley) will win. And that's before you also take into account the patience – and luck – you're going to need with your tee times given the inevitability of the afternoon thunderstorms that will have us on and off the course all week. Not that us tour caddies are allowed to bet on golf these days. A ban that also extends to our immediate family members. Although there are a few grandmas still making use of their online betting accounts to good effect – some long after their death – allegedly.

But no matter where in the world you're from, when you come here you know it's going to be a long week. Amazingly we get through Thursday with no rain delay, but the same can't be said of Friday when a localised monsoon hits as we're standing on the 8th fairway. Actually that's a bit of an understatement to be honest because I have never ever, ever seen as much water fall from the sky in such a short space of time. Literally within two minutes the course was underwater and completely and utterly unplayable. And had anyone been going off the 1st or 10th at that moment, the starter would have switched to say 'Lane 1 …' rather than 'On the tee from …'

However, this being Singapore, within an equally short space of time, thanks in no small part to the engineering and design of this course, all the water had drained away. So thankfully we were back out for another couple of holes while there was daylight. Thankfully, because despite the general whingeing from caddies and players alike, especially when the TD (Tournament Director) decided to dispense with the usual 40 minutes between announcing a restart and the restart itself, those couple of holes proved vital when it came to Sunday.

Because after 20-odd holes on Saturday and a super-early U-draw on Sunday, five minutes after the last group put the flag back in on the 18th the heavens opened again, and this time didn't shut for another two hours. Meaning that those three holes we played on Friday night avoided another Monday finish, which if you've read my previous ramblings, no one out here likes. So here again kudos to the TD, David Williams, and his team: us caddies may not always see eye to eye with them, but we do know they know what they're doing. And this was another case in point. Chapeau. As the Frenchies say.

Not that that last group featured the winner, because by that time Ockie Strydom had already signed for a 63 and his second victory of the season having won in Leopard Creek in December.

But here's the thing. Personally I have always got the distinct impression that the Tour is sometimes less than 'ecstatic' when a guy from the co-sanctioned tour wins a co-sanctioned event: like Ockie was when he won down in SA. It's almost like they're sometimes seen as 'weaker players' taking away spots from Q School and/or Challenge Tour players. But certainly in the case of the current crop of South African guys, like Burmester, like Lawrence, once they win they keep winning. So my argument is that the co-sanctioned events and co-sanctioned event winners actually add strength to the Tour, and too right they should be celebrated. And the large contingent of South African caddies sat watching the final few holes in the Caddy Lounge certainly did just that. Good on you, boys. Not a bad lad amongst them.

As for us, it was one of those weeks when my man played like a knob and behaved even worse. So we leave for Thailand with relations a little strained and in need of a happy ending next week.

One way or the other.

What's in a Tour Bag

Last week you'll remember I narrowly avoided having to carry his tour bag round in the pro-am with a 'slight headache'. Well, here's the main reason why this would have been a really bad thing.

A fully laden tour bag is bloody heavy: weighing in at around 25kg. And we have to lift it up and put it down around 110 times in an average round – all of which equates to a half-decent gym session, or in the heat in places like Singapore, Bangkok or South Africa, something akin to purgatory. Especially as, sadly, not every golf course we go to is flat, so 'goat tracks' (as we call hilly courses) are to be avoided if at all possible. The worst was (was, as thankfully we don't play there any longer) Madeira, where the climbs up the last few holes were the stuff of nightmares. And sadly claimed the life of one of us a few years back.

Now there are a number of reasons why tour bags weigh so much, but it's principally because pro golfers, and sometimes us to be fair, put far too much in them.

Like, fairly obviously, golf clubs. Fourteen of them to be precise. Except during practice rounds (and the odd pro-am if no one is looking too closely) when there may be a good few more if he's testing stuff out. I think my record is lugging 19 of TaylorMade's finest around nine holes once in Abu Dhabi. Sadly I wasn't being paid by the kilo.

Each of these clubs has, unsurprisingly, a shaft in it. But before the golf pervs amongst you get too excited, 99 per cent of tour caddies do not know what make of shafts they are, how stiff they are, where the kick point is, whether they've been pured, or what swing weight they are. Nor do they care. So asking us about stuff is a bit like asking how much we earn: you won't get the answer you were hoping for. And in this case, you'll be announcing yourself as a golf perv. Our interest is only in how far each club goes, and how much it spins into the wind. And that is the first question every caddy asks a player when he hooks up with them. Well, the first question after 'How much are you going to pay me?'

What you might not know about the clubs themselves, though, is the heads on a tour pro's clubs aren't necessarily the same as the ones on your 'identical' clubs, even though they might have the same logos, branding and colours. More likely is that yours have 'customer heads': ones which, if a tour pro hit often enough (the driver head being a good example), would simply disintegrate with the forces they can put through them.

Nor would you necessarily be aware that the order in which these clubs sit in the tour bag varies from player to player. Or that while some tour pros really don't care if the 3-, the 4- and 5-iron are in the same divider, others are completely anal about it and liable to have a head-off if the caddy puts the 5-iron next to the 6-iron in a different divider. Not that tour pros are alone in this weird tour bag OCDness: there's a few of us who make them look like amateurs.

And every tour pro on the planet keeps their putter next to their driver in the bag. That way the face never gets marked the way the irons do. And if you're an amateur reading this, and your putter isn't next to your driver, now you know why it has marks in the middle of the face.

The next heaviest thing that goes 'into' the bag is the umbrella. Award for the heaviest – and therefore most universally reviled – goes to TaylorMade. God only knows what those things are made of but believe me you don't want to be carrying one if you can possibly help it.

And that actually goes for umbrellas per se. And listen closely at the start of any given day on tour, and you'll hear the 'Not going to rain, is it?' question being posed in the hope said umbrella can be jettisoned back into the locker. All very well until it rains when the forecast said it wouldn't, as 'afraid it's in the locker, mate' will not stop your player having a head-off.

Although to be fair, one year at Celtic Manor, round that awful Ryder Cup course, one guy actually didn't have a head-off when the clouds sank over the hills behind the course, the heavens opened, and his 'pass the umbrella' was met with the aforementioned excuse. But he did a split second later when his 'no worries, just get the waterproofs out will you' was also met with 'afraid they're in the locker, mate'.

Because it's not like a tour pro's waterproofs are heavy. Because they're not. Especially not these days when they are literally featherlike. And that's why I always carry my player's waterproofs in the bag: that and for situations like when, despite my guy telling me to leave them in the locker, I didn't; so when he had to play a shot out of thigh-high stinging nettles late in the round, I could suggest he popped them on rather than saying, 'You could have put your waterproof top on, but I'm afraid it's in the locker, mate.' The result was that he didn't end up with arms that looked like a blind cobbler's thumb, I looked smug and he looked thankful.

Oh, and these waterproofs (his and mine) go in the main pocket of the bag. Mine at the very bottom; his where we can get at them quickly should we need to. In the old – arguably more fun – days it was not unknown for a crafty caddy to stick their waterproofs in the bag of the other caddy in the group when they weren't looking. You'd get battered if you tried that these days.

The other thing that goes in the bag is food. Generally it's a mixture of bars, fruit, nuts, occasionally sandwiches if the tee time is before lunch and, increasingly, energy gels. And here again some players are rather more fussy than others. At some tournaments there is a huge selection on the 1st and 10th tees for you to nab, with Dubai being everyone's favourite as there's two or three huge fridges packed with stuff to choose from. And obviously it's not just the players who eat during the round; us caddies, especially in the hot countries, need food too. If you don't eat, then at best you'll be shattered at the end of a five-hour round, and at worst you'll have been carted off on a stretcher.

Also crammed into the bag will be a spare towel for when it's a wet day. Or when you drop it walking off the tee like I'm prone to do, and only find out 304 yards later when you reach his drive. It saves you the walk of shame. Somewhere there will also be the rain cover which, although it feels like we do, we don't actually use that often. Although there was one caddy who used to have his up and on the bag most days on the basis that 'there's no way I'm carrying that in the bag'. I kid you not.

Water goes in the pockets on the outside of the bag. Or at least his does. Mine goes inside as I've no idea where his lips have been the previous evening. And prefer not to take chances. And finally, here's the other bit the golf perverts amongst you have all been waiting for: the golf balls.

A tour pro usually carries nine balls with them each round. They're all marked up with whatever identifying mark your guy uses (everyone is different) using one or more Sharpie pens. And mostly they're kept in their boxes rather than being tipped willy-nilly into the ball pocket as that way they don't rub together and ruin the identifying mark. Some guys only use high-numbered balls (i.e. numbered five to eight), some only use low-numbered balls (numbered one to four), some use balls numbered one on Thursday, balls numbered two on Friday, etc., some don't care either way. And before you ask, if it says Titleist on the ball it is one. No matter what you've heard from Jimmy down the golf club.

Oh, and if your player ever has a ball pre-marked up with a 'P' for Provisional on it, then as a caddy you're probably on borrowed time as that means he knows there's a bad one off the tee in the bag. And that's not good for him or your continuing employment.

How many balls a player uses in the round, and therefore how many you end up carrying round the full 18 holes, will depend on one of three things: firstly, how many he loses; secondly, how many times he changes his ball which can be anything between three and six times a round; and thirdly, on how many of the used balls you give away to spectators. Only if it's the latter, don't give too many away just in case number one kicks in.

And then there's gloves. Typically I'd carry three new ones, in one of the side pockets so they don't get crushed or mangled. Most guys use a new glove every tournament round: hence they get given four new ones every week by whatever manufacturer they are signed to. When caddying for some guys it's also best to have a 'provisional glove' in one of your pockets just in case he has a head-off and rips his current one to bits. That seems to be the head-off of choice these days. And I think we've all worked for someone in our caddying careers who in such circumstances would simply put his hand out expectantly without even looking at you, knowing you'd have a new one handy. And you'd hand it over without saying anything. Mainly because you quite liked your face the way it is.

And finally in a separate pocket go the tees, ball markers, Sharpie pens and pencils. Then you know where they all are, which in the case of ball markers is usually when walking on to the first green of the day.

All of which explains why tour bags are as big as they are. Why they weigh as much as they do. And why we prefer flat golf courses.

The Story of the Week of the Thailand Classic 16–19 February 2023

Sometimes the DP World Tour gets it right. And with this Asia Swing they've done just that. This is the second of three weeks here in Asia and, like last week, this tournament has decent prize money, is on a very decent golf course and, if history is anything to go by, will attract more than decent crowds seeing as they've not seen the European/DP World Tour out here for a good few years now.

Actually this course is more than very decent. It's immaculate. And in the 17th has one of the quirkiest holes you'll ever see. Because you will see it a lot this week, whether on TV (if you can be arsed to get up at silly o'clock to watch it in Europe: we're seven hours ahead here remember) or on social media, as everyone takes photos of it. Or rather photos of the island green and/or the boat ride across to it. And if that wasn't quirky enough, the length of that boat ride changes every day as the green is actually floating and is anchored to change the yardage every day. Thankfully it's usually only an 8- or 9-iron depending on the wind, which on the days it's not flat calm makes this a potentially very tricky hole indeed.

The other thing about Amata this week is that while it's still a strong golf course, this time we're here in the dry season so the rough that was thick when we came here around 2015 at the end of the wet season just isn't there. So my warning my player of how difficult the course would play was utter bollocks, and we're probably in for a lower-scoring week than foreseen.

Hopefully this Asian Swing will become a permanent fixture in the schedule: further kudos to the Tour if they can pull that one off, because personally I'd forgotten what a great place Asia is, while there are a good few 'new' caddies who have never been here before. And they're all loving it too.

Why do we like Asia? Well, for a start the food is fantastic wherever you go, and this week and last we've been eating street food every night, which is as delicious as it is cheap. And that's because it's cooked and served in furnace-like temperatures right in front of you, it's perfectly safe and no one gets food poisoning. Try this next week in Delhi, however, and it would be a very different, and very brown, story. The weather is always the same too: very little wind, steaming hot, with the possibility of an afternoon thunderstorm never too far away. Tour caddies like consistency, and Asia delivers on this one.

The accommodation is almost always reasonably priced. Like this week when we're in a great place for the princely sum of £78. For a single room. For the week. That is basically what we've had to pay for one night across the last four weeks thanks to the strength of the Middle East currencies and the Singapore dollar, and much less than what we'll be paying when we get back to Europe in a month or so. It's also peanuts for taxis here: my 30-minute ride from the airport on Sunday night into the centre of Bangkok was only £7, and it's even less to the golf course in the mornings too. Mind you, the traffic is so horrendous that we're all walking 20 minutes to the course as it's far quicker than getting a taxi, or even a taxi scooter.

Best of all, though, with the exception of KL Country Club where we used to play the week after The Masters every year, the courses out here are usually flat. And as you already know, flat tracks are caddy-friendly. So we tend to like them. Oh, and the massages here are cheap. And much needed as his golf bag isn't getting any lighter these days.

Asia is so good in fact that there's been many a caddy over the years who's ended up caddying on the Asian Tour for exactly these reasons, and with the investment in that tour over the last year, there might be a few more heading that way.

And sooner rather than later in some cases, as this week, as usual around this time of year, there have been quite a few caddy changes. Obviously, as a player, when you miss a few cuts at the start of the season, it's not your fault so it must be the caddy's fault. No mirrors in their hotel rooms, let me tell you. So there's been a few 'I just feel I need a change' player to caddy conversations (which is more often than not code for 'I've lost confidence in you and I'm also frankly sick of the sight and sound of you') and a few where the caddy has legged it to an employer offering better prospects, i.e. they're playing better.

And when you get fired out here, because you will (it's part of the job) best remember that there's no notice periods, no HR, no severance pay, and no unemployment benefit like you get in normal jobs. There's nothing. Not a penny. So it means that if you're ever tempted to pack in that comfortable nine to five job that pays the mortgage, pays the bills, feeds the wife and kids, etc. because you fancy having a go at that caddying thing, you probably shouldn't. Because it can become a very, very bad idea very, very quickly. But we'll talk more about this as the year goes on.

So like I say, come Thursday there's a few new pairings stepping on to the 1st tee at 6.15am. But it's one of the established caddy/player combos who are leading after Round 1, with Valimaki and his long-time caddy taking advantage of a super-soft golf course after Wednesday's torrential downpour and leading with an eight-under 64. But with a bit of breeze springing up into Friday, the course becomes firmer and faster like it was when we got here, making it kind of how they wanted the set-up.

Friday was also interesting because on 17, and I think for the first time in tour history, the Tour provided two lasers on the tee: one in metres, one in yards. The reason being there was clearly some suspicion that the green, which is floating but allegedly moored in the same position for all four days, may have actually moved in the wind. And sure enough, what our book told us was 133m flag was actually 138m flag: so half a club out. Doesn't sound much, but over water, in a wind, to a tight green, believe me it is. Predominantly because golf balls don't float.

Not that any of this stopped the low scoring, with Olesen taking a two-shot lead into Round 4 on 18 under after a flawless 64 on Saturday. And after three birdies in a row from 13 on Sunday he ended up winning by four from Yannik Paul. Arguably his most important win since that court case the other year.

Away from the course though, the other great thing about this week has been that a fair few guys who aren't working this week, but live over here, have made the trip up to Bangkok to catch up with everyone. It's been great seeing them all again, listening to and laughing at their stories for the thousandth time, and realising – not that anyone needs reminding – that caddies, current and old, are part of a 'Caddy Family'. You only really know when you're lucky enough to have been part of one.

Most notable visitor of the week was the legendary 'Ronnie Corbett' who lives out this way these days, and the only tour caddy I'll mention specifically by name in this book, and then only because he's long since retired.

Obviously Ronnie's name isn't actually Ronnie. Just as his surname isn't Corbett. It's just because he was (and still is) small and bore some resemblance to the British comedian and golf nut of the same name; the Ronnie Corbett nickname given to him when he first came out on tour simply stuck. In fact it was years after meeting him for the first time that I eventually discovered what his real name was. In 2023, though, Ronnie is now well into his 70s, and possibly older, still as fit as a fiddle, and is probably the only tour caddy ever not to have ever played golf in his life. Not that it stopped him having a few wins in his career. Or coming up with some absolute classics: the most famous being him reminding someone who thought his player had missed the cut with rounds of 78, 78, that 'the cut is top 65 and ties, and I'm caddying for a Thai'. The thing was, he was serious.

As he was when I overheard him trying to explain to his player in Italy one year how he'd come up with the 157 pin number. His explanation was like something out of the numbers game in *Countdown*: it's this to the pin, then there's five downhill, I've taken an extra three off for the air, and added five because you're not striking it good today. After the round his player mixed the letters and numbers rounds up, and came up with P45. Few people out here deserve the adjective 'legend', but in Ronnie's case it's probably justified. Love the man.

Now, as much fun as it was seeing these guys, it was equally as sad to hear of the passing of John Paramor, the recently retired European Tour Chief Referee. Now I can't say us caddies ever really interact with the referees on the course the way the players do, but what I can say is that John had what not many people you meet in life have: and that was real presence. And not just because he was a mountain of a man. No, because when you saw him heading your way in his referee's buggy to deliver a ruling, you knew no one was getting away with anything: the ruling you were about to get would be fair, and it would be pointless arguing because it would be 99.999999 times out of a hundred correct. Yes, the man had presence all right.

One of the few other people with such presence out here is Tiger Woods. And although obviously he's not playing here this week (he's playing Riviera), even 5,000 miles away his presence is felt. The talk on the range before we go out is about how he's doing, those still in the Players' Lounge are all watching and delaying their exit to the range as long as they possibly can, and the first question coming off the course is 'What did Tiger finish on?' I'm not sure anyone who's ever played this game professionally commands the same attention.

Not that anyone really cares about this or who won today because there are the delights of Bangkok to be sampled, or overindulged in, tonight before flying to India in the morning. Obviously muggins here has booked the cheap just-after-midnight flight so I head to the airport instead, while the potential over-indulgers head into town secure in the knowledge that their flight is on Monday afternoon, and their wives think they're in bed recuperating after a long week.

Anyway, no matter what time your flight is, that flight is heading to a place where even feeling like you're going to fart is enough to engender rising waves of panic.

Yes. It's time for Delhi. Belly.

The Practice Round

I suppose it was about the 12th hole, and granted it was cold and absolutely pissing down, when my then player turned round to me and said, 'God, I detest practice rounds.' Which did kind of beg the question why we were actually out there in the first place that day. And indeed why we ever bothered playing them.

So I asked him. Albeit in the locker room after we'd finished the remaining six holes in, and of, abject misery, instead of as we were walking off – which is what we should have done: if only because that might have meant I wouldn't have had to caddy feeling like death and with a nose like a tap for the tournament days that followed.

Turns out the reason why we carried on that day, and why we carried on playing practice rounds after that, was somewhere between it's expected that you play them, and he frankly had nothing better to do. Not that he exactly put it that way, but that was the underlying reason.

And that's still true all these years later. Because even though today the yardage books are so good most tour pros could actually pitch up on Wednesday night having never seen the course before and still shoot a good score, Monday through Wednesday their lives, and therefore ours, still centre on all things 'practice'. Be that the practice ground, the practice chipping green, the practice putting green or the practice round.

Now there's pretty much no mystery as to what goes on at the first three: you work on stuff, hit balls and smash drivers on the first one; you hit basket after basket of chips and bunker shots to the second; and you do all your weird and wonderful drills on the third. But what about the fourth? Well here's all you need to know about the rounds you never see the professionals play. All of which comes with a 'Golf Pervs Only Past This Point' warning.

Ninety-nine per cent of practice rounds start on the practice ground. Even if it is only just hitting a few balls to kind of loosen up before dispatching driver down the 1st. And from a tour caddy's perspective, or at least mine, ideally the latter will occur within one minute of the 1st tee opening in that morning, which is typically at 7am. Especially if the intention is to play a full 18; otherwise you could find yourself out there for hours behind a whole bunch of four-balls – of which more in a minute.

Because if you're going to do all the things you really ought to be doing to get the most out of a practice round, like carefully looking at the lines off every tee, deciding on landing spots and zones, looking where the best misses are (especially round the greens), where you want to be to certain pin positions, and where you definitely don't really want to be, putting to the likely pin positions on the greens, and hitting an inordinate number of chips round each green, you need time. And the more of it the better. So as a player it's worth dragging your arse out of bed earlier than you really want to on Mondays and Tuesdays: most tour caddies encourage our players to do so. Most of us are ignored.

Because most players have their own routine for the practice days which invariably includes texting each other the night before to agree what time they're going to play. Apart from, obviously, those guys who always try and play on their own first thing for the reasons already stated: these are the ones many of us cast envious glances at (and their caddies) as we're queuing on the 1st tee as they're walking off the 9th green, or worse still the 18th, having done their work.

That said, having a regular practice partner is sensible as you know each other's rhythm, routine and way of working in the practice round, and so there's zero frustration – again, allowing the time you do spend out there to be productive and free of annoyance. With the chief source of the latter for any player being the one guy you always end up playing against in your four-ball, who you know will play out of his skin like he does every week in this game, making birdie after birdie, meaning that your money pays for his lunch for the umpteenth week running, only for you then to see he's shot 78, 76 on Thursday and Friday. For the umpteenth week running. And it's only when you point this out to them that there's the audible sound of a penny dropping.

And then of course there's the Spanish Armada who casually muster and set sail mid-morning. Because you really don't want to be behind them too often. All lovely, lovely guys, but as Captain Scott once said, 'I may be some time.'

Oh and, apart from at The Open, you don't actually book a time: you just pitch up on the 1st tee and queue like at the local muni. Another reason why you really should be first up come Tuesday morning. But no matter what time we actually start the practice round, I always start it with three new balls in my pocket. With up to an extra nine in the bag.

He gets the first one to hit. And is thrown a second if that's dispatched into the shite. But hopefully not the third. All are marked, but differently from how they'll be marked in the tournament: that way there's no possibility of playing the wrong ball should your man end up playing from the deep rough on the left of the third where he hit that one in practice but couldn't be bothered to look for it. Yes, believe it or not tour pros do occasionally hit that off-the-planet shot like we do; the difference being they get their golf balls for free so they aren't going to waste time in knee-high jungle searching for it like we would.

In my other pocket I have two or three 'false holes', which are basically plastic or rubber discs the same size as a normal hole. My personal favourites are the three limited-edition Scotty Cameron ones; my usual ones: three white solid Titleist ones. And no, the Scotty ones aren't for sale.

As we come up to each green, either me or the other caddies in the group chuck these false holes where our combined educated guesses tell us that the pins are likely to be on the tournament days. So once the players finish putting to where the hole is that day, they put down these false holes to, fairly obviously, get an idea of which are the hard putts on this green, where the principal breaks are, etc. After which they'll generally grab the lob wedge and hit some chips to these holes from the spots where we're most likely to miss the green (especially on long par fours), followed by some bunker shots.

Meanwhile, you'll see me, and every other tour caddy, scooting about the green checking things like the carry over that trap to the flat part of the green, where the false front actually ends (effectively this makes the front of the green number more than it is shown in the book), how severe the slopes on certain greens are, the general fall lines in the green, where the best misses are to certain pin positions, where we will want to finish to others, etc. All the while, throwing the balls he's putting or chipping back to him or rolling them to other parts of the green/surrounds for his next set of putts/chips.

Technically speaking, the number of putts, chips and bunker shots you're 'allowed' to take around the greens is restricted to, if memory serves me rightly, four per green; although the last time anyone ever stuck to this number or was sanctioned for exceeding it, no one can remember. Probably because (a) it's ludicrously too few; and (b) thankfully, at least from a player's perspective, not enforced. Tour caddies would, however, be delighted if it were, because then we'd be out there for about 30 minutes less, but hey.

What we're allowed to mark into the book has changed over the last couple of years in terms of denoting lines and slopes, but the idea behind it hasn't changed, which is to make sure we have all the information to hand come Thursday morning.

Then just before, and only just before, whoever is behind us playing their practice round starts firing balls at us for taking too long, we hastily pick up all the balls and holes, rake the bunkers, put the flag back in and leg it to the next tee. Ready to do it all again on the next hole.

After nine holes I tend to swap out the (hopefully) three we've used for three new ones. That kind of mimics the use a ball gets on the tournament days (my current player swaps after three holes maximum), but more importantly contributes to my stash of balls the next time I play at home.

Done like this, an average practice round takes around five hours, which to be fair is about the same time it takes on Thursdays and Fridays; it just seems longer. And the longer we're out there, the more likely it is that your player is going to lose interest. And believe me, a lot do. Especially if that guy is doing his usual and he's five down already in the match with his mates. We still have to do our work though, but add on to that trying to keep him, even slightly, focused on what we're actually out there for – and there's the reason why tour caddy practice nirvana is nine holes' practice on the Monday afternoon, and the other nine holes on the Tuesday morning. Either that, or when your man doesn't play a practice round at all, preferring instead just to walk round, maybe even with just a putter, and take everything in without the baggage of remembering his bad shots in practice at this hole. More importantly, though, doing this means that your man will never ever have to pay for that annoying guy in the four-ball's lunch.

And, I suspect, was the real reason my then player hated practice rounds so much.

The Story of the Week of the Hero Indian Open 23–26 February 2023

Unlike 90 per cent of my colleagues, I love India. It's vibrant, colourful, completely safe, the people are lovely, and you get to see stuff you don't see anywhere else in the world. Like cows in the road. People playing cricket in the road. And people shitting in the road. Which is why it's sometimes unkindly referred to as Smelly Delhi.

Anyway, we land early morning out of Bangkok, and take a taxi straight to the golf course in an attempt to ward off any jet lag. I say 'taxi', but I suspect our driver was just some guy posing as a taxi driver because as well as the fare being ridiculously low even for India, the car was hardly big enough for the three of us, never mind our luggage, which ended up being tied to the roof John Cleese style. And that was before we drove half the way on the wrong side of the road with none of us wearing seat belts because there weren't any. Nevertheless, we arrived safely at DLF Golf and Country Club no more than 90 minutes after landing. Unlike anyone landing in Delhi from the West later in the day who weren't even close to the front of the queue for Passport Control after 90 minutes.

This week there's none of the usual Monday rush to walk the course as he's not coming until Tuesday night as we're in the pro-am Wednesday and intend using that as this week's practice round. Not uncommon practice at the end of a good few weeks on the road.

And what the amateurs in our pro-am group will never suss is that at some holes we'll not be aiming at the flags, rather we'll be aiming at where we think the trickier flags will be come the tournament days. Again not uncommon practice. So the next time you play in a pro-am and think the pro is playing crap because he's 45ft away every hole, he's not, believe me.

The DLF golf club itself is a throwback to the days of the British Empire in terms of its clubhouse, and when I first came here a decade or so ago the course was great. But that was before Gary Player got his hands on it and ruined it with some of the most ridiculous changes to perfectly good holes, turning them into ones that wouldn't look out of place at your local crazy golf centre. I'm not the only one who suspects that, the minute he passes away, they'll send the bulldozers back in, level the place and return it to what it was. And if they could then head down to SA and do the same to the cambered fairways round Sun City, that would be great too. Controversial maybe; but required, definitely.

So it's actually just as well I have a couple of days to wander round and shake my head at some of the changes.

Or 'butcherings', depending on your point of view. All I see is severe run-offs, very slopey greens, some very funky holes, and a course that will be impossible for the amateurs in the pro-am: it's hard enough for the pros.

Off the course, a fair few of us opt to stay in apartments this week. Ours just happens to be round the corner from a shopping mall with a whole host of different food outlets, and when the one we choose the first night doesn't give anyone food poisoning, this is nominated as the place we'll all eat at in the evenings this week. With the added bonus being that we'll have the option of something other than the traditional Indian food that will be served up in the Caddy Lounge which, by the way, borders on fine dining; it's that good. Our apartment is also just a short tuk-tuk ride from the course, and as we are obviously the only passengers for several thousand miles who pay in notes, by Tuesday morning there's a whole gang of drivers right outside the apartment block as word has got around. Everyone else stays at the IBIS across the road from the course, where out of the front you can see the ornate gates to the golf club and the leafy driveway down to the clubhouse; while out the back you can see squalor and a good few animals that looked a wee bit close to the back door of the hotel kitchen for comfort the last time I stayed there.

Fairly obviously the hot topic of conversation early in the week here is Thomas Pieters and Dean Burmester hightailing it to LIV Golf. Personally I'd thought something was up when Pieters was bleating about not getting into Riviera despite being 34th in the world. Which was a fair point. But I'm not sure I saw him heading to LIV. Same with Burmester. Super-talented and hugely long, we'd all envisaged him doing really well, and winning, on the PGA Tour this year. Well, clearly that's not happening now.

But, as ever, I say good luck to both of them. Petty jealousies are not uncommon out here, so both will no doubt be cast as pariahs when in fact they're both nice guys. As are their caddies. So again, I say good luck, lads. You'll end up being on the right side of the argument. Might take a while, but you will be.

Anyway, by Wednesday I've sussed out the course and how I think we should play it, which is just as well as due to 'fog' the pro-am ends up being only nine holes. The Tour use the word 'fog' in their blurb, but we all know it's actually smog. And it only shifts when the wind picks up late afternoon.

This is also curiously around the time my health seemed to start picking up. Because up until then my sinuses were completely blocked, my eyes felt like I'd been rubbing a Carolina Reaper chilli into them, and I'd had the worst headache since the one I had the morning after my guy won the other year. In fact things had got so bad I'd been on the phone to my GP in the UK a few times to see what I should do. Although to be fair I wasn't expecting him to prescribe a liberal dose of 'get yourself to the nearest mall as they have air conditioning there, and that will help' medicine; nor did I expect that to work, which it did for my eyes and nose. But nothing seems to be shifting this headache.

I'm not the only one with health issues this week. There's been a fair few last-minute withdrawals due to guys getting sick and so the Entry List has gone down much lower than it might have. Now for those guys getting the call that they're suddenly in the field, the whole army of local caddies here has been a godsend. There are so many of them employed by the golf club that there's even a room in the basement of the DLF clubhouse with bunk beds where every other week of the year the guys sleep between rounds. Not this week, though, as those that haven't been lucky enough to pick up a player coming last minute are out on the course working as spotters, which given the amount of bundai just off the fairways, we're all really glad about.

And of course at the end of the week we all give them anything and everything that we don't really need, like balls, gloves and clothes. Not that any of ours actually fit any of them, but it's the least we can do.

Speaking of health, fortunately my guy, who hasn't been here before, has listened to my advice and has stayed healthy. Advice that was based largely on some bitter experiences here in the past. Although thankfully they were all bitter for my then player rather than me. Uppermost being my counselling him that boasting you've stayed clear of vegetables and instead have just eaten fruit is never a proud boast; in fact it's a one-way ticket to, if you're lucky, the loo, where there's toilet paper; and if you're not, the bushes at the side of the fairway, where there isn't any. This will also stop me having to run to the medical tent to grab an emergency supply of Imodium; you having to duck into those bushes at the 3rd, and then get a visit from the Tour doctor on the 6th. All best avoided. But also why we have half a roll of toilet paper in the bag. Just in case.

And on the subject of advice, this week is one of those when the experienced caddies are 'straight into their guy's head' the minute he gets there. Like me for instance. From the minute he turns up I'm on him psychologically, drilling it into him that this week is as much about attitude as it is anything else, because two-thirds of the field are mentally gone before they even tee it up. They're too busy worrying about the poverty you see outside, whether they're going to get sick, and how shit some of the holes are, rather than focusing on the fact that it's a short 120 field this week, and out of them only 90 can actually play, so you have a better chance of a decent finish than any other regular week. Our mindset is to really focus, avoid the trebles and quads that you can quite easily rack up round here, and ignore the fact that next week the beach is calling. If we do that, we'll be okay; if we don't, we'll be spat out like two-thirds of the field.

And after 36 holes it looks like Yannik Paul's caddy has been doing a fair amount of the psychological drilling I was talking about, as he's leading by five. Over the weekend, though, Marcel Siem emerges from the pack, and in the end, despite Paul going bogey-free in the last group on Sunday, Siem shoots 68 in his last round for his first win since 2014.

We do okay in the end, but as the winning putt is being rolled in, I'm already thinking about turning left as I get on the flight home tonight and how good that seat in Business Class (courtesy of some expiring Skywards air miles) is going to feel. And that when the doors do close, it'll be time to say goodbye to Asia for another year, and hello to my new friend: Mr Six Weeks Off. Which actually is a shame, because looking at who just won, I suspect there may be a fairly decent celebration going on somewhere in downtown Delhi tonight.

But on the bright side, despite the odd tense moment recently, we've had a pretty decent start to the year, meaning that we're not now going down to the tournaments in South Africa in March, or across to the ones in the Far East in April.

At least that is the plan as EK515 takes off bound for Dubai. Whether it changes over the next six weeks remains to be seen.

When We're Off, We're Off

I left India on Sunday night pretty much straight after the tournament, and thanks to that left turn into Business Class as I got on the plane in DEL, followed by a second one in DXB, I'm way more refreshed than usual when I land back in London town on Monday morning.

And just like that, rather than picking up the golf bag out of a bag store, I'm picking the kids up from school, while ensuring that I keep my eyes open long enough not to crash the car or fall asleep before 9pm as when you go east–west jet lag can be a real issue if you're not careful.

At least the two wee blighters actually still recognise me despite me being away for the best part of two months and seem pleased to see me. As is their mum, which also never fails to astonish me if I'm honest: there's not that many women who will tolerate their husband being away half the year. In fact, on the evidence of the number of my colleagues who've shelled out lots of their hard-earned cash to divorce lawyers across the years I've been doing this job, I'd say she's as unusual as I am lucky.

So here's me who's travelled around 6,750km in the last 24 hours (Delhi to Heathrow is 6,715km, Heathrow to our house makes up the other bit) doing my washing, making a family dinner before she goes off on night shift, and putting the kids to bed, instead of meeting in a hotel lobby and heading out for dinner with the boys like I would on a normal evening on tour.

And as I do so, my transition from tour caddy to house husband is complete, and so begins six to eight weeks of this shite as my man is not playing in Kenya or the two in South Africa, and is doubtful about Japan and South Korea despite his name ominously still being on the Entry List. Which might yet make my assertion to the missus that he'll definitely pull out before the deadline for entries closes look 'ill-judged'. At best.

But my shite is significantly better than some colleagues' shite because, whereas I can afford to earn nothing on my weeks off, they very definitely don't have that luxury, and have to find work where and when they can. That is one of the harsh realities of being a tour caddy, especially if you're married and have people who depend on the money you bring in. Like children, for example.

And so there are a fair few guys I know who have already swapped their Callaway or Castore polos for DPD or Evri-branded ones, and are out on the road delivering parcels in all weathers from dawn until dusk. Others have opted for stacking shelves at their local supermarket. For others it's labouring jobs. While the really desperate (?!) plump for the bête noire that is Amazon, which for all its faults does seem to provide the best repertoire of stories: with one guy regaling us with tales of all the drug-taking, fights and shagging he'd seen over a month's worth of shifts in his local centre last Christmas. Now I'm prepared to admit that a fair few of these may well have been embellished, but it was enough to keep us royally amused one evening a few weeks back. One that suddenly seems a lifetime ago for some reason. Probably the kids.

Yes, you might think our lives look glam when you see us on TV at the end of a week, but there are weeks when the reality is somewhat different, especially if you are married like me.

Which is a long-winded way of saying that it's kind of better being single when you're a tour caddy because then you can go do some of the things some of my colleagues are currently doing. Not that I am jealous, obviously.

No, I mean the two-week trip that six of the lads are taking down to Sri Lanka to go surfing sounds utterly horrendous, what with its wall-to-wall sunshine, sandy beaches, cheap accommodation, beautiful food and stress-free relaxation. And as for the guys who headed straight down south from Delhi to watch their beloved Aussie team play India at cricket, well they look like they're having a terrible time too. But spare your biggest and most sympathetic thought for those that have headed off, on their own or in small groups, to some of the few really unspoilt corners of the earth that remain: ones that even the most vacuous of social media influencers haven't heard of. And even if they had, couldn't spell. Yes, they're the ones having the best time from what I can see. And no, I'm not going to tell you where these are.

But no matter how good or miserable a time any of us were having on this first week off, that was put in perspective by the news from South Africa that one of our colleagues, Tiny Tim, had suddenly died. Tim might have been tiny in stature (hence his pretty unimaginative nickname), but there was nothing tiny about his smile, his personality, and his love of carrying that massive tour bag round after his man: a bag that was pretty much the same size as he was to be fair. We mourn any of our colleagues who die, but in Tim's case, we'll mourn him a little bit more.

But life goes on. Especially ours. And bizarrely, part of that is something that we all feel in this job/life: the moment when no matter how big your wanderlust, no matter where you are in the world, no matter how good a time you're having, and no matter who you're having it with, you're ready to go back to work. Mainly because we all love what we do. And so with the Seven Dwarfs' 'Hi Ho, Hi Ho' song reverberating around my house husband brain, it is, some would say finally, time to go back to work.

In my case this will involve flying halfway across the world to Japan as he's now decided to play the ISPS Handa tournament in Omitama and then maybe Korea the week after. Oblivious obviously to the fact that the prices of the flights are now way more than they were a few months back when he told me he almost certainly wouldn't play, and I naively, stupidly and expensively believed him. A proper rookie mistake. Even after all these years.

But nothing that a few shifts at Amazon won't cover.

Chapter 4

The Months of Africa and Asia

The Story of the Weeks of the African Swing
9–26 March 2023

This week the Tour starts a three-week run down in southern Africa: the first week in Kenya followed by two in South Africa itself.

Me, I'm still in snowy southern England in full house husband mode. But try as I might I still keep looking at the golf scores from Thursday morning onwards. Mainly because a few friends are down there caddying, and you obviously want them to do well. And constantly looking at their players' scores has got to help, hasn't it?

Not according to the kids or the missus, though, who keep bleating about me being on my phone all day. But I still can't help looking.

Now if ever there was an aptly named tournament on tour, it's the Magical Kenya Open. Because Kenya and the tournament are both magical.

For starters the golf course is one of those tight old-fashioned layouts that are sadly a dying breed these days, so in a sense it's a shame not actually being there. And there even seems to be universal praise for its condition, which is also a bit of a rarity these days.

But for me, being a bit sentimental at heart, it's also magical to see how many local caddies get a bag this week, if for no other reason than the chance of earning some serious cash if their man ends up doing well. They get bags mainly because (unfairly) this is seen as one of the lesser tournaments on tour, so the field goes 'right down' as we say. In fact, right down into Category 20, which is about as low as the cut-off for entries ever goes out here, meaning a very rare start for guys who made the 72-hole cut at Tour School but didn't get a full card.

And if you're that far down the list you almost certainly won't have a full-time caddy, and instead just 'take a local', which is the term for hiring a caddy who works at the host golf course or one of the members, etc.

Taking a local is actually a bit of a win–win really, because the player doesn't have to pay the same kind of money he would ordinarily have to for a caddy in Europe, and for the local caddy it offers the opportunity to be paid far more than they would ordinarily get paid in a week, the opportunity to get that money in euros, and the opportunity to earn a very, very healthy bonus payment if their man does well.

And that does happen. In 2022, for example, Ashun Wu won (he missed the cut this year by the way), but did so with a local caddy carrying the bag in the last round as his regular caddy was so sick he couldn't actually get out of bed that day. A bad day for him, but a very good day for the local caddy. Actually scrub that: it was a life-changing day for the local caddy, because Wu's sick caddy is a decent guy with morals and scruples, so he paid the local a fair percentage of the percentage Wu paid him. He'd literally never seen that much money in his life.

The scoring is pretty magical too, with Hisatsune at it again with a 63 in Round 2, which included two bogies, although after 36 holes it was Nacho Elvira who led on minus 10. But the highlight of the first two days was actually provided by local professional Mutahi Kibugu who drained a huge putt for birdie on his last hole to make the cut, which made it a life-changing week for him, never mind his caddy.

And while that was kind of his tournament over (he finished T65 in the end), it very definitely wasn't tournament over at the business end of things, where after a five-under 67 on Sunday, Campillo prevailed over another Japanese player, Masahiro Kawamura. All of which meant a good week for his caddy, but not really a life-changing one money-wise if we're honest.

And so ended arguably the year's most magical week so far according to my spies who were there, and to cap it all the snow stopped in London which made house husbandry a bit easier. Even better, though, was knowing I'm one week closer to getting back out on tour. Not that that was helped by messages from the guys who headed from Kenya to South Africa.

You see, there are some weeks when you've got a week off that you wish you hadn't. And this first week in South Africa is one of those. Nothing to do with the golf really. No, it would have been an opportunity to travel to a part of South Africa that I've certainly never been to: the Eastern Cape.

And I think that is actually why there are a fair few people in the field this week who you wouldn't ordinarily expect to see in an event boasting a pretty measly $1.5m prize fund. But by all accounts the golf course is pretty decent so that's an added bonus.

This makes it slightly surprising that a few caddies who were there last week haven't made the trip this week: after all, you're down there anyway. And it's not because they've been fired. Instead it's because, and this has been the case for a few years now, they've started playing the 'I don't feel safe down there' card. Now South Africa may not be the safest place in the world and, yes, not being able to walk back to the hotel after dinner in a few places definitely starts to grate on you after a few days, but seriously? No, I think we all know the real reason why they're not going.

But their loss is another's gain, as their player's bag will be picked up by one of the caddies from the South African Caddies Association, who normally work on the Sunshine Tour, for whom working these two weeks means a substantially higher wage than they would get on an ordinary week on that tour. And then you might even get as lucky as Lucky in Joburg, and end up caddying for someone who nearly wins, meaning your bonus will also be enormous.

Then of course there's also the possibility that if their player likes them enough, he might ask them to caddy for them across Europe in the summer. In doing so they'll be following in the footsteps of a whole bunch of South African caddies who have made that jump in the past. To a man these guys are universally popular, and are very much part of the furniture on tour. It obviously also helps that to a man they're really good caddies.

That is just as well, because as beautiful as the Eastern Cape and St Francis Links look from all the photos – on the practice days it's 30 degrees, not a cloud in the sky, with no wind – it looks like they both have a sting in their tail with the weather guys forecasting 50kph winds from the east on Thursday, and then 60kph winds from the west on Friday. This basically means that whatever game plan you had worked out on those flat, calm, warm practice days is about to go up in smoke once the tournament starts. Not ideal. And requiring every caddy to do quite a bit of extra work on Wednesday night to come up with a revised strategy once the weather forecast is confirmed.

Mind you, by the sounds of things not everyone will have been able to play a practice round anyway. Apparently the guys who flew down from Kenya via Joburg on Sunday night arrived only to be told 'no bags', i.e. none of their bags had made it on to the SAA flight at all. Bang went their early

Monday morning practice round. And the guys who flew down from Heathrow didn't fare much better. A couple of hours' delay out of the UK meant a missed connection in Joburg: not in itself the end of the world, but it is when you eventually get to that connection and find that your bags didn't even make it on to the original BA flight from London in the first place, which is the reason everyone has AirTags in their luggage these days, because in these situations at least you know exactly where your luggage is, unlike the routinely useless baggage staff at the airport.

And so began a few days of refreshing the Find My app on the off-chance that those bags were on the move. And you thought refreshing the scores to see how your mates' players were doing was a fruitless exercise. But eventually for the lucky few it paid off. Bags moved. And bags were delivered just before Thursday's carnage began.

And for once the weather forecast was spot on. Because if anyone thought Thursday was windy, then by Friday afternoon everyone was off the course due to gale-force winds ripping their way across the course making it completely unplayable. Play was called for the day shortly afterwards, but not before some horrendous scores from guys who had to start at the height of the tempest.

A tempest so bad that from reading the various opinions on the caddy messaging group, the consensus in the Caddy Lounge seems to have been that this was some of the worst wind experienced on tour in many a year, if not ever; certainly the worst since around 2018 in Dubai when play was called for the day as trees were flying across the fairways on the Friday afternoon.

But as ever there's always one dissenting voice in these things. Now sometimes dissenting voices say sensible things, but this definitely wasn't one of those times. Because this dissenting voice had the temerity, or should that be stupidity, to opine that the wind wasn't actually as bad as the wind at the Irish Open in 1990-whatever. That might have been a fair point had this clown not been a paid-up member of the 'I don't feel safe down there' brigade and sitting at home in Aylesbury (or wherever they live) rather than on-site in Africa. Proof if ever it were needed that sometimes it's better not to type and have everyone think you're objectionable than to type and remove all reasonable doubt.

Not that any of these winds seemed to bother Matthew Baldwin who ended up winning by seven, which is about as close to a stress-free first win out here as you're ever likely to get, and just reward for never giving up after losing his way so spectacularly a few years ago. And a very popular win it was too – mainly because his caddy, who was actually only standing in for the week, is the salt of the earth (despite supporting Liverpool) and the huge irony that had Baldwin's regular caddy bothered coming, his regular boast that 'I'm only doing a few just to get some more money, then I'm quitting' might well have borne fruit. It was also a healthy reminder that if you see a caddy on TV and they're over 40, then they're really, really good. Because Baldwin's caddy is. And is.

Baldwin's caddy was one of the lucky ones though. Because 30-odd other guys ended up going down with stomach issues, with one guy ending up in hospital having a throat cyst operated on. Now in such circumstances no one ever really knows what the cause is, but whatever it was, a lot of guys obviously had it in common. And as they hadn't stayed in the same hotels or eaten in the same places, then the spotlight of suspicion seemed to fall on the water in the unrefrigerated water containers on each tee in Kenya the week before as being the source of whatever bugs or bacteria was causing the mass illness: after all, they are sat in the blazing sun all day.

Being a bit old-school I'm still not sold on this idea of water containers, because at least with a sealed bottle of water (like we used to get on every other tee) I know where it's actually come from. That said, though, this new system of everyone having their own metal bottle and refilling it when they need to does dramatically reduce the number of plastic bottles used each year. And that's probably a good thing in terms of sustainability. Or whatever this month's buzzword is.

Had I anything to do with the European Tour Caddies Association I'd have been tearing the door of the Tour Office off its hinges at another example of being thoughtless when it comes to caddy wellbeing, and politely 'suggesting' they do something about it. But I'm not. And so instead nothing appears to have happened. No one appears to have done anything. And that sadly is not untypical. Anything that requires them to confront the Tour, they shy away from. Any criticism of the Tour on any public forum is stamped on. Any chance of anything getting done – in this case about caddies' health which they rely on to keep working and therefore keep earning – is lost. I call that being in cahoots.

Anyway, if last week was a 'Wish You Were Here?' week, the third one in the African Swing is a 'No, Not Really' week. It's just that Joburg is somewhere we've all been so many times that there's nothing really new about it. It's always a kind of week to hunker down a bit, accept that the power might go off in the middle of the day, and basically be sensible. So don't buy Rolex watches in shops and expect to get back to the hotel with it still on your wrist. Don't wander the streets at night. And don't believe the guy who tells you this cashpoint machine isn't working but the one beside it is.

And definitely don't fall foul of the fake police car scam, which seems to be emerging as the go-to scam of choice on Joburg's roads over the last few years. Basically it involves a fake police car stopping you for some made-up misdemeanour, the policemen in this fake police car holding you up at gunpoint, then driving you round for a few hours rinsing your credit or debit card at the city's cashpoints, before (most of the time) letting you go. All of which actually happened to one unfortunate player a year or so ago: bloody scary and not something I would like to happen to me, or even my worst enemy. But it does explain why no one down here stops for police cars. Well, certainly not in Joburg, you don't.

Anyway, it looks like everyone is staying at Monte Casino again this year, which is where the England rugby team stay when they're on tour in South Africa. And where you remember you only have a few more days of steak and all the sides you could wish for washed down with a healthy glass of South Africa's finest red for less than £15. So that should be safe enough.

And definitely safer than a certain English pro playing on the PGA Tour last week by all accounts, who, if you believe all the messages flying about from my caddy friends, would have been 'knocked the fuck out if he'd talked to me like that on the course in front of the cameras'. Bravado or not, it's a fair point well made. And just as well his current caddy is the epitome of French coolness. And forgiveness.

Not that any of my friends are actually in Steyn City this week, because the entry list isn't exactly stellar if we're honest. But as ever in these weeks, that means there is a stellar opportunity for (and this sounds awful) one of the not-so-well-known players to make themselves very well known in the shape of a win on the DP World Tour, a one-year exemption, entry into all the Rolex events in the summer, and a pretty tidy sum of money.

Mind you, a few of these candidates ended up doing a screeching U-turn on their way to the airport when five under actually made the weekend after looking like, even late on Friday afternoon, that it wouldn't sniff it. At least no one was actually on their flight yet, as did happen a few years ago at The Open when a good few people got off the EDI-LHR flight on Friday night, and got straight back on the return leg.

In true Steyn City style (the course isn't the toughest) it turned into a last-round shoot-out with Nick Bachem turning himself from someone basically no one had ever heard of outside the Tour into someone, as we said before, who is now known as a winner, with an exemption for next year, entry into events he wouldn't have got into on Thursday morning, and a bank account about €250,000 fatter.

Arguably none of which he would have got near but for having another experienced over-40s caddy on the bag. Just like last week. A caddy whose experience came to the fore down the stretch where he left the rest of the field for dead. Just like last week. A caddy who was prepared to make the long trip down to South Africa for these 'lesser events'. Just like last week. Food for thought for players and caddies alike.

And just like that the African Swing is over for another year, and with it the majority of guys' thoughts turn to what to do for the next month before the European season starts in earnest at the start of May.

Me? Well, if I'm honest, I just think avoiding Africa was, on balance, a good thing.

The LIVerdict

My final week of house husbandry and the week of The Masters was also the week of the verdict of the DP World Tour and LIV arbitration hearing – which kind of went exactly how we all thought it would, i.e. on the point being argued, the DP World Tour was being reasonable in not granting those players permission to play in a conflicting event, and that when the guys ignored this and played anyway, they laid themselves open to a fine.

Now all this was pretty clearly set out in the Membership Regulations, which I guess explains why a few of the original plaintiffs pulled out before the arbitration hearing itself. What does seem strange, though, is the lack of rejoicing on social media by the vocal anti-all-things-LIV minority within the playing membership: in stark contrast to their wailings when this first kicked off.

Maybe the stark reality is dawning on them. Because when you read some of the informed commentary within the European golf media, they have spotted the problem here, while the PGA sycophants within the US golf media choose to ignore it because it doesn't affect the Tour over there. And therefore doesn't matter.

And the problem is this: ask any tour caddy to rank the world's tours (for men) in April 2023 and they'll give you pretty much the same answer:

1. The PGA Tour
2. LIV Golf
3. The DP World Tour
4. The Asian Tour

Lil guys get pts on tour

So effectively this means that the DP World Tour is down one place from a year ago, and if the LIV guys go hunting World Ranking points on the Asian Tour, then it's highly likely to drop down another place fairly soon. And that's bad for business. No matter what nonsense gets spouted about the strategic alliance with the PGA Tour. And what do you do about that? Nothing quickly is the obvious answer.

not DP any more

So it's no surprise that the DP World Tour has indicated they're going to take six weeks or so to consider what sanctions to now impose and how to deal with the same problem if and when it happens again. And even less of a surprise is that the end of this six weeks conveniently coincides with the week of the PGA Championship at Oak Hill.

The smart money in the (virtual) Caddy Lounge is therefore already on some form of joint statement from the DP World Tour and PGA Tour that week that talks up the opportunities of their Strategic Alliance, so pandering to the vocal minority of the DP World Tour membership.

Whereas what they really should be doing, at least according to the guys I hang about with, is to slap the guys who brought the case against the DP World Tour on the wrists financially, and then say, 'Fuck it, we're going to invite the top ten players (say) from LIV to play on the DP World Tour after The Open.'

Because a few of these tournaments, like in Northern Ireland, like in Czechia, are the arse end of the schedule, so have poor fields, and are, at best, background viewing in golf clubs up and down the land. And the harsh reality is that they would massively benefit from having some star names playing in them.

It's just that, Mr LIV Golf man, you have to play in these tournaments to get your invite into the bigger events like the Irish Open and Wentworth later in the summer, and these have the World Ranking points that might be handy to you. And all of this would be a sponsor's dream: you get a load of top players at your, frankly second-string, tournaments. For free. What more could you want?

Yes, the vocal minority of DP World Tour players might be pissed off. Yes, the guys at the very bottom of the rankings might be very pissed off at an opportunity to play being taken away. But they're not the ones who will sell extra tickets on the gate, or add viewer numbers. The DP World Tour can afford to take their criticism.

They just need the balls to do it.

The Story of the Week of the ISPS Handa Championship 20–23 April 2023

I suppose it was halfway through my period of enforced house husbandry when I got a text off his manager saying that we're now going to go to Japan: best get your visa sorted.

This went down very well with me; less so with the missus and offspring.

One of the two actually suggested it was nice having me around and couldn't I just skip the trip. I took this to be pretty close to a football manager being told he had the full confidence of the board, so headed straight up to the spare room to search out flight prices and what to do about a visa.

And that's because it's always our responsibility to get ourselves to a venue on time and have somewhere to stay where we can get to the course on time every day: no one else's. And we incur the expense up front. Which is great for my collection of Emirates Skywards and BA Avios points, but little else.

The early signs for both flight and visa were not encouraging. My eyeballs popped out when I saw the price of an LHR-NRT-ICN-LHR round ticket. And then my brain went numb reading what we were being told about the visa for Japan. Maybe I should just stay home after all.

But fortunately, after 20 minutes bemoaning my rookie mistake in believing that when he said a month or so ago that he wasn't going to play that meant he wasn't going to play, and a further 20 minutes on Skyscanner and Google later it was obvious that the impending cloud had a silver lining. Two in fact.

First up I remembered he pays half the flight if it's outside Europe, and that would bring the ticket price down to something almost sensible. And second, that history would suggest that there was a fair chance that as a caddy I wouldn't need anything other than a tourist visa, despite what we were being told.

And that is actually how it all panned out. Because it turned out that it was actually just the players who needed a Japanese 'Entertainment Visa' rather than everyone per se. And they only needed this to enable them to get paid for competing in the tournament. Whereas, because the rest of us caddies, physios, managers, etc. would effectively be paid outside of Japan, we didn't need this expensive visa.

Something that me, and a fair few other guys who'd also smelt a rat, discovered after doing some hard yards and researching what the visa requirements for Japan actually were – simply a normal tourist visa allowing you to conduct something referred to as 'Business Tourism'. Which cost rather less. Too late for those guys who'd blindly accepted the original visa email and forked out way more than they needed to; but at least they'll know for next year.

Anyway, after a few hours in the spare room I've got a return ticket from around Japan, Korea and back to Europe at a sensible price, and have checked all the entry requirements properly. Just as well as Japan appears not to have caught up with the rest of the world yet, and you still need to show evidence of your COVID jabs an arrival, so I've had to reinstall the UK COVID app on my phone as it's a long way to go to get refused entry on arrival.

And it's also just as well I shared the COVID info around some of the guys who I know are also going as those who have yet to be triple-jabbed need a PCR test (remember them?) less than 72 hours before landing. Again, that would have shortened a couple of trips.

It takes a little longer to find anywhere to stay at a half-sensible price. Mainly because the players' hotel is unsurprisingly fully booked, while the one that's been nominated as the caddy hotel for the week appears to be three times the price it is the week after the tournament. And even then the twin rooms look so small that even the most talented of cat swingers would struggle to swing theirs in them, even if their roommate would let them. But eventually I've sorted that too, and we're somewhere decent not far from where the transport to the golf course will leave from. Job done.

So that left me with a couple of weeks' worth of house husbandry to endure (once the flights are booked every tour caddy in the world starts mentally counting down the days, although not out loud in case the wife hears), and we're off again.

And one of those weeks was Masters week so at least there was something decent to watch on TV. And although the back nine of Sunday wasn't exactly enthralling, the best guy won and his words afterwards about his caddy were heartfelt as well as giving you some insight into the value we add out there each and every week. Apart from the days when we couldn't club a seal, obviously.

Masters Sunday also meant that my mental countdown to going back to work in a week's time was well and truly underway, unlike some colleagues who were actually nearly on the start line, having decided to go across early, ostensibly to get over any jet lag, but also to travel around a bit and see some of the sights.

But I'm not joining them, tempting though it is, having not been to Japan since the days of the Dunlop Phoenix tournament. Mainly because after all this time at home, leaving is going to be hard enough on everyone, never mind announcing that you're leaving nearly a week before you actually need to. Even though I think that after 20-odd years together and 20-odd years of me doing this, my missus would have taken it all in her stride. Something for which I am forever grateful. Because it's genuinely not easy being married to a tour caddy.

And then just like that my house husbandry is over for a good few months, and I'm suddenly at Heathrow checking in for the trip over to one of the most amazing countries I have ever visited, or am ever likely to. It's impossible to see and experience everything this country has to offer when you are just there for the week, especially with the effects of an eight-hour time difference that needs to be behind you by Thursday morning. So no doubt at some stage this week I'll be messaging home saying that we'll all have to come out here on holiday when the kids are a bit older to do just that. Before falling fast asleep the minute I get back to the room.

But falling fast asleep seems to do the trick as by Thursday I'm 100 per cent adjusted to the time, unlike a few colleagues who always seem to struggle going west to east. Although to be fair, they've had a right result with it being an hour's journey by bus from the hotel to the golf course, because that allows them more sleeping time. Especially on Thursday and Friday when the first bus to the course leaves at 3.30am.

Once you do get to the course, though, you immediately notice how well everything has been organised. I mean it's not like things aren't well organised each and every week out here, they are; it's just that this week it's noticeably a notch up on a normal week. Everything is in place, everything runs like clockwork, nothing has been left to chance. The smoothness of everything is palpable: and not just because Pelley and Dr Handa from ISPS (the title sponsor of this and a fair few other events on tour) are here. It all points to a real desire to get this event established on the schedule for 2024 onwards: something which is confirmed by the end of the week when I'm writing this. And something which we all very much support, despite the early alarm calls.

And as for the course itself, it's a Nicklaus design, which I'm always a big fan of for some reason, and is just immaculate. Stunningly immaculate, just like Japan itself. The start-of-the-week-caddy-consensus seems to be that it's very scoreable, but only if you've brought your A game, or something approaching it. If you haven't, then the tight tee shots are going to get you at some stage, and if they don't, then the deep bunkers will: both hallmarks of a Nicklaus design. And with grainy grass throughout, if we were betting this week, it would be on a host of the Japanese guys doing well.

First week back after the break and it's obvious from the off that he's also a little off. But he's got enough game to avoid enough trees and bunkers to make the cut, so come Saturday morning it's time to try and get somewhere nearer the leaders who sit at ten under after two days. Only he appears to have not woken up properly after falling asleep on the 4.30am bus to the course on Saturday, and that sets the tone for our weekend.

A weekend that also starts with only one Japanese player lurking in the top ten despite our earlier predictions, and finishes with Lucas Herbert winning in extra time. Due in no small part to his caddy who had everything planned out and figured out in time for him actually arriving in Japan literally just a few hours before teeing it up on Thursday: something he graciously and fulsomely acknowledged afterwards, proving that some weeks the good guys win, but some weeks, like this one, the really, really good guys win. And also that sometimes our predictions are a bit rubbish as only Iwata finishes in the top ten for the home nation.

Anyway, that's it for our first trip to Japan in years. And my, oh my, did it set a high bar in terms of organisation, golf course, off-course sights, sounds and, most of all, food.

No wonder everyone is looking forward to coming back here in 2024, and for a good few years after that: what a country.

And let's hope that this time next week we're saying the same about Korea as that's where we're off to next, for a brand-new event: the Korea Championship presented by Genesis at the Jack Nicklaus Club in Incheon just west of Seoul.

The European Tour Caddies Association (ETCA)

I have long suspected that within the ranks of the powers that be who run the world's professional golf tours there are some who regard professional tour caddies as something of a necessary evil. Not that it was always like this. Actually it was worse. Far worse.

In fact, from what I hear from guys who were out here in the very early days of (what was then) the European Tour, caddies were little more than a bunch of undesirables. And treated as such. Admittedly in some cases this may have been more than deserved, but I suspect this attitude to us has its roots back in the 'rats' label given to the club caddies who worked at some of the golf clubs around Sunningdale and

Wentworth from which many early tour caddies came. Rats being vermin. Which of course we are not.

Now as time went on and the European Tour grew bigger and better, the full-time caddies on tour got together with the aim of getting a better deal for themselves, forming what is now called the European Tour Caddies Association. Or the ETCA for short.

All very laudable and well intentioned. And without doubt caddies on the DP World Tour are now treated far, far better than they were at that time, which is in no small way down to those individuals who over the years have created and organised a unified front with which to go to the Tour with their colleagues' concerns and suggestions.

Less laudable, but well and truly intentional, however, was that the guy who actually set the ETCA up (gaining some notoriety and publicity in so doing) allegedly then helped himself to a fair few thousand of pounds of caddies' money, largely to pay for what appears to have been a prodigious alcohol dependency. Obviously, though, and as always when dumb people do dumb things, he got found out when someone eventually looked at the books, and realised that they'd been well and truly cooked.

Now usually in a situation like this in the real world, you would be talking police, lawyers, court and he who perpetrated the fraud ending up in jail, hopefully in the same cell as someone with a pathological hatred of petty fraudsters, and an insatiable desire to roger them at every chance he got. But ours isn't the real world, and instead he was just asked to pay the money back with no more being said. And had he lived to approximately 357, he might well have done so.

But that was a long time ago now. The ETCA survived. And continues to do a great job liaising with the DP World Tour for things like our yearly accreditation, caddy hotels and transport, as well as things like day-to-day tournament updates. And while, since COVID, a lot of this information now comes direct to us from the Tour's Portal app, caddies' accreditation badges for the year still come through the ETCA, which is reason enough in itself to be a member.

The ETCA is run by the ETCA Committee, or 'The Committee' as it's known out here. This is a group of colleagues who give up their time to try and make things easier for the rest of us: looking after things like our accreditation, organising caddy transport and caddy hotels, and talking to the Tour about things that impact on our lives out here. They might not always get it right. But they do a great job. Not that that seems to stop a vocal minority (who it has to be said are predominantly UK-based and 'of a certain age') trying to find fault with them at each and every turn. Which is frankly a bit churlish. And unnecessary.

Personally I'm not sure I could ever be bothered with being on the receiving end of any of that, so I'm 'in the background' on this one: grateful to those colleagues who put themselves out, but in absolutely no rush to join them.

Not that there's a lot of rushing to join the ETCA itself these days either. To the extent that guys can join immediately they come out on tour rather than having to caddy a certain number of tournaments before being eligible to join as was the case up until very recently. Hopefully that will help boost our numbers, but from what I'm hearing from a few of the younger guys, this might not actually work.

And it's really down to the fact that the younger guys coming out to caddy are just much less likely to want to be a member of any representative organisation than, say, guys of my age, which I totally understand. They are, dare I say it, more 'educated' than some of us veterans, and see the wood from the trees rather more easily than we might, having been in the metaphorical golf course woods so often for so long. For example, and again I've heard this said on a number of occasions when the subject has come up, they are really concerned about their names being on a membership list of any type. Full stop. Or their personal details being held somewhere where they could potentially be shared or, worse still, studied. Like by His Majesty's Revenue and Customs, for example.

Because it is true, and I hadn't really twigged this until recently, that if someone high up in HMRC was to be watching the golf one Sunday afternoon and started thinking, 'I wonder …', the ETCA might subsequently be required to submit its membership list to HMRC, resulting in every UK-based caddy on that list being investigated, which has happened before, albeit not en masse.

Now this wouldn't be an issue for me. I have an accountant. And a very good one at that. Meaning that in addition to not paying a penny more in tax than I need to, I'm also squeaky clean. But for Silly Bollocks over there, for example, who is very open about the fact he hasn't paid tax in years, well, he's getting invited in for a 'chat', and when they find out that he's actually been telling the truth about not paying tax for years, and hasn't the money to pay the fine, he could end up swapping his ETCA membership for membership of D wing at HMP Golf and Country Club. At which point that £50 ETCA subscription doesn't look like a sensible investment.

And this is not me going off on some conspiracy-theory tangent. This is actually what might well have happened to a colleague a good few years ago had his then player not stepped in and paid his then caddy's outstanding tax bill. And it wasn't just a few hundred pounds.

The trouble is that these days we're all much more visible out here due to the wall-to-wall TV coverage and social media, so if you're on a list somewhere, or on someone's radar, it definitely pays to have a good accountant.

It's just that no accountant I've ever dealt with is ever going to let you get away with putting a receipt through on your expenses from AllAboutCoffee.net, which is what the annual uplift to the very basic annual travel insurance from the ETCA comes through as being from. Although to be fair, this is a gripe from ETCA members rather than those who aren't joining in the first place.

I'm also pretty sure, though, that some of the original incarnations of the ETCA Committee wouldn't have countenanced things like this being offered to us. And certainly not without knowing who was actually behind the company, or knowing who exactly was making exactly what from the deal – which, by the way, is carefully hidden from public view. Because they were a different breed. To the extent that the (then) European Tour openly admitted that their annual meeting with the ETCA was always 'difficult', mainly I suspect because they were facing off against tour caddies who had some backbone. And rarely took no for an answer. Maybe we need them back. And their transparency.

Because with some of the things that would benefit every caddy out here (irrespective of whether they're an ETCA member or not), but are going to require some pretty steely negotiations with the Tour before they do, we kind of need these old-school guys. Without them, I suspect those negotiations will be more of a meek agreement, and from a tour caddy perspective, a case of what might have been. Like those around finally delivering a single title sponsor for us all: after all we are walking advertising boards, and the PGA Tour caddies got themselves a broadly similar arrangement a lot of years ago now. And like ensuring that we actually get paid a proper fee for completing the stats cards on those weeks when we're still required to: one that ends up being a percentage of the annual revenues they help generate, and not just a measly few pounds per round. Caddy Lounge bravado, of which I hear plenty, isn't going to cut it here.

In fact what we (and admittedly by 'we' I mean we, the silent, even lazy, majority) need is guys leading the ETCA who aren't in it for a misguided sense of power and importance, which, someone recently pointed out, a good few of the current ETCA Committee certainly give the impression they are. For them it's all about that strut into the Caddy Lounge or on to the bus home, when they see (or think they see) all the younger caddies thinking oooh there's so-and-so the secretary, or there's so-and-so the ETCA whatever: something that they would absolutely never get in a real job in the real world. And once you see it, you can't unsee it. And then you also suddenly realise they're also really on the ETCA Committee to get first sight of any jobs that come up. Because until recently, player managers always went through the ETCA when their clients were looking for a new caddy; until of course they started realising that not everyone who applied for these bags actually got their names put forward and that their players were being conned. No wonder they now increasingly use trusted independents or just go to caddies face to face.

Where I do think the ETCA is right, though, is to take offence to being criticised in various WhatsApp message groups, and beyond, by those caddies who have chosen not to be members. And call them out on it. Because as full-time caddies we need to look united if we're to keep changing things for the better out here. And in late spring 2023 the vehicle for this is the ETCA. And only the ETCA.

And while, like I say, I may wish that this was done slightly more forcefully at times, and by slightly more well-intentioned people, until I'm prepared to do something about that (and I'm not), then arguably I should keep shtum too.

The Story of the Week of the Korea Championship Presented By Genesis 27–30 April 2023

Sunday night is flight night. So we all pile to the airport straight from the golf course in Japan for what, to the untrained eye, must look like a DP World Tour charter flight up to Incheon in South Korea.

Golfers and caddies on a flight after a good couple of hours' wait in an airport: what could possibly go wrong? Actually, on this occasion, the answer is very little. No one put their bag on the luggage belt and scanned the tag that was in their hand not attached to the bag (bye, bye bag, never to be seen again). No one got left behind. No one got refused on to the plane. No one was too loud once they were on it. No one refused to get off at the end. No one got off at the end but didn't have a visa. Oh, was it always this way on Sunday-night flights between venues. And that's just the players.

It's also not like anyone is saving themselves for a big Sunday night out in downtown Incheon either. By the time we get through immigration, our bags off, find a Kakao T (Korea's equivalent of Uber) and get to the hotel, it's nearly midnight, and with his 'I'll meet you up there around 11' still ringing in my ears, I know from bitter experience that bed is the only sensible option. So I take it, knowing that I'll still feel shattered in the morning, but way less so than had I succumbed to (much younger) peer pressure and wandered out for 'a few beers'.

And even then it's not great having to drag myself out of bed early Monday so as I at least get to walk nine holes before he gets there. Hopefully these will be the nine he actually chooses to play today.

They say first impressions are everything. And so, as an unashamed fan of Nicklaus courses, mine is that this one is really good. Even though I'd have frankly rather been tucked up in bed back at the hotel, which, by the way, is superb and, in stark contrast to last week, only five to ten minutes away from the course, so shortening everyone's week considerably.

When I say the course is good though, I'm mainly thinking good in terms of its layout, because April in Korea is maybe a little early for it to be at its very best, condition-wise, but it's still more than decent. Risk-reward holes abound, and as it's a Nicklaus course, it goes without saying that the greens are slopey, have plenty of tiers and are defended by deep run-off areas.

But the course has one other defence up its sleeve: the weather or, rather, the wind. Because while we walked the course on Monday in lovely temperatures with the wind off the Yellow Sea to the west, by the time we got to the Wednesday pro-am (or divot-watching day, depending on your ranking), the wind had switched to the north. Or to be more accurate, from Siberia – which meant it was on with every layer as you had to try and keep warm in the kind of dry, frigid, bitter cold we don't often get in Europe. After their pro-am round, a colleague described it, through chattering teeth while clutching a cup of tea in each hand to try and get some feeling back in them, as, 'Horrific, man. Worse than being on the range at Carnoustie at the Dunhill,' and he wasn't wrong as, apologies to the range at Carnoustie at the Dunhill, but you just lost your title as the coldest place on tour. Albeit just until October time when we'll no doubt be back to saying, 'It's colder here than Korea,' while shivering on the range at Carnoustie at the Dunhill. And this wind is forecast to return at the weekend, possibly with rain, so that'll be a joy if we make the cut.

Yes, one thing for sure, it'll be a proper player who wins, and probably a European one, because, to use the slightly less-than-PC phrase we all give to tracks like this one, it's a 'big boys' golf course'. Short hitters need not apply.

Anyway, we walk nine on Monday morning then retire to the excellent Caddy Lounge, where lunch is absolutely top-notch like last week, then have a mosey around all the photos and memorabilia from the Presidents Cup, which was played here in 2015. All the while reminding ourselves that the only two team events in professional golf that actually matter are the Ryder Cup and the Solheim Cup. That, and that none of us could afford to be a member here, with a $1m debenture required just to get through the members' locker-room door.

The odd thing about this Monday is we're the only professional caddies walking the course: our colleagues who work on the KPGA Tour are bound by some very different rules set by that tour. For example, their pro-am day is a Tuesday with Wednesday being the official practice day (the opposite way round to most other tours), and while professional caddies are allowed to walk the course early on the Wednesday, they are not allowed on the course when their player plays their practice round, nor are they allowed on the course during the pro-am (club cleaning and so on is done by a small army of local lady caddies). And yet, they still get around the same money as we do, for only working four days a week, while playing for only slightly less prize money than a 'normal' DP World Tour event.

From a caddy perspective, what's not to like there?! Money-wise, nothing; lifestyle-wise, quite a lot actually: as, although food and accommodation are cheap and you travel everywhere by train (also cheap), it does make Monday to Thursdays 'challenging' if you don't like your own company, especially if you're European or African and don't speak the language.

Off the course, though, this week is already looking like a way more sociable one than last week. Mainly because everyone has now adjusted to the +8-hour time difference, and so is now out for dinner after work rather than being out for the count.

All of which has allowed us to have proper catch-ups with some of the caddy fraternity out here who we've not seen for a couple of years now, thanks to COVID. And with there being plenty of fantastic restaurants close to the hotel, and no hour-long trip to the golf course the morning after, there have been some fairly 'substantial' catch-ups.

I'm guilty of one of these early in the week, which just reminds me of how tired I actually am all of a sudden. Something which is not going to be helped by the biting energy-sapping wind forecast for later in the week: another example of how the lifestyle of a tour caddy can sometimes sound very glamorous, whereas the reality is sometimes very different.

Because as well as feeling tired, you just feel all out of sync on weeks like these two. It's even mundane things like there being no Champions League or Premier League on the TV at night because of the time difference, which seems to make the time off the course pass slower; while some guys haven't been able to talk to their young kids for a week: when we're getting up, they're in bed; when they get up, we're at work; and when we finish work, they're at school. Which can't be easy. For him, the kids or his wife. Thankfully mine are all used to it by now, and don't seem to care. Or at least that's what they say.

The other off-course highlight this week was the Caddy Championship put on by the DP World Tour. Thankfully, on a simulator. Inside a nice, warm building. And complete with proper signage. And sponsorship. All of which meant that a fun time was had by all, especially the guy who won with a pretty decent under-par score. And I know we occasionally whinge about the Tour doing this or forgetting to do that, but we're sometimes equally as guilty of forgetting that they do stuff like this for us; in this case right in the middle of their day job of actually running a $2,000,000 golf tournament. They really don't have to, but they do. And we all appreciate it enormously.

But on the proper course in the proper tournament it was Larrazábal who won with a pretty decent five under in the cold and wind on Sunday, to win for the eighth time on tour. And the fourth or fifth with his current caddy, making them everyone's favourite Spanish team. His winner's speech was a classic, very obviously dropping the word 'Callaway' in at every opportunity as that secures him a sizeable bonus from Callaway for doing so. We all knew he was going to do it, but it was still funny when he did.

That only leaves us to say that although these two weeks out here in the Far East have been absolutely fantastic, there's not a single caddy who's not headed back to ICN for the ball-ache of a minimum 14-hour (ours is nearer 24) journey back to Europe (generally Rome or London) with something of a spring in their step.

Why? Because the European season proper is about to start. And for us that means it's Destinazione Roma.

Tournaments Don't Just Happen

Golf tournaments don't just happen. Although as tour caddies, if we didn't know any better, we could be forgiven for thinking that they do: all we do is show up on a Monday morning fresh from the previous week's venue, and magically everything at that venue is there ready for us.

But for that to happen requires an unbelievable amount of work to have been done in the weeks leading up to whichever tournament it is: most of it completely unseen by us tour caddies and players alike, not to mention the spectators who show up Thursday morning to watch the opening round every week.

And literally all that work is coordinated out of Wentworth which, as well as being the venue for the BMW PGA Championship each September, is also the DP World Tour's official home. And has been ever since the inception of the European Tour in the early 1970s.

But whereas the first original schedule was just a handful of tournaments so presumably relatively simple to organise and run, today's global schedule of nearly 40 tournaments in 26 different countries is anything but simple. Yet it's still all done out of the unassuming offices that sit at the back of the main Wentworth clubhouse and to the left-hand side of the range that you might be standing behind if you are coming to watch the BMW PGA Championship later this year. You'd actually be forgiven for not even knowing they are there.

But it's from this pretty tiny footprint that the entire DP World Tour operation is run. And something that we tour caddies occasionally forget when we're raging because the bus to the caddy hotel is ten minutes late, or any other of the myriad of first-world problems we encounter from week to week out here. Because what the Tour actually does is in fact nothing short of remarkable.

And while it's true that managing the set up of the tournament infrastructure such as hospitality units and spectator grandstands is the responsibility of the tournament promoter, basically everything else to do with the tournament each week is the responsibility of that week's Tournament Director, or TD for short.

They are basically 'in charge' on-site that week. The buck stops with them. And that buck can involve tricky things like, for example, being the public face of the Tour when, say, a high-profile player is DQd, deciding exactly when to suspend play and when to restart it, explaining difficult calls in such situations to the media, right through to managing sponsors' and promoters' expectations when, on the rare occasion, a tournament has to be shortened to three days.

Although, to be fair, most of the time they are 'just' in the background making sure everything runs smoothly, and on a good week basically the only time you ever see them will be in the background at the presentation ceremony on Sunday afternoon. But without them, there 'just' wouldn't be a Sunday afternoon.

For example, last week's tournament in Korea might well have been halfway round the world from the office of the TD that week in Wentworth, and the tournament itself is significantly smaller in scale than Wentworth will host later in the year, but basically the same things have to happen every week for the tournament to even start on time on Thursday morning. First off, fairly obviously, the tournament requires players. And any player with a status on tour can enter any DP

World Tour event, but whether they actually end up teeing it up in that tournament is another matter. Because that is determined by their position on something called the Entry List, which you can see as a tab on the week's tournament feed on the DP World Tour's website. Everyone above the cut-off point for that week in the Entry List gets to play; everyone below it doesn't.

And for what's referred to as a 'full field' event, this cut-off point comes after the 156th eligible player who has entered; while for tournaments impacted by the amount of daylight available (like in the early-season events in the Middle East and the autumn events in the UK) this cut-off point may vary from 144 to 126.

Now, where a player actually sits on the Entry List basically depends on how well he's played in the past on tour. So Category 1 for example is for guys who have won majors or the Race to Dubai rankings; Category 2 is for guys who have won WGC events or Rolex events; winners of tournaments in the last three years with elevated prize funds slot in after this; followed by winners of tournaments with lower prize funds in the last two years; Category 10 (the largest category) is for guys who finished in the top 110 in the Race to Dubai the previous year (or whatever the cut-off point is as this number does vary from year to year, for reasons that are too complicated to go into here); and after that comes a Medical Extension and Legends category, followed by the top 20 on the Challenge Tour last year in Category 14, with guys who got their cards through the previous year's Qualifying School making up the fairly low Category 17. So fairly obviously, the lower your category, the less tournaments you play. And the less tournaments you play means the less likely you are to make enough points to get into Category 10 for next season. Again, who ever said golf was meant to be fair?

Interestingly enough, on the DP World Tour, players actually have to pay an entry fee each week: much to the consternation of anyone coming over from the PGA Tour, where you don't. And you also get to pay a fine if you withdraw within a certain number of days before a tournament starts, which the last time I heard was a good few hundred euros.

Fortunately for the TD, all of this is managed by the Entries Department, which is itself housed deep in the bowels of the Tour's offices in Wentworth. So one less thing to worry about.

Next the players need a golf course to play on. Its conditioning has typically been worked on for a good few months before even the TD gets there the week prior to the tournament week, usually in conjunction with the DP World Tour's own agronomy team. And generally, unless the weather has really not played ball, every course we play on is in great condition. But the way that course is then set up for the tournament itself is all down to the TD and his team of referees.

The 'set-up' is the general term given to how the Tour, well, set the golf course up for the tournament. And that includes things like the height of the rough, where that rough is in relation to the fairways, whether any of the tees are, or might be, moved up in one or more of the rounds, and where the pins are positioned in each of the tournament rounds.

Additionally the team of referees any given week will, along with the TD, assess where the drop zones will be located, where the hazard lines will be (no one I know out here calls them Penalty Areas yet), what colours those hazard lines should be, whether any areas of the course should be deemed GUR (ground under repair), and whether the weather or course condition means that Preferred Lies need to be played. And if they are, then what length they should be set to.

Day-to-day set-up on the tournament days is devolved, under the watchful eye of that week's TD, to two of the Tour's full-time referees: one does the front nine, and the other does the back nine.

And while ultimately the set-up is down to them, it's relatively common for either players or caddies on the practice and pro-am days to highlight to the TD or referees possible areas of concern for things like potential rulings, where hazard lines actually start and end, etc., so saving them time and hassle during the tournament. And proving that there are actually times when tour caddies do make the lives of the Tour staff easier, rather than the other way round.

Not that the course set-up always goes according to plan. There have been occasions where the TD has decided, with all the best intentions, to take Thursday and Friday's preferred lies off on the Saturday, only to have to put them back on again for the Sunday after asking for 'feedback' from players and caddies after their rounds. Because no one ever gets everything right all of the time, not even tour caddies.

Now generally before the tournament starts the Tour knows where the pins will be on all four tournament days, or rather where they intend having the pins. But fairly obviously there are days when Mother Nature intervenes, for example the original idea of having a right pin tight to the water isn't such a good idea now the forecast is for the wind to be blowing at 25kph, wind off the left. Or when it's due to rain heavily so having that pin in the little bowl on the front-left corner also isn't a good idea. So some weeks pin positions get changed during the morning set-up (done long before anyone gets to the 1st tee that day), we get issued with a revised pin sheet, and the commentators end up referring to their being a 'new pin position' on this hole.

A good TD always listens to the players; in fact they actively go out to get their feedback. So again using the Tour's flagship event at Wentworth as an example, the players' feedback from recent editions of the tournament seems to have been that they'd like the rough much thicker to put more of a premium on accuracy, so expect there to be thick rough only just off the fairways when we get there. And with there being traditional bottlenecks on the West Course on holes like the 4th, 12th and 18th, expect those tees, certainly in the first two rounds, to be 50 yards up to try and alleviate some of the delays typically experienced round there; while the pin positions on those bottleneck holes will also likely be set in the flatter spots on the greens, again just to try and speed things up.

And overall I think this year of all years, up to now there's been pretty unanimous praise from players and caddies alike at how the Tour has been setting the courses up, especially when it comes to the slightly tighter and trickier pin positions we've been seeing.

So with the players present and correct, and a tournament-ready course, the tournament can start: again all under the watchful eye of the TD. And with any luck the only time we'll really see him again that week is when he's in the scoring tent on Sunday, suited and booted, and thrusting the pre-written winner's speech into their hand just before the prize giving. Yes, sorry to disappoint but the winner is just reading out what he's been told to say. Apart obviously from the bit where he mentions his equipment supplier's name. Which he does because he knows that nets him a hefty bonus payment from that supplier, on the basis that a lot of people will now go out and buy the clubs he's using in the hope that their game will magically improve. Which of course it won't.

After that all that's left for the TD to do is to presumably sit down with something cold and refreshing if it's been a stress-free week. Or in a dark room just gently rocking in the corner if it hasn't been. But either way knowing that in a few weeks' time they get to do it all again.

But finally it's worth remembering that while they're doing this on the DP World Tour, there are other TDs doing the same on the other tours run out of Wentworth. So alongside the BMW PGA Championship in September for example, there is the Open de Portugal on the Challenge Tour and the

WINSTONgolf Senior Open in Germany on the Legends Tour: both of whom will also have their own Tournament Directors. With pretty much the same responsibilities and workload. And so you begin to get a sense of the scale of the DP World Tour operation.

No. That golf tournament you're watching definitely didn't 'just happen'.

Chapter 5

Europe in the Springtime

The Story of the Week of the DS Automobiles Italian Open 4–7 May 2023

In the 27 torturous hours since we all left the course in Incheon, I've flown a total of 6,397 miles, crossed seven time zones, been home (very briefly), consumed enough sleeping pills to put a glass eye to sleep, and at various stages sworn blind that I'm never doing this again.

But finally, finally, finally, we're back in mainland Europe for the first time this season.

And that means it's Airbnb season for a lot of us: a huge change from when I first shouldered a tour bag when we basically used to arrive in the nearest town to the golf course, and two people would guard everyone's luggage, while everyone else fanned out and tried to find a suitable hotel or hotels for the week, and even from ten years ago when the default option was the official caddy hotel for that week.

So this week we avoid the hotels situated to the north of Rome, on the basis that they're (a) expensive, (b) just that little bit too far out of the centre of Rome to be able to go there at night, and (c) an equally fair distance away from the golf course itself, and Airbnb it in a lovely big apartment in an equally lovely small village.

All of which makes a huge and very welcome change from the monotony of the hotels we've been predominantly staying in so far this season. And while they absolutely serve their purpose in the likes of the Middle East and the Far East where the language barrier makes it virtually impossible to communicate with the likes of an Airbnb owner, they do mean that more often than you'd like you're in the same bar and restaurant as people you'd rather not be anywhere near, watching them do the things that people you'd rather not be anywhere near tend to do after they've had one too many, like in Ras Al Khaimah. And although there's something deeply satisfying about watching people you'd rather not be anywhere near get the comeuppance like they did that day, personally I'd rather just not be anywhere near them in the first place. A thoroughly repugnant little individual.

Even allowing for this, our journey from one continent to another and from one culture to another is really only complete once we all walk into the local bar around the corner from where we're staying. Because there is football on the TV, there is fantastic food on the table, even better wine in the glass, and a whole bunch of (what to me are now) kids looking like a cross between some boy band and an inner-city gangsta sat drinking very expensive Barolo wine. Or civilisation as it's also known. Sometimes it's just good to be 'home'.

Although less good was waking up at 4am on Tuesday morning for a meeting with Mr Jet Lag like I did. But on the bright side, or very light side, that did give me time to catch up on inputting his stats from last weekend in Korea, before heading to the course to walk around as the sun was starting to rise and long before he got there for a practice round.

And it was just as well I did walk the course rather than just relying on what I'd seen last year. Because back then I think it's fair to say that none of us were impressed: although one caddy's social media post saying that it was a 'Shocking design, shocking area, shocking traffic around, shocking clubhouse, shocking locker rooms … That's it.

Shocking overall to have the next Ryder Cup here' was maybe a little OTT.

This year, however, it's a bit of a different story. Because while it's still relatively early in the year in the northern hemisphere, they've done a great job with the conditioning and set-up, especially when you take into account that most of the fertilisers used on golf courses around the world are actually banned in Italy: as if a greenkeeper's job isn't hard enough in the first place. The rough has all been thickened, graded and really brought out in places; virtually every fairway bunker has been deepened and their lips raised, making them proper hazards and meaning the 5-iron you could clip out last year isn't happening this year, and a fair few holes have been lengthened or shortened to make them driveable. In both cases this is designed in conjunction with Dodo Molinari's StatisticGolf programme to effectively take wedges out of the hands of the Americans in the Ryder Cup, removing what is one of their key advantages over the Europeans.

Added to this, a bit of the Ryder Cup infrastructure is already in place on the course; for example the 1st tee has most of its 5,000-seat grandstand already positioned there, and while it certainly won't be full this week, it does add to the atmosphere of the tournament. The hospitality units are also all pretty much in place; the other grandstands dotted about add even more definition to the amphitheatre-type holes out there, and obviously you still get to see the Vatican and the Seven Hills of Rome as a backdrop.

It's just a shame that there aren't many of the world's best players here to see them this week, although given that it's the Wells Fargo at Quail Hollow over on the PGA Tour and they're playing for $20m, that's not too hard to understand. But what, at least for me, is hard to understand is how a DP World Tour player gets a release to play on the PGA Tour this week, but wouldn't get one to play on LIV: because to me that has more than a faint whiff of double standards about it. Or maybe even player power. That said, most of the top European guys did play here last year so at least they will have had some sight of the place before this September.

Reverberating around the Caddy Lounge on Thursday, though, was the word 'brutal'. And not because all the hills make it a bloody long way round this course. No, the consensus was that the set-up was definitely a Ryder Cup week trial with the rough eating balls for breakfast, making even the supposed 'easier' holes tricky if you missed the fairway – which my man did too frequently for anyone's liking, let alone his, and requiring one fairly hefty 'sorry if you heard any bad language' apology from the TV commentators. Enough said.

Not that he was the only one. Because as the course dried out after the rain early in the week and the wind got a bit more blustery, it got more and more tricky, and the swearing count seemed to rise accordingly. In fact, any day you shot under par you moved up. And that is the hallmark of a difficult golf course and a great set-up.

Moving up on Saturday was Langasque with a course record 62, making it an all-French last group on Sunday. It was just that Meronk's two-under Sunday was enough to move him to a one-shot win, a fair few hundred grand, and what's got to be the shittiest little trophy for such a big event.

But really they should have awarded a trophy to the knees of every caddy who managed 72 holes round there this week. Because by Sunday afternoon mine were shot, but safe in the knowledge that if my man gets a shot at playing here in the Ryder Cup come September, they know what's in store for them.

But let me tell you one thing: their owner won't care.

What You Hear on TV

TV loves to try and capture what caddies and players talk about. Whether that's over the shot or between shots. Thankfully in my experience they only broadcast the former.

Because some of the stuff me and him talk about between shots would get us both banned from tour, especially in these days where people seem to be actively looking out for things to be offended by.

So like I say, while there's no caddy on this planet who will reveal what they talk about with their player between the tee and the fairway and the fairway and the green, what isn't a secret is what we talk about over the shot.

First up, fairly obviously the player wants to know how far it is. This involves us first pacing off the distance between his ball and the nearest marked spot in the yardage book, which may be a spot painted in the middle of the fairway; a run-out, again marked on the side of the fairway; a bunker; a hazard; a tree: you get the drift. That will allow us to calculate the yardage to the front of the green, and then to the pin itself using the pin sheets that are produced for each round showing, unsurprisingly, where the pins are located on each green.

And as an aside, these have two columns: one showing the number of yards on the green the pin is, and a second showing the number of yards the pin is from the nearest edge of the green. So 13/3R means the pin is 13 yards on the green, and three yards from the right edge; while 13/3L would mean the pin is 13 yards on and three from the left edge.

While I'm doing this I'm also calculating any other numbers he might need, such as how many yards there are between the pin and the back of the green, how much room he has on both sides of the pin (one is obvious, one is not), and how many yards there are to the top and bottom of any significant slopes on the green.

Additionally I'll already have worked out the night before where we ought to be trying to pitch the ball on this green from the fairway; where we absolutely do not want to end up; and where the best miss is, i.e. if we do miss this green (or any shot in fact), where offers the best chance of getting the ball up and down. Just in case he asks.

And at this stage is normally when the commentators say 'let's listen in to their conversation' and you get to hear something along the lines of:

Player: What we got?

Caddy: Four off red. 178. Up three. That's 181 front. 13 on. 194 flag.

Literal translation: We're four yards behind the red spot. That makes it 178 yards to the front of the green. It's three yards uphill to the green. So that makes it 181 yards to the front of the green. The pin is 13 yards on the green. So the total yardage is 194 yards.

Player: Wind?

Caddy: Off the right and in. Two o'clock.

Literal translation: It's wind into you slightly off the right.

Player: So it's playing?

Caddy: 194 playing 199.

Literal translation: The wind that is into and slightly off your right is going to make this shot play five yards longer than it would if there was no wind. So it's half a club more. As it has been on every hole this afternoon, and we're on the 15th, you do know that, don't you?

Player: Where are we pitching this?

Caddy: It's 185 over the corner so pitching 188.

Literal translation: You need to hit this at least 185 yards or else it doesn't get over the false front. So you need to pitch this a minimum of 188 yards.

That's here. See. Look at my yardage book here.
It's marked with a big P.

Player: What have I got behind it?

Caddy: 13 behind. 207 back edge.

Literal translation: There's plenty of room behind
this flag so long is okay.

When I first started caddying I freely admit I marvelled at
how the experienced guys had all this information to hand
without seemingly having to look again at their yardage book.
And a bit of me still does. You only get that through real
experience. And that comes with years of caddying.

Now hopefully in this imaginary situation we have added
when we should have added, and subtracted when we should
have subtracted: otherwise you end up with what is commonly
referred to on tour as 'a mystery'.

A mystery is where a player hits what he thinks is a perfect
shot only for it to finish either long or short of its intended
target because the yardage he's been given – by the caddy – is
wrong. Often so wrong that it's frankly a mystery how the
caddy came up with that number in the first place: hence the
title 'mystery'. Too many mysteries and it's no mystery why
you got fired.

But let's assume you've done all your numbers correctly,
and that we're agreed that it's 194 pin playing 199. Now I
always reckon that armed with information a tour player's
hand is already somewhere near the top of the bag ready to
pull the club out. At which point he may go, 'Six gets there,
doesn't it?' Basically looking for confirmation that his 6-iron
is getting there, i.e. it's the right club.

If you think it does and it is, then that's fine. But if you
think otherwise, you need to have the balls to say so – and
bear in mind that there could be a huge amount of money
riding on that shot – because you might not be right. And

even if you are right, you disagreeing might put doubt in the player's mind for which you'll get the blame if he whiffs it. Believe me, there are times when the latter is not easy and absolutely not for the faint-hearted.

But the very best caddies aren't faint-hearted, and whether it's on the first hole on Thursday or the 72nd hole on Sunday with €1m on the line, they 100 per cent trust their judgement, they say what they think and they aren't afraid to be wrong. And it's this kind of quiet but total surety and confidence that filters through to their players, allowing them to commit 100 per cent to the shot. We're all great caddies out here, but like in, say, football, there are some guys who make what is hard look ridiculously easy. And they're a joy to watch.

But I do think that no matter how long you have been caddying out here, the times when you disagree with what he's thinking of doing, you tell him he's wrong, he listens, ends up taking your advice, and the ball ends up next to the hole, or simply just dry, are still very satisfying. And if he grunts something along the lines of 'good club' or 'glad I listened' afterwards then so much the better. Even though it's what we're actually out there to do.

Whereas an incredulous bog-eyed 'how the fuck did you know it was that?' is code for I'm really, really, really glad I listened. And usually that's the time when the club you've insisted that he hit (to the point of walking away with the bag) lands five yards on dry land, instead of 15 yards short of it like the one he wanted to hit would have done.

And to this day, that is still the best club I ever pulled. Mainly because it kept him his card.

The Story of the Week of the Soudal Open in Antwerp 11–14 May 2023

If you thought the Entry List was a little light on 'big names' last week, then spare a thought for Soudal, whose event is the week before the US PGA Championship. Because only two out of the top 100 in the world are here in Belgium.

That, unfortunately, is the harsh reality for these events in the early season in Europe: they simply cannot compete with the likes of the Wells Fargo (last week) and the Byron Nelson (this week) in terms of attracting the top players, especially the week before a major. Which must be soul-destroying for the sponsors, not to mention poor business.

But at least they've managed to fill the field this week, albeit the Entry List has gone all the way down to Category 19, which is the category for those guys who finished between 134 and 155 on the main tour rankings last year, alternated with those guys who finished between 31 and 45 on the Challenge Tour rankings last year.

But a start on the main tour is a start on the main tour, and with it comes the chance for these lower-ranked players, all of whom are, by the way, bloody good players in their own right, just not as good as the ones who aren't playing, a chance to maybe have that career-changing week that means they too can skip this week next year as they prepare for the US PGA. It's happened before. Whether it happens this week remains to be seen.

But whether it was entirely necessary for a particularly cynical colleague to sound off to anyone who'd listen this morning that 'the starter on the 1st tee had better have a good microphone, otherwise you'll not hear him for the noise of barrels being scraped' also remains to be seen.

Anyway, where are we this week? Well, for starters, we're in another nice Airbnb around 10km away from Rinkven Golf Club, which seems to now be the permanent home for this event.

We'd chosen this Airbnb carefully knowing that Monday was likely to be a day off. And a much-needed one at that after three weeks without one, although to be fair that's not unusual for a tour caddy. Mind you, I could think of better ways to spend one than hunched over my MacBook sorting out flights and accommodation in line with his newly revised schedule, doing laundry and, hardest of all, looking for a place to get a haircut (which in a foreign country can be a challenge, risky, and doesn't always go according to plan), like I had to. All of this was made easier as our Airbnb had good Wi-Fi, a washing machine and a dryer, and was less than a par five away from an English-speaking barber, rather easier than it might have been had we chosen to stay in one of the hotels on offer. Missions accomplished, before you knew it we were all back at it Tuesday morning, heading up to the course at silly o'clock in the peeing rain to get the course walked before he got there at lunchtime.

The course itself is pretty short by modern standards, measuring just less than 7,000 yards, making it a very welcome change from the type of 'bombers' tracks that we tend to see more and more these days. And meaning that strategy (which we can help with) and straight hitting (which we can't help with) will be the order of the day. So a few guys had better be practising the 50-yard pitch out sideways that can't get above waist height between now and Thursday morning, else that Friday night plane home beckons. That we know already.

The other thing that walking the course allowed us to do was, for what seems like the 37th week in a row, have a right laugh about the latest Sunday night Twitter spat between golfers or, in this case, golfer and TV presenter. Surprisingly, though, it doesn't look like alcohol played any part in this one, which is also surprising in its own right. But unsurprisingly, it's about LIV. And even more unsurprisingly, once again the vitriol and lack of objectivity seems to be coming from one side, not the other.

And for all the endless (arguably sycophantic) words typed, this, and every other DP World Tour v LIV argument, ultimately boils down to one thing. And one thing only. Ultimately what every golf fan (and that includes some, though not all, tour caddies) wants is to see the best players in the world play against each other as often as possible. And in 2023, as close as you get to that is the PGA Tour and the four majors.

After that, I'd argue, comes watching guys who used to be amongst the best playing against guys who also used to be amongst the best, with a few guys who could rightly claim to still be amongst the best thrown in for good measure. And that's currently LIV Golf.

In third place, comes watching golf where few people have any real interest or connection with the guys they're watching: they just watch it because it's on TV, and they like watching golf. And that's basically, certainly outside the Rolex events, the DP World Tour.

All of which has led to this (our) tour being labelled a 'feeder tour': a term that a lot of people, especially it would seem Keith Pelley, really, really don't like. Mainly because it's designed to be evocative and dismissive in equal measure. Our suggestion to bring the curtain down on this one was dreamt up while we walked the course this morning (somewhere between the tee and green of the par-five 17th to be precise), and was that maybe the term 'stepping stone' might be less inflammatory as well as being spot on, especially given that top ten on the Race to Dubai rankings next year will step through the stone door marked 'PGA Tour'. Mind you, this would give us less to talk about when we walk the course on a Monday, or a Tuesday as it is this week, so maybe that's a poor idea.

What we were talking about come the weekend, though, wasn't that the caddy facilities and food this week were light years better than they have been in previous years when we've been herded away in what could actually pass for a farmer's shed and fed accordingly, but whether Forsström could hold on to his slender one-shot lead, which he did with a bit of help from the rest of the field who got close after his stutter at the start of the back nine on Sunday, but not close enough. And made it kind of a life-changing week for him, and propelled him straight into the unofficial 'might be skipping this week next year' category.

And while this week wasn't our best by any means, mine next week looks half decent as it'll be spent at home combining house husbandry with celebrating my latest (but hopefully not last) birthday, and getting tutted at for looking at the scores from the US PGA Championship on my phone from Thursday onwards.

Tuts that might turn into tantrums if I end up getting a late call to caddy at the US Open Qualifying down the road at Walton Heath. Actually, make that 'will'.

Caddying in the US of A

I love caddying in the US. Not because the caddy facilities are any better than in Europe: some weeks they very definitely aren't. Not because everything is laid on travel-wise: it isn't – over there you do everything yourself as there's no caddy hotel and no caddy transport laid on by the PGA Tour or their Caddy Association. Not because you rarely play in the rain: I mean when was the last time you watched the PGA Tour on a Sunday night and saw an umbrella up? Exactly.

Not even because the conditioning of the courses is generally better: as it should be given that the Tour basically follows the sun round America. And absolutely definitely not because no matter where you go in the States, it feels pretty much the same each week: you eat in the same chain restaurants, stay in the same hotel chains, and get to shout at the same helmets in the crowd yelling 'babbabooey'. All of which I quite like doing.

No, the real reason I love caddying here is that every single tournament on the PGA Tour still feels like it's a really BIG event. And that's because basically every state is the size of a small European country, and when that state hosts a tournament, to them it's like THEIR major. So the week has a real atmosphere to it. People flock to watch in their thousands. There are literally hundreds and hundreds of volunteers, whose connection with 'their' tournament makes the whole thing palpably different in terms of atmosphere. The only tournament in Europe that can match (and arguably exceed this) in Europe is Made in HimmerLand, which is extraordinary. And if you ever get the chance to go, then you really should. Oh, and then what's also good is the fact that, especially with the advent of these new 'elevated' events, there's pots of cash to play for whenever we do come over here. Which always helps.

But while there's a lot to like, what I still can't quite get used to is the PGA Tour yardage book. It's very different from the ones in Europe. Because, believe me, when you caddy your first tournament over there and pick up the book for the first time, it really is a 'WTF?' moment. Just ask those guys heading across to Oak Hill this week for their first sortie on to US soil.

And it's not because the yardage books on the PGA Tour have mistakes in them. Anything but: they're 100 per cent reliable on that score. Rather it's just that the way the holes are drawn in the book, and the level of detail provided, is so completely foreign to us, well, foreigners. And it's all quite hard to get your head around, let alone like. Especially when you compare it to what we're used to in Europe – basically the hole drawn on one page, with a page above for writing in your notes, and recording the distances, clubs, wind, carries, pitch numbers, etc. across the practice round, pro-am and tournament rounds. All nicely set out. Very simple. Very clear. Very logical. And very easy to use.

Not something you can say about the PGA Tour yardage book. At least I don't think so. Because open up that book and you find holes split across two pages in the book, sometimes three. There are separate insert drawings for where the second shot (or third shot) is likely to be played from. There are no pictures in the standard book to allow you to see where the run-out lines are. There are significantly less numbers. And there is precious little space to make your notes or record the numbers. It's just not that user-friendly; again, at least to these bespectacled eyes.

And the numbers that are in the book are taken from sprinkler heads rather than from painted dots or markers in the fairways like they are in Europe. This means you really do need to go out and walk the course to get an idea of which sprinklers are where on the fairways, which is something you don't need to do this side of the pond because those dots make it much easier to orientate where you are on a fairway. The same is true in the rough where sprinkler heads tend not to be marked, making getting a yardage off a marked sprinkler head more of a chore. And why you will see caddies going out to walk the course with chalk pens and marking sprinkler heads in the rough themselves. It just makes things easier.

Now I totally get the argument that having a book with less information in it means that you're obliged to put in more work yourself, and that that ultimately benefits the caddies who are prepared to put in that extra work. Because absolutely you have to spend more time walking the course, adding numbers from places you think you may lay up to and from, looking more carefully at lines and run-outs than maybe you would in Europe where basically everything is there for you, to the extent (as we've said before) that it is entirely possible to just turn up on Thursday morning and compete without even seeing the course before – which, and yes it's getting another mention because it really was a caddy masterclass the likes of which isn't seen that much these days, is what Lucas Herbert effectively did in Japan last month.

But that's kind of not the point for me. This yardage book hasn't really progressed in all the time I've been pond hopping, whereas everything else in the world has moved on. So maybe it's time for this to move on too, with more numbers, more photos of lines, more finesse; although to be fair there seems very little drive coming from the PGA Tour caddies for this, which is odd when so many of them come to Europe these days to play the likes of the Scottish Open, The Open and Wentworth, and see the difference between the two books. Maybe the reverse of all this is true for them?

But it's not all doom and gloom as the yardage book over here is effectively free: unlike in Europe where we buy ours each week, on the PGA Tour you get given yours when you sign in in the Caddy Lounge each week. Along with, quite often it has to be said, some gift from the tournament sponsor such as tournament T-shirts, tickets to see the likes of baseball, basketball, etc. Not something we ever get in Europe.

I say 'free', but it's actually only the basic yards version of the yardage book that is free. If you want a yardage book with the kind of pictures (of lines and run-outs) that are standard in Europe, then that's going to cost you. As it will if your player works in metres, which at the last count was zero per cent of Americans. Because if they do, then you'll be handing over around $200 for the privilege, quadruple the price of the equivalent in Europe, where yards and metres books are both £40. There would be a riot if they weren't. And even then there are still a few, mostly it has to be said people that have been out here as long as I have, who still whinge about this being too much. Which every time I think about it, beggars belief.

But while we might think the PGA Tour yardage books are 'back in the day' books, we're stuck with them every time we pond hop. And in the same way that if you had to use a persimmon driver instead of the latest Paradym, while it might look okay, if you've not used one for a while, it takes a bit of getting used to.

And given that the 105th US PGA Championship starts in just three days, that doesn't exactly leave much time.

The Story of the Week of the Second Major of the Year, at Oak Hill, Rochester, New York
18–21 May 2023

Touching down at Heathrow after an early exit from Rinkven last week, my phone bleeped with an offer of a job at the US Open Qualifying at Walton Heath. Practice round Monday; 36 holes Tuesday; £500 plus expenses.

Tempting. But quite liking how my face looks, and fearing that the wife would 100 per cent alter this with a frying pan if I said yes, I politely declined. And instead recommended a colleague who I knew was available and looking for a bag. I knew he'd have done the same for me had I been looking, which is kind of how tour caddies work in situations like this. Always best help your colleagues when you can, and the nice ones will reciprocate that time when you really need them to: usually after you get fired.

In this case the guy I recommended ended up working the qualifying. So that worked out well. Even though the young lad he worked for didn't get one of the seven spots that were on offer. So he won't be caddying at the year's third major. And neither will I as my man didn't bother entering – which, with the benefit of hindsight, was a bit dumb as with seven spots available from a field of 84, he'd have had a near ten per cent chance of qualifying had he bothered teeing it up, which is pretty good odds in anyone's book. Shame he was at home reading one instead. And shame on me, who'd been sounding off for months that the USGA have been actively engaged in trying to limit the number of Europeans getting into the field across the last few years. Clearly not the case.

But with him being at home and (obviously) not being at Oak Hill this week either, that leaves us basically with only The Open left as a possible major to play in this year. And because he's not exempt yet, we'll only get into that via the Final Qualifying in July or securing one of the three spots available at each tournament leading up to Hoylake.

Not that not being at Oak Hill in person stopped me hearing all about it from guys who are (lucky enough to be) there with their players or, for that matter, getting involved in some of the debate about the fines handed out to the likes of Stenson and Otaegui by the Tour last week for playing on LIV Golf.

As I found myself ranting to a golf journalist (under the strict condition of anonymity), irrespective of what anyone thinks of whether the 'punishments' handed out are justified or not, having the likes of Westwood resigning their memberships ought to be a huge concern for any organisation and its members (and it's kind of worrying that it doesn't appear to be), and secondly, making up the (huge) fines after the event looks very iffy and the kind of thing a Sunday morning football team would revel in. And get away with it. Because nowhere in the Players' Handbook (which is the document that effectively outlines all the conditions of DP World Tour membership) does it refer to this sliding scale of fines. But rather than challenge this legally, which would ultimately benefit everyone, those affected will likely take the easier option, and also just resign their memberships, which will just make it way more cringeworthy when at some point in the future the Tour does an about face and 'welcomes' them back. Because 100 per cent that will happen.

Oh, and speaking of the Players' Handbook, there's a section specific to caddies, which refers to caddies as 'he' but not 'she', which is kind of interesting in itself.

Anyway, LIV was only a minor start-of-the-week distraction for me, as there was plenty of chat about the US PGA too. That and, come Thursday, the early coverage to watch and scores to scroll through.

Getting through immigration in the States, specifically in New York, appears to be as torturous as ever, with guys standing there for up to 90 minutes at JFK. The standard of American driving on the roads, again especially in New York, appears to be as chronically hopeless as ever, with tales of narrow misses and stars being thanked that fully comprehensive insurance had been taken out. And the American yardage book appears to be as head-scratchingly complicated as ever.

And expensive if you wanted a yardage book with pictures in it like the ones we get in Europe every week. Unless you think that around $200 isn't expensive and that the yardage book in Europe should cost about the same. Which no one ever does.

Aside from this, what was also interesting this year is that caddies (and players) are again able to use lasers in the tournament itself. Now, while they'll never be a replacement for the yardage book, even the purist of purist caddies has to admit that if you're way off line because he's whanging it everywhere off the tee, or just off line and needs a number to a lay-up, then they're certainly a useful addition to our arsenal. Not that we would ever give one obviously, but it does reduce the chance of a 'mystery' in such situations. As well as saving us a lot of time and hassle. Maybe one day they will get around to giving this a whirl in Europe: perhaps in the big, late-season events when daylight is at a premium. Or would that just be too sensible an idea?

And judging by some of the photos I've seen of the course, you'd better be checking the battery level of the laser before you go out as the fairways aren't exactly wide and the rough isn't exactly sparse so you might be using them more than you anticipated. If only because it looks, at least from my living room, pretty much like a US Open set-up, although no doubt the best players in the world will find a way to get round it way under par when, to the untrained eye, level par would win by five. Especially as, on the eve of the tournament, and apparently not widely publicised, they cut down the rough by one inch across the entire golf course. Might make things a little easier. But as a caddy mate just texted, 'It's still brutal mate. Absolutely savage in fact.' So maybe not.

And that was before Saturday which for me, as (still) the world's worst wet-weather caddy, would have been a nightmare given that it started raining basically before play started and never really let up. As you'll see in the next chapter, caddying in the rain isn't easy unless you have at least three sets of hands and arms: and I don't.

At least the rain had stopped on Sunday. But what didn't stop were two things. Firstly Koepka, who looked like the relentless major machine he was a few years ago. And secondly, the drain of talent to the PGA Tour with Special Temporary Membership Status being quietly granted to another two DP World Tour members, allowing them unlimited sponsors' exemptions for the rest of the season: potentially very good news for their caddies' bank balances, and definitely very good news for their air miles. But arguably rather less good for the DP World Tour.

But my immediate thought as Koepka was tapping in for par on 18, apart from it was good to see his caddy adding another 18th flag to his collection because he is genuinely one of the nicest people you'll ever meet out here, was that being sat in my front room was way better than trying to watch it en route to US Open Final Qualifying in Texas (like some of the guys are doing) or sat in a hotel room in Holland (which is what I should have been doing). And that's because, as you'll see, a lot can change in a few days.

But no, I've not been fired.

Caddying in the Rain

But before I explain why I'm writing this at home and not Holland, seeing the guys caddying in the rain at Oak Hill last week did remind me of perhaps the wisest off-course statement made by any tour caddy ever. And that was: 'Thou Shalt Not Start Golf in the Rain.'

And from the day I first heard him say it to this one, I have followed his advice to the letter. Because I hate playing golf in the rain. There are few things less enjoyable in life. One of those, however, is caddying in the rain. Which I hate even more. With a passion in fact. Mainly because I'm shite at it. But also because, as anyone who was watching the Saturday at Oak Hill last week could clearly see, tour caddies only have one set of arms. When on rain days we need at least three.

And need them we do, because unlike in the US where the PGA and LIV Tours tend to follow the sun, rain is always a distinct possibility on the DP World Tour no matter where we are: it can even rain in places like Abu Dhabi and Dubai as you've already read my bleating about this year.

So sooner or later each season we have to go out to caddy in the rain: preparing for this starts the night before when we typically write tomorrow's pins into the yardage book in pen, rather than pencil. Because that way there is less chance of getting to the 12th hole and discovering that page is already soaked and you can't see what you dutifully wrote in last night. And to make matters worse the pin sheet itself is so wet that you can't decipher that either. Oh, and carry a spare pen in case your first one gets waterlogged to the point where it stops working.

Now obviously we'll be wearing waterproofs on a rain day. But what you wear under them depends on the temperature. The worst are windy, cold rain days where half the time it doesn't matter how many layers you wear under the waterproofs – you're still getting freezing cold; while the best (not that any rain day caddying is good) are the ones in the warmer climates where you just need a polo under the rain jacket, but then you sweat like a cow in a slaughterhouse. No, you basically can't win.

But at least this means we're wearing the waterproofs rather than carrying, in order of priority, his and mine. The cloud to this silver lining is that in the bag goes at least one extra towel so we can keep the grips and his hands dry during the torture that awaits. So what one hand takes away, the other gives in equally heavy measure.

And where your player is one of those (and there are a few) who refuse to wear a waterproof top, then there's a further darker cloud, in that it's likely you'll be packing between three and six spare polos, which he'll change into every few holes when the one he's wearing gets too heavy with the wet. And yes, the used ones go guess where, to be carried by guess who around the remaining holes?

So the bag's all packed, and that means I can no longer delay going to the range to meet him, which is usually a minimum of five minutes before we've arranged to meet. But today being a rain day is more likely to be 50 seconds. It just means I get slightly less wet and cold.

But however much time we do spend on the range obviously means you're wet before we even tee it up. And that's despite me being able to cower under the umbrella while he works his way through his warm-up. Personally, here's where I remove the headcover from the driver on the basis that it's going to be under the rain hood all day anyway to protect it, and not having to pop the headcover on every hole will save a few seconds because life is about to get complicated as we leave the 1st tee.

Fortunately the next five hours, 20 minutes (rounds take longer in the rain) start with him splitting the first fairway. I'm slightly ahead of him when we get to the ball so, as usual, I pop the bag down and pace off the yardage to the red spot seven yards in front of us. By the time I turn around to walk back he's beside the ball holding the umbrella: I'm dispensable in that I get wet, while he stays as dry as possible.

As he's decent on rain days, he holds the umbrella over us both as I fish out the yardage book and do the numbers which, as the rain is coming straight down today, isn't too bad. But it is when the wind's coming in horizontally and you have to morph into a part-contortionist, part-tour caddy, and turn your body away from the wind to at least attempt to keep the book dry.

Equally as fortunately, today is not a lift-clean-and-place day because that would mean I also have to fish the 'wet' towel out from under the rain cover, then clean and dry the ball, hand it back to him, as well as getting the number. Start to see where the need for extra sets of arms comes from?

Once we've decided on where on the increasingly wet-looking green we're going to pitch it and what club will pitch it there, I take over holding the brolly as he's got to now get his glove out of his pocket and on without getting it wetter than he has to. He'll then open the rain hood, pull the club out vertically and then use the 'dry' towel, which we keep in the front pocket of the bag, to make sure the grip is again as dry as it can be. After that, I back away, leaving him to hit the shot: book in one hand, umbrella wedged between my arm and side, with the other hand on the bag to make sure it doesn't move or, worse still, fall over while he's hitting the shot.

Shot hit, straight away he gets the umbrella back. I get the club cleaned and back in the bag as soon as I can. Get the rain hood zipped up. Get the dry towel back in the dry front pocket. Get the divot. Get that back in the ground. And get a move on after him up the fairway. Getting wetter as I do.

Because we're on the green, and on rain days I'm needed there a lot more than usual. Yes, he still marks the ball and chucks it at me to clean, using the 'wet' towel that sits on the top of the bag. But after that, at some stage I get given the umbrella, and have to either stand over him while he lines the putt up to give him five seconds less in the rain, or over the ball once it's down and lined up to give it five seconds less in the rain.

The trick is to be able to move away just at the right moment so as he's not standing in the rain for a second more than he needs to, and not a moment after he pulls the club back, which would incur a penalty. With a new player this can be a tricky balance to achieve, but we've played enough rounds in the rain to know precisely which moment is the moment for me to move.

And obviously I'm hoping he holes this early birdie chance as, if not, then we have to go through the same rigmarole all over again. Anyway, on this occasion it's easy, the putt goes in, he gets the brolly back, and I get the ball to dry off, the putter back into the bag as soon as possible and, if I'm lucky, a few seconds under his brolly while the other guys putt. But only if he's feeling public-spirited enough to let me.

And that is the pattern for the rest of the round really. And because we work in partnership and follow a kind of set routine every hole in terms of who does what and holds what when, then apart from getting piss wet through, it is normally tolerable. It also helps if he plays great and sees his name on the board as that tends to stop the mind drifting on to how shit playing golf in the rain is.

And unless the course gets flooded or there's a threat of lightning, we just have to get on with it. Meaning by the time we trudge off our 18th, we'll have (on a really rainy day) used at least four towels, trashed about five new gloves (because nine out of ten times he'll have forgotten to bring his rain glove designed specifically for days like this), probably need a new umbrella (the spokes on which one of the towels sat all the way round easily become warped), and, for definite, need a new pair of golf shoes (one round in the rain and the shoes typically get donated to the locker-room attendants to be replaced by a brand-new pair next week).

As for the tour bag, clubs and waterproofs, they won't dry themselves. So it's up to me – typically – to take them home and dry everything off ready for tomorrow. And when you're sharing an apartment with three other guys who've also been out in the rain, that puts paid to any space you might have had in your living room. And the place doesn't smell too good either.

But if you're really lucky, then your apartment will have two hairdryers so at least you can take it in turns to use them on your own shoes (which definitely aren't binned after one round in the rain), the inside of the tour bag, and the individual pages of our respective yardage books which now likely resemble papier mâché.

And if you're really, really lucky, then the forecast for the next day will be for sunshine. Or failing that, no rain. Because a dry tour caddy is a happy tour caddy.

Chapter 6

Clogs and Cars

The Story of the Week of the KLM Open 25–28 May 2023

Last-minute changes to schedules can be the bane of our lives as tour caddies, and this week is a case in point. Although technically it was last week, but let's not split hairs.

I had been all set to say goodbye to my latest-attempt house husbandry at the weekend, fly to Eindhoven, pick up a hire car, drive up to Cromvoirt all ready for the KLM Open, only I get a message from him last week saying he's pulling out with a recurrence of a wrist problem. Fortunately I can say things like 'you want to get yourself a girlfriend, mate' to him without getting fired. So I did.

But anyway, that was that one out of the window. Unless I had decided to go out to Holland anyway and pick up a 'one weeker', which is the term we use for when you caddy for someone other than your regular player for, you'll never guess, just the one week.

Personally I try to avoid doing this like the plague because unless it's someone I really know, like or have caddied for before, I'd frankly rather be at home. But obviously don't tell the wife that. Or the kids. That and I know there will be guys wanting that 'one weeker' who might need it more than me, assuming obviously their regular player actually lets them work for someone else. Because over the years there's been many a caddy fired for working for someone else on their man's week off. And also many a caddy who is actually 'not allowed' to work for anyone else as part of their deal with that player. Not that my player puts any such restrictions on me: he's practical – and decent – enough to know that if he's not playing, I'm not earning. Which is actually kind of irrelevant as I'm not going anyway.

So straight after dropping the kids at school I'm straight on to changing my arrangements: trying to get a refund on the flight (it's Ryanair so that won't be much), letting the guys who I was meant to be sharing with know so they can get someone else in, cancelling the hire car, and rearranging the travel from the KLM to the Porsche the week after – which won't be in a Porsche obviously.

Oh, and don't think that any costs I incur from these changes will be reimbursed by anyone other than me. Because they won't. It's all part of the cost of being a tour caddy: reason 1,245 why it's not like any other normal job. And reason 1,246 why you shouldn't try this at home.

That done, I settle back for another few days of enforced house husbandry, interspersed now the weather is a bit warmer here with a couple of rounds of golf with friends. Friends who are lucky enough to be members at a very well-known leafy course to the west of London, and generous enough to invite me along as they know I gave up my membership there a good few years back as £500+ a game each year just didn't make sense. And as they're friends I disengage caddy mode, and refrain from any head shaking, eye rolling, tutting or sarcastic 'good club' when they come up woefully short for the fifth hole in a row; look the other way when they look like they're about to take a drop at the nicest point of relief and not the nearest; and refrain from shouting 'Quiet Please' at 200 decibels when the old boys in tweed insist on shouting away to each other while we're trying to tee off. But God, it's hard.

As is the golf. Mainly because I'm at best a five handicap, and at worst (like this week) about a 15. But there again I've not touched a club, or rather not played because I've touched plenty of clubs obviously, since before Christmas. All of which puts me somewhere in the lower-mid-range of the current crop of tour caddies. Because a lot of the guys coming out on tour to caddy now are decent players in their own right: a few have dabbled in the pro ranks, while a good few others are good county standard amateurs with handicaps around the scratch mark. That's in contrast to a lot of the elder statesmen tour caddies out here who tend not to be members of golf clubs, and those that are boast double-figure handicaps. All of which gives a lie to the myth that you need to be a good player to become a tour caddy.

And looking at the scoring and a few messages from guys who are actually caddying at the KLM, one thing you needed round Bernardus Golf Cromvoirt was to be caddying for a good player having a good week. Otherwise, with all that coarse grass just off the fairway, a fair bit of breeze and plenty of water to boot, it was always going to be a short one.

But irrespective of how your man played, it seems to have been a very good week off the course for the caddies, with the Caddy Lounge offering up restaurant-class food all day, so hats off to the KLM people for organising all that. A far, far cry from yesteryear when we were lucky to get a voucher for a sandwich in the public catering tent at the likes of Zandvoort. Long may that continue.

He who had the best good week on the course though was, once again, Larrazábal, who got his nose in front late in the back nine Sunday, and generally when he does that he wins – which he did, edging out Otaegui, who'd benefitted from a last-minute 'well seeing as you paid your LIV fine early with no fuss, go on then' invite into the tournament.

And so that was that: back-to-back wins in Europe, a fourth win in the last season and a half for one of the, if not the, longest player/caddy partnerships out here, and one very happy Pablo. Oh, and by the way, the other half of the winning caddy partnership kind of proves my point about how the younger caddies out here are decent players. Actually in his case, a bit more than decent. As in good enough to play on the pro mini-tours in Spain when Pablo has time off. And clean up. To the point where Pablo regularly and openly says he's a better player than him. And he's not joking either.

But it's not just him that is happy come Sunday afternoon; I am too. And that's because as my man's wrist appears to be better, I won't be having to make more last-minute revisions to my already revised travel arrangements for next week.

So that's me back on the tools. And straight back into tour caddy mode. And just in the nick of time too, as it's time for one of my favourite weeks on tour: the Porsche European Open.

The Yardage Book

With his wrist mended I'm back on a plane to get back on the tools at the Porsche, which means I'm back using the yardage book: the basic tool of every tour caddy in the world, no matter what tour they're working on. Only every tour caddy I know shortens this to 'the book', so that's what I'll call it from now on.

Except our book isn't like the ones you can buy in the pro shop; instead it's custom-made for that week's tournament, basically because the level of detail required in professional golf is so much greater than anything an average club golfer will ever need.

To the point where, and it's worth saying this (yet) again, the book is that detailed and that good that it is absolutely possible to turn up on Thursday morning having never even seen the course before, and still shoot under par. While it's also true, as I've also said before, that it would be perfectly possible to have a Tour event without caddies, but you could never have a Tour event without the book. So it's pretty important. And, fairly obviously, it's where all the numbers we talked about in the 'What You Hear on TV' section all came from.

So when our caddy said, 'Four off red. 178. Up three. That's 181 front. 13 on. 194 flag,' that's because he (because he was me) has paced off four yards from a red spot painted on the fairway to where the ball is sitting; looked in the book to see that from the red spot it's 182 yards to the front of the green, so it's actually 178 yards to the front of the green from where the ball is; then added the number of yards uphill from this spot to the front of the green, which in this case the book tells him is three. All of which equals 181 yards. On to which he has then added the pin position (i.e. the number of yards between the front of the green and the flag), which in this case is 13; all of which comes to 194. And written all that down in the book. And relayed to his player in the order he likes it relayed. All within five seconds flat.

How I record all this in the book is individual to me: every tour caddy does it slightly differently. But in a nutshell, before the round starts I would already have, for our pretend hole, have written the following into my book:

    3R
/ +13 = [   ]

Because then on the course tomorrow all I have to do is fill in the bottom of the two lines with (left to right) the yardage to the front of the green from our ball, a second number to the right of the '/' which is this yardage + or − the elevation to the front of the green, to give the yardage to flag, which goes after the = sign.

Right of that I will write in the wind direction, and a final number (in the brackets) which is how far we think the shot is playing, which for a shot into the wind will be more; and for a downwind shot will be less. And finally to the right of that will go the club we end up hitting.

Most caddies, especially these days, also record where each shot actually pitches and finishes. This is so when we have 154 into the wind on the 15th and he asks, 'What did we have on 4?', because that was an almost identical shot, I have all the numbers to hand. And I also know what we did here yesterday, and on Thursday. Because being a tour caddy you almost have to be able to second-guess when your man is going to ask these kinds of questions, and have these numbers immediately to hand instead of thumbing back through the book, while he looks on impatiently all the while muttering something about how his previous caddy always had these numbers to hand.

After that, the book also tells me the carries over any prominent knuckles or slopes of the green itself for this shot, how far we have behind the pin to the back of the green, what the carry over every greenside bunker is: all of which he may yet ask me, and I need to be able to tell him. Just like on the tee when I've already been able to tell him how far off the tee the bunker we needed to stay short of was, and what the run-out to the tree on the left corner of the dogleg was.

These are just a few of the 1,500-plus numbers that are in the book we use each week. So you can see how lucky we are to have this level of detail available to us for only £40 a week: which is the current price of the book: which in turn is ridiculous really as the true value of the product is minimum £100, given how much money we're playing for and how much time it saves each caddy, who would otherwise have to go out and laser many of these numbers themselves.

And yet there are still those who complain about the price or that the book has too much information in it, pining for the days when it didn't and was very basic. But in the same way I don't pine for my first car I ever drove, I'm not one of them. Because better things are available now. And anything that makes my job easier is fine by me.

So Dion Stevens gets my appreciation every week. Not just because what I've just said, but because I think his yardage books are the best in the world, especially since for a few years now I've been able to pay for it online, which means there's no longer the issue of what to do if you've forgotten to go to the cashpoint after landing at silly o'clock the night before, and don't have any cash. I can even stomach that a small percentage of my £40 goes to the old caddy whose payment engine Dion uses. Just.

Actually, just at the moment I don't care about that, because my current player pays for my book as part of our arrangement, which is quite generous of him, as most tour caddies end up paying for their own book. But no matter who pays for your book, the one thing every tour caddy doesn't want to do is lose it somewhere during the week. Or for that matter to have it fall out of your pocket into the on-course toilet as happened to one colleague 15 years or so ago. I mean it's one thing for your book to get soaking wet in the rain, quite another for it to get soaking wet in piss.

And for that reason mine stays in my pocket from the minute I leave the hotel room in the morning to the minute I get back, when it goes into my hat along with my credentials so I won't forget either the next morning. It also comes with me the next time I come to the same course so I can quickly see any changes from my previous visit, remember where we hit it to which pins, etc.

So, as you can probably guess, this means I never throw my old yardage books away. And why we may soon need a bigger loft at home.

The Story of the Week of the Porsche European Open 1–4 June 2023

You might remember I said that this week is one of my favourite weeks of the year on tour. And yes, it absolutely is. But don't be thinking it's got anything to do with the golf course. Because it hasn't. It's all about Lüneburg, which is the town where we're staying this week. It's towards the top, if not at the top, of the list of most beautiful places we stay all year. A proper chocolate-box gingerbread town. One part of it is a series of winding little streets alongside the river, each one comprised almost entirely of restaurants with open terraces perched virtually over said river; and the other is a huge long cobbled square. Both bits magically avoided being flattened in the Second World War, unlike its industrial neighbour Hamburg just 55km to the north-west, which is where the players and the Tour staff stay. No doubt cursing, for the fifth year in a row, the exorbitant hotel prices and the horrendous traffic getting to and from the course. Poor club, that one.

But as usual we've pulled a great club: a lovely little Airbnb pretty much in the middle of the windy streets bit of Lüneburg, so we're no more than two minutes' walk from a schnitzel whichever way we turn out of the front door. That is to say that sitting by the river eating one and watching the world go by becomes our nightly routine from basically the minute we get there: me by car, the others by train from Den Bosch yesterday afternoon straight after the tournament finished.

I've grown to really like Germany over the years. Everything is super-efficient, well organised and, most importantly, you can eat schnitzel and chips until it comes out of your ears. Possibly my favourite, albeit unhealthy, European menu option. Another reason to love this week.

It's also been great to catch up with everyone again over (you guessed it) schnitzel, and first on the chat agenda was the two big winners at the weekend over in the States. No, not Grillo or HV3. No, we were all talking about how good it was to see two guys we all know really well from this tour caddying for them. That, and how much money they earned relative to the winner and winning caddy on this tour. Because

Grillo's caddy on the PGA Tour took home more money than the guys who finished T3 at the KLM, while Harold Varner III's on the LIV tour took home $60,000 more than Larrazábal got for winning the KLM. If you were looking for evidence why the top talent on the DP World Tour (players and caddies) look stateside, then look no further. And if you're still unsure, take a moment to try and get your head around the fact that the $4m Harold Varner won was twice the total prize fund of the KLM. Yes: exactly.

More fun, though, was hearing what everyone has been up to since we last all did this. Some of us have been at home, some of us have been continent hopping, some have been on holiday (again), some have been working on the likes of the Challenge Tour, while some are only just starting caddying again now the Tour is firmly back in Europe. And from memory the record seems to have been 14 flights across three different continents in the last three weeks. All of which made my day trip to Chichester with the family (the furthest I got) seem fairly tame by comparison.

One trip we do all have to make this week though is the 20-minute coach ride from the caddy hotel for the week to the golf course itself which, as I alluded to already, is not one of my favourites. Although it's improved enormously from when we first came here in 2017 when the course was somewhere between forgettable (if you were being charitable) and shit (if you weren't). The latter being the answer given by one former Ryder Cup player that year when he was asked what he thought of it. The only trouble being that the guy asking the question then said, 'Shame. Because it's my golf course,' again proving the old adage that you should never ask a question if you might not like the answer. Especially if you own a golf course and ask a tour pro what they think of it. Or worse still, what they think of your swing.

But there again that was then and this is now. Because since then the owners seem to have – thankfully – stopped obsessing about their course being the longest on tour, although ironically, because of holes like the two 630+ yard par fives on the back nine, the length back then actually brought the short hitters into the frame: witness Siddikur Rahman (the shortest hitter on tour at the time) finishing T3 in 2017 and Richie McEvoy winning in 2019. Instead they appear to have listened to the feedback from both players and the Tour, notably by redesigning a couple of holes (for example the par-three 14th, which now has a proper lake in front of it) and dropping any insistence that the course is played from the very back of the back tees. The resulting flexibility this has given the Tour in terms of the set-up has been increasingly obvious over the years; for example, we now play off a good few forward tees, and so play a much better course which is a much, much better test of golf than five years ago when it was anything but.

In fact I'm almost warming to the place to the extent that leaving Lüneburg every day isn't so bad after all. Not that that made it an enjoyable week on the bag if we're honest. Mainly because, aside from him not having a great week, my body is wrecked first week back. Yes, some of the holes might be shorter yardage-wise, but the length of the walk round remains the same as we still have to walk off the green, past the now-redundant back tees, and 50 yards up to the tees we're actually playing off. It's an absolute killer. All 7,500 yards of it. So if there was ever a week we could have done with physio just for caddies, then this was it. But there wasn't one. And neither did we have access to the players' physios either. Meaning a fair few of us resorted to good old-fashioned liquid physio instead – which, oddly enough, didn't really work.

On top of this, throw in a bit of wind (like on Thursday for example), flyer city out of the rough when in previous years it's been a hack out, water in front and behind a number of greens, and golf balls that refused to float, and you have the recipe for some fantastic caddy errors, some big (double-digit in the most notable case of the former) numbers and a stressful week. What we thought would be a good test of golf actually became a brutal one. And all a bit of a ball-ache to be honest.

No ball-ache for young Tom McKibbin, though, who pulled off one of the shots of the year so far to birdie 18, take his first DP World Tour win, and again prove that caddies over 40 (in this case over 60) really can make the difference. And good on him.

Also good was that after four days fighting that wind and avoiding all that water (or two if your man didn't), for the second time in its history, Lüneburg was the site of the signing of an important international peace treaty. In 1945 it was between the Allies and Nazi Germany (something I didn't know until this year); in 2023 it was between me and my player after what could best be described as a 'tetchy' week. Not as newsworthy I grant you, but equally as required. Fair to say I wasn't the only one in this position, though.

But for the first time in a long time it did leave me thinking, 'Do I really need this hassle?'

Eighteen Things You Didn't Know about Tour Caddies – The Front Nine

At the last count there were 18 holes on a golf course, so here's 18 random things that you didn't know about tour caddies, starting with the front nine.

1. We're not all on ten per cent

If I had €1 for every time I get asked this, I wouldn't still be carrying a bag for a living: instead, as one of my colleagues so eloquently put it, 'Son, I'd be living on a beach somewhere doing what I liked when I liked surrounded by hookers, beer and chocolate.'

I'm more subtle, though, and lately just answer this question with a simple 'no' because I now know that that is usually enough to kill the conversation there and then.

But in case you've forgotten what I told you earlier: yes, generally if your man wins a tournament, he will pay you a bonus of ten per cent of whatever prize money he received.

It's just important to confirm when sorting out terms with your player (especially if they happen to be from one of the southernmost European countries) that ten per cent equals ten per cent of the gross prize money, and not ten per cent of the prize money after he's paid tax on it. Because that sum will be significantly smaller.

2. We don't play golf every week

'Get tae fuck do we.' That's my standard response to the following often-asked question: 'Do you get a chance to play when you're out on tour?' Because believe me, the last thing any tour caddy wants to do after they've been, for example, watching their player practice for five hours on a Wednesday morning is be anywhere near a golf course, let alone playing on one. No, instead we're all headed on the next bus to the hotel for an afternoon snooze. Or an afternoon libation. Depending on your predilection.

3. We're not all great golfers

This is another popular misconception. Obviously we all love golf, but that doesn't mean we're necessarily any good at it. In fact, there's probably only half of us who actually possess active handicaps – mainly because not all tour caddies are actually members of golf clubs. Yes, some choose to maintain their membership, but for the majority there's pretty much no point being a member back home (wherever that is), especially if you spend most of the year 5,000km away from that home, and only get back a few times a year. That and the fact that if you show your DP World Tour caddy credentials, that's generally enough to get you a free round of golf, especially if you let them take your photo and stick it on their social media.

4. We don't all fly private

Tour pros do fly private. Not all of them, obviously. But some of them do. And amongst them, there are even some who have their own private planes.

And yes, some caddies also fly private. And don't we fucking know about it when they do. Cue celebratory photos plastered over social media with them posing at the steps of whatever brand of jet they're flying on. Or cadging a lift on, to be more precise.

Obviously none of us who might be queuing for Scumbag Airways to the same destination – via the arse end of nowhere as it's cheaper – are in any way jealous. Post away lads.

5. We don't all work for nice people

Golf on TV looks lovely, doesn't it? But don't necessarily be fooled by what you see. Like in any office in any company in any part of the world, or in life itself, there are some nice human beings and some not so nice human beings.

But that doesn't stop us saying that some of the not so nice human beings who play professional golf for a living have, in the past, done things like putting a cigarette out on their caddy's arm, not bothered paying their caddy until he went to the Tour to complain, refused to pay an agreed share of a hole-in-one prize, refused to pay ten per cent of a season-ending bonus payment that ran into millions, and that's before we get into all the verbal bullying on the course. I mean, in what other workplace can a boss say to his employee, 'I don't give a fuck what you think' and get away with it?

So next time you see that personable not-a-care-in-the-world kind of guy being interviewed during or after his round, just remember he might be one of them when the cameras stop rolling.

6. We make a living on the back of their talent

Whether our players are nice human beings or not very nice human beings, we make a living off the back of their talent. It's as simple as that. Without them and their talent we'd all be somewhere else doing something we wouldn't love as much.

This is arguably why over the years there has been this 'caddy omerta' where what happens on tour stays on tour, where what we do has a bit of a cloak of mystery about it, and where the entry in is so fiercely protected. And why, when you get a 'good bag' you try really hard to keep it.

7. We get fired

Scarcely a week on tour goes by without a caddy getting 'fired' – the term we all use when, for whatever reason, a player/caddy partnership ends.

This is part and parcel of the job. But anyone who tells you they don't care when a player 'fires' them is almost certainly lying. If nothing else, it does tend to bruise the ego. Especially if it comes out of the blue when you've been with a guy for a long time and think everything is going well.

Part of being a tour caddy, though, is that you have to be able to bounce back. And some caddies have more bouncebackability than others. Like for instance the guy who, in a moment of extreme lack of self-awareness, once announced his 14th anniversary on tour on some social media site by name-checking each of the 25 players he'd worked for in those 14 years. Only to be brought down a peg or two by one of his particularly forthright colleagues who pointed out that this meant he'd actually been fired by 24 different players. Hardly an enviable record. Imagine having that on your CV when looking for a 'proper job': I have been sacked by 24 employers in the last 14 years, but honestly, I'm really good.

But our world isn't the real world, and so pretty soon every fired caddy ends up being a 'hired' caddy, and is back to work with a new player. Until the next time they get fired obviously, which in the case of this guy wasn't that long.

Oh, and don't be thinking that there's any redundancy pay or statutory notice period out here when you get fired. Because there isn't. Yet more food for thought if ever you're tempted to sack off that nine to five stable job that pays the bills every month.

8. And why you won't get hired

My virtual pot of €1 coins for every time I get asked, 'You're on ten per cent aren't you?' would be at least doubled if I also got €1 every time I hear, 'Get me a bag on tour, will you?' and 'How do I get a bag on tour?'

My answer is always the same: the harsh reality is that, pretty much, unless a tour pro on the DP World Tour knows you, or knows of you, he won't hire you. So in terms of food for thought, if you're thinking of trying to caddy for living, it's the hors d'oeuvre.

Because the chances are you don't know a tour pro given that they are a pretty rare breed: at the last count there were only 250–300 actually active in Europe. And like I say, if they don't know you, they will not magically be picking up the phone and asking you to come caddy for them. And just like that your dream is dead in the water before it's even begun, I'm afraid.

There's also the small matter that, as per my sections on the yardage book and caddying in the rain, on your first day on the bag you could be having to do both with a grumpy tour pro you don't really know shouting at you because you're not doing the first one quick enough and the second one poorly. The harsh reality is that you'd be found out within 20 seconds and fired. Because that's how long some new guys last out here.

We, however, probably will get hired after getting fired. The reality is that if you are a tour caddy, you're bloody good at caddying. And the talent pool is small. So usually, thanks to a call from a manager or player who's heard you've been fired or by word of mouth, it's not long before you've picked up a new bag.

9. The afterlife

There comes a time in the career of every tour caddy when they don't get hired after getting fired. And generally this comes with age – kind of understandable in one sense, even just on the grounds that what does a kid fresh out of college have in common with, say, a middle-aged bloke like me? Frankly, not a lot.

Not that that is necessarily the be-all and end-all of course, because what you get with someone who has been out here a long time is experience. And you can't really put a price on that. Nor is there any fast-track way of getting it: you learn by often bitter experience. And years of it. But hiring that experience can make the difference between losing your card or keeping it, or finally winning after all those near misses. Which is why people like me still have a job out here. And why I genuinely think all my similarly aged colleagues are just the very best in the business. Even the one who, every bloody year, is 'only doing a few'.

But for the other 'older caddies' there is always 'The Seniors', aka the EU Legends Tour. Here they often hook up with former employers who have now passed the magic 50 mark at which point they can start to play competitively again, and who better to have alongside them than the guy they probably hired and fired several times when they played the Tour full-time?

It really is the caddy 'afterlife'.

The Story of the Week of the Volvo Scandinavian Mixed 8–11 June 2023

This week we get to mix it with the best. Albeit the best on the Ladies European Tour rather than best on say the PGA Tour or LIV. But no matter, we're in Stockholm playing one of only a couple of events across the world of pro golf where men and women professionals play on the same course for the same prize money. Although obviously not off the same tees.

On the downside, though, although we might be playing for the same money, we are all also having to pay the same money to stay anywhere near the golf course. Given that this is Sweden, it's a lot. So your man (assuming you're a DP World Tour caddy) had better make the cut this week, because if he doesn't, you're at best breaking even, but more likely taking a loss.

That's like traipsing into the office from Monday to Friday, working your ass off, and then on the way out on Friday stopping to hand over a few hundred euros to your employer, only for the boss to then get you back in on Saturday and Sunday too because there's some other stuff that needs doing. Well, that's what approximately 70 caddies did this week. Name me another job in the world that offers you this kind of opportunity!

Anyway, we arrive safely in Stockholm; our luggage, however, doesn't – one of the perennial hazards of being a tour caddy: at some stage in the year (usually at three or four stages) the baggage belt will stop without your bag appearing. And absolutely always when you're in a hurry to get to where you need to be. Like this week, for example.

Fortunately I have foreseen something like this happening and had my trainers, a pair of shorts and a clean golf shirt in my hand luggage, which meant that at least I have something to wear when I walk the course early on Monday morning with only the birds and greenkeepers for company. What's immediately apparent is that you don't want to be hitting too many errant shots round this place. And that this week an errant shot might actually bizarrely be one that finishes dead centre of the fairway, as it looks to me like there are certain holes where you'll be blocked if you are. The number of manufactured hooks or slices this week could therefore be off the scale. You're also going to need to put plenty of spin on the ball to hold some of the tiers on these greens, and bring your short game with you for when you miss them.

But whether all this will favour the ladies over the men or the men over the ladies remains to be seen. And with the previous history in this event showing one male winner and one female winner, that's not helping much either. As ever it'll be down to the set-up on the tournament days, especially because if they stick pins on those small tiers or have a lot of front pins (both of which require more spin on the ball to get close to), that would 100 per cent favour the men.

The dynamic is a bit weird this week though. Not necessarily for the caddies as we kind of know quite a few of the guys who work full-time on the Ladies European Tour, but for the players, as although they do the same thing for a living, their lives are really quite different. And as ever it's down to money. There must be some envious glances at the DP World Tour players as the next time they tee it up (in Germany) the winner will get around €360,000 whereas the next time the ladies tee it up (also in Germany), they play for a total prize fund of just €300,000. Not a single DP World Tour player will be doing shifts in Amazon in the off-season; but that won't be the same for some of the LET players. Right or wrong, that's the reality of the two top-level professional golf tours in Europe.

This makes this week arguably way, way more important for the ladies than the men. A good week here and not only is your card secure for next year at the start of June, but you're also potentially opening the door to a couple of months of warm weather practice over the winter rather than cold weather work to make ends meet. Or it gets you that deposit on a house. Or whatever. But a bad week is maybe not a disaster, but definitely a huge missed opportunity.

But for the men, a good week here is just a good week. Nothing more, nothing less. And a bad week is just that: a bad week. And definitely not a disaster either as there's plenty of tournaments left with the same prize fund on offer to keep your card, get that first win, or definitely finance two months' warm weather practice. So the money may be the same, and the course may be set up to offer the same challenge to both the men and the women, but come Thursday morning the pressure to do well definitely isn't the same.

Before all that, though, came Tuesday's announcement that the PGA Tour and the people behind LIV seem to have decided to act like adults a few weeks ago, and have patched up their differences by actually talking to each other like, well, adults. A few of us had long predicted something like this would happen, but the speed and impressive secrecy of it took everyone by surprise, not least it seems the PGA Tour players. All of which signals, it seems, the end of all ongoing future legal action, the likely reinstatement of memberships to both the PGA Tour and DP World Tour, and the wiping of a lot of egg from a lot of faces. What precisely this means for the future of our tour remains to be seen, but my initial thought was (a) it's a good thing if you're in, say, the top 150 in the world, (b) the DP World Tour tournaments that have traditionally had weak fields will continue to have weak fields, but the weak field will be playing for way more money, and (c) any time we play for more money, that's a good thing, and it looks like we might be playing for a good deal more money if this all comes off. Win, win, win, I'd say.

Meanwhile, back at the tournament, our week actually starts with optimism in the air. He's arrived like last week was a walk in the park (which it wasn't), full of banter (which was conspicuously absent last week) and in a positive frame of mind (also a paradigm shift from last week). Cynical me thinks he's been talking to a few of his mates out here, and has realised that everyone struggled last week, and that maybe his caddy isn't the bête noire after all.

Maybe I'm the lucky one, though, as one colleague was informed by his player's manager that this week would be his last on his man's bag: it appears he's the lowest rung in the ladder of a whole bunch of post-Porsche caddy/player changes. But massive kudos to the lad: he basically said, 'Fuck you. Last week was my last week on the bag,' got straight on a plane and fucked off home, leaving his now-former player with no caddy for the week. You reap what you sow sometimes out here, and not having the bollocks to fire your caddy to his face this time got its just dessert.

Meanwhile, my bête noire status has definitely been in abeyance since he arrived on Tuesday afternoon. But who knows how long that will last. It might be as soon as the first errant shot on Thursday, but we'll see.

And arrive it did. But not until Friday's round. Because as well as pitching up in a good mood, he appeared to have pitched up with his game magically in great shape. Not in quite great enough shape to really contend come Sunday but a great deal better than of late.

Not that this mattered as Dale Whitnell won easily enough in the end, with a stand-in caddy. The very same one who won with Baldwin earlier in the year at the SDC down in the East Cape. So cementing his position as the number one choice for anyone needing a caddy for a one weeker. On top of which he's also (fairly obviously) a great caddy, and an even nicer man. And, it has to be said, proof again that you can't buy experience, which he has in spades.

So after a pretty momentous week it's Sayōnara Stockholm, and because there's no tournament next week, it's hello to us all scattering to the four winds of home, holiday, the US Open or Copenhagen for the Challenge Tour event.

I've pulled a hybrid. And am heading off for a few days at home followed by a few days somewhere sunny with the missus. Hopefully that's the right club.

Eighteen Things You Didn't Know about Tour Caddies – The Back Nine

After a quick stop at the halfway house that was the Scandinavian Mixed, it's time for the back nine of things you didn't know about tour caddies. Starting at the tricky 10th hole.

10. We're constantly tired

Some weeks back I spoke about getting back to London after a good few weeks on the road. What I omitted to say was that my house husbandry was put on hold for a while as on about the second night back I just zonked. Completely zonked.

This is not uncommon for tour caddies on weeks off. Because what you don't see on TV is that scrapping for the cut each week (which I had kind of been doing) or being in contention (I wish) is bloody tiring. I mean the job is physically tiring anyway – as a reminder, a fully laden tour bag weighs 25kg – but the mental stress can be different level. And at some stage, both will catch up with you. Usually the second day into a week off. And I was a case in point.

In my case I'd sat down after dinner and just fell asleep. Next time I opened my eyes I was still on the settee (albeit with a blanket on me), and it was nearly time to take the kids to school the next morning, but that was only the start of it. Because my nap on getting back home turned into a sleep from which I woke up six hours later, about 20 minutes before I was meant to be picking them up again. And the same thing happened after dinner that night. And the same thing happened with my morning nap the day after.

Fortunately my missus is well used to this, hence the blanket over my snoring slobbering belly on the settee rather than a set of divorce papers.

11. An average season

As I've already said there's many a tour caddy who ends up spending a chunk of their week(s) off, well, asleep basically, because they're so tired. Because, make no mistake about it, irrespective of whatever stresses they go through actually caddying, carrying a tour bag is a physically demanding way to earn a living. And here's why:

An average tour caddy probably goes to around 30 tournaments each year. I say 'average' because not all caddies caddy for the guys who play a max of 18–20 events each year because they're that good.

So this means that in an average year, a tour caddy will:

- take around 70–80 flights (most people take four a year)
- walk the equivalent of Land's End to John O'Groats … and back
- put down and lift the tour bag around 25,000 times
- wait in airports (preferably in airport lounges) for a full six days
- spend around nine full days actually flying

And that is why come the end of the season I'll be having the mother of all zonks. Just like I did last year. And the one before that, come to think of it.

12. We're not allowed to bet

Tour caddies are prohibited from betting on golf. Basically because, theoretically, we can adversely affect the outcome of a score or a tournament. And because, theoretically, we know who's injured, who's playing rubbish, etc. So when you think about it, that's kind of not too surprising.

And obviously, therefore, every single tour caddy on our tour absolutely completely, unfailingly and unquestioningly complies with this no betting rule. Similarly not one mother, grandmother, dad, grandfather, brother, uncle, nephew, niece, etc. has ever bet on golf since they introduced this ban a few years back now. And don't let anyone ever tell you differently.

13. We're not sponsored

'You tour caddies are walking billboards, aren't you? You must be raking it in from sponsorship?' The answer to the first question is 'yes'. The answer to the second is 'are we fuck'.

And the reason for the latter answer is that on the DP World Tour caddies are basically barred from being sponsored as a group thanks to a sneaky little clause in the Players' Handbook which states that no more than two caddies can wear the same sponsor logo(s).

However, the Tour did finally agree a few years back to work with the ETCA to relax this rule and find a mutually acceptable and beneficial sponsor for every tour caddy. In the intervening years, nothing has ever come of this, despite, and I have this on very good authority, the ETCA chairman personally turning down in excess of £300,000 of sponsorship opportunities. Not that obviously he ever admitted that to those of us he's meant to represent. Meaning that caddies on the DP World Tour remain logo- and sponsor-free in 2023.

14. We're not all earning fortunes

Not being sponsored is not ideal, but that said, these days if your player is in, say, the top 50 in the Race to Dubai then you're doing okay financially. And if your player is in the top 50 in the World Rankings you're doing even better.

But if your player isn't, then it can be a very different story. Take the guy who caddied for the Spanish guy who got the last card in 2022, for instance: his bonus that year would have been in the region of €16,000. Half decent yes, but then there's whoever was caddying for the 159th-ranked player, because they will have earned in the region of €8,200 bonus. They'd have been better off stacking shelves in Tesco. Some might say that it's a shame they weren't, but I couldn't possibly comment.

No, caddying is not your instant gateway to a fortune: reason 1,287 why you really shouldn't try to become a tour caddy.

15. Winner pays the room

Each week on tour most of us share hotel rooms, or more frequently these days apartments or Airbnbs. And we share the cost.

The cost is not shared, though, if your roommate or someone in your apartment/Airbnb happens to win that week (or rather their player wins that week). Because in that case he or she picks up the cost of the digs. It's a time-honoured caddy tradition. Hence the phrase 'winner pays the room'.

16. Chiselling

If the time-honoured tradition of winner pays the room is at the top of tour caddies' moral codes, then 'chiselling' must be at the very bottom.

Chiselling is the term given to the practice of trying to go after a specific bag – or bags – while a fellow caddy is on that bag. People who do this are labelled 'chisellers'. As in someone who chisels away at a player with a word here and a word there, etc., all in the name of undermining their current caddy to the point where that player decides that the chiseller is right and they would do a better job than his current caddy.

Hand on heart I can say I have never indulged in chiselling, mainly because I have mirrors in my house and I like to look at myself in them without the revulsion that I would feel seeing a chiseller's face looking back at me. To me it's reprehensible to go behind a colleague's back knowing that, if you're successful, he'll be out of work. Most guys out here also draw the line at chiselling, thankfully.

But we all know who the chisellers are. And secretly rejoice when they're either unsuccessful or get fired themselves.

17. Getting fined

If you forget to rake a bunker on tour and a referee spots this, then your player will get a €500 fine – which he will pass on to you. If you don't replace a divot and a referee spots you, then your player will get a €500 fine – which he will pass on to you. Similarly, if you refuse to fill in a manual stats card, then your player will get a €500 fine – which he will pass on to you.

Yes, there are plenty of traps us caddies can fall into across the season. And that's just on the course. Perils await off it too. Because let's say as a caddy you decided to swear and gesticulate at a local's car in Qatar while getting a lift home in a player's courtesy car, only for the Qatari in question to get the police involved, then you'd probably get fined for that. Similarly if you tried to fight a statue in an Italian clubhouse in front of a whole bunch of pro-am guests, then as well as looking pretty stupid, you'd be looking at a fine for that too. And just say you exhibited the kind of behaviour on a tour charter flight that would see you banned from a commercial airline for life, well you could hardly complain about being fined for that either. Or about being fined if your Napoleon complex kicks in after too much alcohol and you end up leading a midnight rampage ending up at the door of the Tournament Director's hotel room in Cyprus. But at least that drunken rampage would only result in a fine, rather than six months inside.

No, it's best to behave like an adult out here. Especially as when the Tour issues fines to players it seems to act as judge, jury and executioner. And get away with it. In the way no other organisation on this planet would.

18. Yes, we do pay tax

A veteran caddy now long, long retired once told me, 'Tax, son: that's what they use to put carpets down.' And while there are Caddy Lounge rumours about that lad who's never paid a penny of tax yet, these days 99.9 per cent of us pay tax in whatever country we live in. Mainly because a lot of players now insist on it.

And that's why a lot of caddies absolutely have their own accountants because (a) it shows you are legit, and (b) having a good one can save you a fortune, especially when your man is having the kind of season mine is having this year.

But more importantly, it also means that you have nothing to worry about the next time His Majesty's Revenue and Customs decide that 'it's a while since we looked at professional golf; let's see if they've cleaned up their act'. And you definitely won't have to go cap in hand to your player to see if they will pay off your backdated tax bill with all those noughts on it like one guy had to a good few years ago now. Although quite why his player ended up agreeing todo so is still a matter of some conjecture.

Or maybe he did have an incriminating photo after all.

Chapter 7

Major Season

The Story of the Week of the US Open
15–18 June 2023

Not being exempt and having decided to give the qualifying
a miss this year, fairly obviously we aren't at the LA Country
Club for the US Open this week and so have the week off.
He's headed off to see the coach for a top-up; I've headed back
to the UK and then off to sunny Spain for a few days with
the missus. Shame really as he found his game last week and
played some lovely stuff. Was it ever thus?

But what one lost another gained, because instead of
going on about thick rough, impossibly quick greens and the
usual amateur set-up by the USGA that is the US Open, I
get to go on about last week's news that the PGA Tour, LIV
and DP World Tour have seemingly come together under a
new organisation funded by the Public Investment Fund (the
PIF) of Saudi Arabia.

As we alluded to the other week when all this was first
announced to an unsuspecting world, there's a large amount
of people with a large amount of egg on their long faces. And
without naming names, there's not a single one of us not
enjoying watching the squirming and backtracking of some
of those who have been very public in their views on LIV to
date. Which kind of serves them right. And in a few specific
cases, a case in point (yet again) that 'sometimes it's better to

keep your mouth shut and have everyone think you're stupid, rather than opening it and removing all reasonable doubt'.

Now as you already know tour caddies are all professional clairvoyants on and off the course, so you'll not be surprised to hear that we'd worked out a good few months ago that some form of entente (maybe not very) cordiale was always going to be the end result. Even for no other reason than it would stop a few law firms getting immensely richer the longer the slanging match went on. And here it duly is.

And kudos by the way to all parties for keeping everything secret: the world of professional golf is notoriously 'porous' when it comes to things like this. That in itself was some achievement: I mean, there's many a caddy who gets to hear he's being fired before his player (or if they're a coward, their management) tells him.

But if nothing else, it at least junks the whole notion of the PGA Tour's line that LIV was bad for 'golf's eco-system', when what they actually meant was that it was bad for their business model, which everyone who didn't swallow this, or the hostile coverage by the majority of golf journalists, knew from the off. The Saudis were never ever, ever going to just go away, and at the end of the day money talks: always has done, always will do. So once all parties had dialled back the emotion and stepped back to look at the numbers, some form of joint venture was always inevitable, no matter how many people that upset. And although he now faces being labelled 'the Chief Hypocrite', Jay Monahan is right in saying that it's good for business.

And actually very good business if you're in, say, the top 60 in the world, as the Caddy Lounge is predicting that at some stage in the future there will be some form of new (say) 14-tournament series plus the majors (something we just named the 'world series of golf'), in which all the top 60 players in the world have to play. Yes, have to. Gone will be the option of choosing your own schedule in this series: a series that will feature tournaments right across the world, including fairly obviously Saudi. That way, the best play against the best more often, which after all is what golf fans across the world want to see. And with innovative TV coverage where you can watch every shot of every player, there ought to be a real surge in the number of people watching and engaging with golf. Each tournament will effectively be like an F1 Grand Prix where all the teams 'play' every 'tournament': no one turns up at an iconic place like Monaco only to find that, for example, Ferrari and Red Bull aren't bothering that week as they don't like the 'course'. In short, it's not a million miles away from the exact format Premier Golf League, who must be spitting feathers watching all this by the way, was proposing a few years ago now.

Below this would likely sit what is now the PGA Tour. Where the best of the rest play. Just for far more money than they do at the minute. With the prize at the end of the season being 'promotion' to the 'world series of golf', swapping places with the guys who have been 'relegated' from the 'world series of golf'. And again, once these players put emotion to one side, they really ought to take the view that currently in a PGA Tour event they have bollocks all chance of winning anyway, so to have 60 players automatically out of the potential field while playing for more money has got to be a good thing. It's still golf at the elite level, just not quite as elite as the 'world series of golf', which is what they are too: elite (golfers), just not quite as elite as the elite.

This leaves the DP World Tour. Currently it apparently has no seat on the board of this new venture – not that surprising seeing as they appear to have turned down overtures made by the Saudis a few years back, in favour of a 'Strategic Alliance' with the PGA Tour. Who, true to form, have to all intents and purposes ditched them when faced with a choice between loyalty and self-interest and money. But from a tour caddy's perspective, and I suspect from a player's perspective too, over here we ought to see a healthy increase in the prize funds from 2024 onwards, if not the quality of the fields in some of the events. And any increase in prize funds is ultimately an increase in our bonuses across the season. About which not one tour caddy will be complaining. Or frankly be bothered where that money has ultimately come from. But if you do or you are, then there is always the option of swapping the greatest job in the world for a not so great job in the 'real world'. No. I didn't think so.

This 'pecking order' mirrors what's been said in these pages already about golf fans wanting to see the best playing against the best more often than they do now. And to watch that in the not-too-distant future (2024 is too early we think), you'll be turning on the 'world series of golf', which would relegate coverage of what was the PGA Tour down a peg. And put it more on a par with the 'because I like golf and because it's on' reason for watching the DP World Tour these days. But our Sunday nights will definitely be more interesting, that's for sure. As will the average golf fan's. And that's got to be a good thing.

One other thing all this does mean, though, is an important paradigm shift as to what it means to be a professional golfer. Because from what I understand, we finally get to the point (or certainly closer to it) where the tours no longer own the players. Instead the players are what they always should have been, free entities: free to play on whatever tour they are eligible for, at any time. And that has got to be a huge step forward for them. For years the players with cojones have regularly had to remind the odd officious member of the Tour staff, 'Remember you work for us, not the other way round,' and now that's beyond argument. And not before time if you ask me.

What definitely remains to be seen, though, is whether the adults return to the room (i.e. the Players' Lounge), and remember that they were friends (and in some cases teammates) before LIV started, and just because someone made a different choice from yours really isn't a mature reason for stopping liking them. Instead, take a leaf from the Caddy Lounge: no DP World Tour caddy fell out with a mate or colleague because they went to LIV. Which, not for the first time, makes us tour caddies look like the sensible ones in all this.

But to go back to the US Open, which this chapter was meant to be about, apparently Wyndham Clark won, keeping his nerve nicely after two late bogies, and winning by one in the end. I say 'apparently' because this side of the pond it was literally the middle of the night, and no one bar the odd insomniac golf perv would have still been up watching it, ensuring no one bar the odd insomniac golf perv will remember it. What was noticeable waking up to the news was that in this major it didn't seem to matter which tour he normally plays on, or what he thinks or doesn't think about LIV, so hopefully that is also a sign of things to come. Maybe it's also players recognising that keeping shtum and not getting involved in the politics keeps your stress down and your focus on your job up.

My Sunday was similarly stress-free, with an early-doors fond farewell to the missus for a week or so, a nice lunch, then a wander to the airport, albeit to then have to navigate the human jungle of AGP (Malaga Airport) sober, which put me very much in the minority.

But at least I wasn't having to navigate LAX in a mad dash to get the Sunday-night flight from LA to Munich after the US Open like a few of the guys were, safe in the knowledge that the distinct possibility of a week's worth of mind-bending jet lag awaited them.

No, my progress up to Munich was much more serene. And by 9pm I'm in the hotel in Erding, our perennial home for the week of the 2023 BMW International Open. Another of my favourite weeks on tour.

A Wait Well Spent

Tour caddies spend a lot of time travelling. And waiting. And when doing either it's always best not to do it with someone who would send a glass eye to sleep or make you want to jump off the nearest bridge. Otherwise both can be purgatory.

Fortunately my well-known disdain for football bores and *Daily Mail* readers is enough to deter all but the most un-self-aware of my colleagues from plonking their boring asses next to mine should they fall into either of the aforementioned categories.

Indeed, waiting around in Stockholm airport the other week, myself and a colleague (who very definitely doesn't fall into any of these categories) mused this very predicament, in the company of a well-known golf journalist. Thankfully he didn't print any of our conversation. Actually, we only mused it after he asked, 'What *DO* caddies talk about over a pint?', which took care of the rest of the two-hour wait. And then some.

Our answer went something along the lines of the following: 'A pint? You're having a laugh. Half of those guys are raging alcoholics. They'd never just stop at one,' said my colleague without even a hint of a smile. 'But if you really want to know, here's a few examples ...'

The Boring One

Boringly, but I guess predictably, the subject that comes up most is the travel and accommodation arrangements for the upcoming tournaments: where is the best place to stay, what's the best way of getting there, is anyone looking for a roommate, etc.

But there is always that one guy who has found the cheapest way of getting from A to B, who has found an unbelievable deal in an unbelievable hotel once you get to B, and who is pretty keen to let you know you've missed out.

There is of course a catch. Or several, in fact. Usually starting with the fact that getting from A to B for that price involves a flight at a time of the morning I only see when my prostate is playing up. And then that unbelievable deal is only unbelievably good because the hotel is unbelievably basic. And no one does basic hotels out here these days, because that was the old way.

And if there's one thing that the young lads out here don't do, it's the old way. And I admire them for it.

The Great Issues of the Day
Like in every golf club across the land, and across the world for that matter, there are a few guys who really do know everything. And it's no different in the Caddy Lounge.

But if you did happen to be casually sat at a table next to them 'discussing' (or rather talking your own wild theories over the wild theories of the others) the likes of Brexit, strikes or COVID then you'd be forgiven for wondering why more haven't put down the bag and gone into fields like political theory, climate change or immunology.

Or wondering why the leading scientists and politicians of the world don't make a beeline down to the closest Irish Bar to a tournament one week and give some of these guys a good listening to. Because if they did, most of the world's socio-economic issues like post-Brexit trade deals, Ukraine or even the Arab/Israeli conflict could be sorted out before the winning putt was holed that Sunday.

Either that, or you'd be left thanking the planet's lucky stars that the lure of an itinerant life on the world's fairways put paid to these intended career paths.

Brexit
If I were to generalise, I'd say that a fair number of the older UK-based caddies could be described as 'right wing'. (If you haven't read Lawrence Donegan's *Four-iron in the Soul*, then you should.)

And like all good turkeys who voted for Xmas, many are not shy to say they voted for Brexit: it won't affect us; they need us more than we need them; and all manner of other soundbites straight out of the right-wing (social) media.

But facts are pesky little things. And mean that things like the ending of Freedom of Movement for UK citizens really will affect their, and obviously my, ability to travel, and possibly even work, in Europe. No matter how deep you choose to bury your head in the sand. Or however neatly your colleague with similar views then rakes it behind you.

Cue an audible gulp from the aforementioned turkeys.

Young Caddies

A few, though not many these days to be fair, of the older caddies on tour are prone to harking back to the 'old days' on tour: these young guys have no idea; they shouldn't be out here; couldn't club a seal; and so on.

The world, however, is changing. And more guys who get their cards out here are bringing their friends out to caddy. Because you can teach your friend to caddy; but you can't teach him to be your mate. It's a trend. And a growing one at that.

But as I've said ad nauseam right across the season, you can't buy the experience that comes with someone who's been out here for 20 years like a lot of the over-40s you see on TV. And that will never change. Because when they say it's a hard six and not a smooth five, it is.

Not that that stops the ones who you don't see on TV whingeing. While turning green with envy.

How the Fuck did he get that Job?

Being fired is part and parcel of being a professional caddy. But so is being hired shortly afterwards.

Not that that stops the hushed 'how the fuck did he get that job?' question being posed around the Caddy Lounge table equally as shortly afterwards. Usually it's asked by a caddy who wished they had been asked. But hadn't been. Or had asked about the job but were politely declined: not that many caddies let on about that one.

Cue a whole list of wrong clubs, bad lines, crap advice the caddy in question has pulled/made/given across his entire career. Half of them massively embellished; half of them true. But hey, they've got the job and you haven't.

This then quickly descends into the 'yeah, but who got them that job?' question. And the answer is usually that one particular person: the one who put their name to the player or the player's manager. Sometimes from a list of caddies who have put their name forward. Sometimes from a reduced list of caddies who have put their name forward (i.e. the original list minus people that individual doesn't like). But always someone they like. And always someone who isn't a threat.

'As fucking usual' then ends this ten minutes of lively debate. And that 'will the last remaining three passengers …' call over the airport tannoy ended our debate too. We scurried one way; the journo the other.

All three happy in the knowledge that the two-hour wait had been a two-hour wait well spent.

The Story of the Week of the BMW International Open 22–25 June 2023

The good weeks on tour don't stop coming at this time of year. And out of all of them, this is probably my favourite. And for once not just because it's schnitzel for dinner every night.

No, there is 'something' about this week. Maybe it's the lovely town we stay in ten minutes from the golf course; maybe it's because the weather is always warm with generally very little wind; or maybe it's because of the huge crowds; or because the course is pan flat; or maybe even just because 'I've' always done well round here. I don't know. But whatever it is, it's got something.

What we've definitely got this year, though, are a couple of changes to the course: primarily to the 2nd hole. And about time too, as the second green at Golfclub München Eichenried used to be one of the most dangerous places on tour. Why? Well, for no other reason than it was located only around 280 yards in front of where the finest golfers in Europe were pounding drivers on the range. A fair percentage of which cleared the flimsy net at the back of said range and rained down on anyone on the green. How no one has been nutted by a ball in all the years we've been coming here I'll never know. And neither will I ever know how many pitch marks we've all had to repair on this green over the years ... from those drives.

Anyway, this year the old green has gone, replaced by a brand-new one 40 yards closer to the tee, which is now the old tee because we're playing off a new one about 50 yards further back. The hole isn't any shorter, more characterful or indeed better; but it's a damn sight safer.

What's also safe to say is that with it having been so warm here in the run-up to the tournament there's bugger all rough this year, and with storms forecast on Thursday and Friday afternoons that will soften everything up, making the fairways wider and the greens more receptive; this year more than ever round here, it's all about the scoring clubs.

This is the term we all use for the short irons. Because round here, apart from a couple of holes, the majority of the time you're going in with a lot of 8-irons, 9-irons or wedges to some pretty flat greens. Dial them in and you have a real chance round this place. Dial them out, and it's dial a Friday night flight home – which for some guys is only a couple of jet-lagged days after they flew in from the west coast of America, adding to their misery.

Any jet lag and lingering daytime tiredness also isn't helped by the food we get here at the course. Some weeks we eat on our own in the Caddy Lounge, but this week there's a huge marquee-type tent at the back end of the tented village where we eat with all the tournament volunteers. And what it serves is traditional German fare, so vegetarians need look away now. Or rather look elsewhere for food. Because it's all substantial stuff, and very nap-inducing. Bad news if you're off straight after lunch. But actually this is another thing to love about this tournament.

But it's not only us caddies who love this week. The players love it too. In no small way due to the fact that BMW lay on a load of (very fast) cars that they can take out for a leisurely drive round the country lanes around the course, or more likely a blast up and down the nearest autobahn, where the speed goes up and the video on the phone goes on. Of all the weeks on tour, this is the one where the smell of professional golfer testosterone hangs heaviest in the air. And why not? They're (mostly) young, can't really drink, definitely can't take drugs, so the odd adrenaline-pumping blowout can't hurt.

Yes, it's a strange, strange life being a tour pro. For a start you can go to work on Monday, work really hard the first three days of the week, perform as well as you possibly can, but then make a few mistakes late on Thursday afternoon that mean you're not getting paid that week, but still have to get up at silly o'clock Friday and go to work anyway. What other job offers such an opportunity? And if you're really unlucky, you get to do it all again the week after.

You also don't really have a boss to answer to either being a tour pro. You're effectively on your own out here. There's no one to give you a bollocking if you deserve it, an arm round the shoulder when you need it or that pat on the back when you've earned it. Yes, you might have a coach or a teacher, but professional golf at the highest level is not like sports such as tennis or athletics where the coach is king or, more obviously, football where you answer to the manager. It's up to you to manage your own performance: no one else.

And performing means beating a whole bunch of guys whom you travel with, practise with, and in a lot of cases are friends with. Okay, you might have done this at amateur level in the past, but now you're playing for money, and lots of it. And that can really get into your head.

A head that, believe it or not, might already be full of demons. Lots of them. All negative. Now, the best players basically stick two fingers up at them, and play with no fear: they really don't care if the flag they choose to go for down the stretch because they need to to win costs them an eight that drops them to eighth place: winning is all that matters. But for the rest, controlling these demons is an ongoing fight. Speak to virtually every tour caddy and they'll tell you they've worked for at least one player whose natural talent was incredible, but it's just that they play like they're driving down the road with a police car behind them.

Hence you now have a fair few sports psychologists out here; when I started there were precisely none. And, while it might not be everyone's view, personally I think they're invaluable. And invaluable to the point where there's many of us caddies who could also benefit from seeing them: if they can help the players get more out of their talent, then maybe they can do the same for us.

Now I don't actually know whether Thriston Lawrence has a sports psychologist as part of his team, but if he has, he or she will be one pretty happy sports psychologist tonight as his client played with zero fear down the stretch for his second win of the season, and his third in less than a year. Pretty impressive by anyone's standards. So much so that, irrespective of whether he uses a sports psychologist or not, his caddy better make sure the one thing he is using is a damn good financial advisor. Because his man is fast becoming what tour caddies refer to as an 'ATM'.

And speaking of ATMs, it's finally time to draw some £s out of one, as it's destination Birmingham for our first tournament in the motherland in 2023: the 2023 British Masters.

Eighteen Things You Didn't Know about Tour Caddies – Oh Fuck, We're Going to Extra Holes

Play-offs can be a right pest in terms of missing your flight on Sunday. Although obviously not that much if you end up winning that play-off. But it's arguably far worse when you've come out of nowhere with a low one on Sunday and then have to hang around all afternoon in case you make the play-off, only for right at the death someone to birdie their 72nd hole to pip you by a shot. Usually around the time you should have been boarding the flight you just missed.

So in honour of the dreaded play-off, here are the extra holes of things you didn't know about tour caddies.

19. We're not out on the piss every night

Back in the day it is true that after a round all the players and caddies basically went to the bar like every club golfer does every time they play. How long they stayed there varied. For some it was one drink; for some it was for one drink too many; while for some it was basically until they got kicked out or their next tee time: whichever came first.

But this was before my time. Because by the time I first shouldered a bag in anger on the European Tour, the Tour had already become a way more serious place, mainly due to the likes of Faldo preferring practice to pints, and that culture had gone forever.

And it's continued to evolve over the years I've been out here. For example, when I started there was basically no internet, then there was internet accessible by Wi-Fi in the hotel lobby on a laptop, whereas now everyone has tablets, iPads, iPhones, etc., so it's possible to stay in your room all night all week without going stir-crazy.

And in the same vein of there being more to do of an evening, then you're more likely to see the younger caddies out here in the hotel gym than the hotel bar, and then in their rooms filling in their player's stats for that day, and heading to the salad bar rather than kebab house.

And while the 'last to leave' brigade with their varying degrees of alcohol dependency still exists, at least in the days of Airbnb they get to do it somewhere other than opposite the players' hotel like they used to. Which in itself is also progress.

20. Losing luggage

At some stage during the season you'll arrive at your destination, but your luggage won't: it's an inevitable consequence of the increasing number of flights we take combined with the decreasing amount of time between connecting flights.

With the advent of things like Apple AirTags at least you know where it is (which in one case was Los Angeles on a flight from Malaga to Charles de Gaulle: explain that one), but that doesn't always mean that the airline does or, crucially, can tell you when you're likely to be reunited with it.

And that's why most tour caddies pack at least a few golf shirts, spare shorts, spare underwear and their trainers into their hand luggage on every trip to a tournament. You just never know when you'll get that sinking feeling at the baggage carousel. But at least when your worst fears are confirmed, you'll have something to go to work in the next day.

21. It helps if you're funny

Given how much time you spend with your player I always think that it helps if you can make him laugh. And from the Scottish caddy who told his player that 'Lassie would nae find that ball if it was covered in fucking bacon' after he'd hit it deep into the woods, to the guy who on reading a *Sunday Times Magazine* article describing 70 per cent of caddies on the (then) European Tour as 'brothel hands' wrote them a letter of complaint based upon the figure being 'much closer to 95 per cent', they come up with stuff that you just can't make up if you tried.

It's things like these, and a thousand and one others, that mean I can honestly say, and say it with some pride, that my colleagues are some of the funniest people to walk this earth – which is just as well because when things get tense on the course, as they are prone to do from time to time, being able to make a grumpy, highly strung athlete laugh always comes in handy. And is occasionally essential.

So if you've never made anyone laugh in your life, caddying definitely isn't for you. Reason 1,256 not to give up that day job.

The Story of the Week of the British Masters 29 June–2 July 2023

Finally, finally, finally, we're back in the UK for a tournament. And wow, is it nice to be back. Personally my 'back' starts with actually getting home on a Sunday night for a change thanks to the ultra-efficient MUN airport where getting from the taxi to the departure gate takes minutes as opposed to centuries in the likes of CDG – which, by the way, everyone avoids like the plague as no matter what time you turn up for your flight, although you might make it on to the plane, your luggage almost certainly won't.

However, being back only properly starts the minute I walk into the house. Because, and it's the one tour caddy life thing I'm absolutely anal about, that's when I do my laundry. It all has to go in the washer the minute I get in the house. At whatever time of the day or night.

And then it all has to be hung up to dry: golf shirts together on separate hangers, likewise my collection of

T-shirts. My collection of golf shorts go on one clothes maiden, and fill it; my collection of Falke Hidden Cool golf socks on another. And fill that too with, I have to admit, left sock followed by right sock, followed by left sock followed by right sock order and so on. Because I am slightly OCD as you might have guessed. After doing this, home life can begin; but not before.

And in this week's case, home life begins with being 'back' to being a Monday house husband as I don't have to be at work until mid-morning Tuesday. So that means I get to do normal dad/husband things like take the kids to school, complain about the traffic, do everyone else's washing when I get back, pick the kids up again and have dinner as a family.

Not that this 'normality' lasts long as I'm (back) on the road at silly o'clock Tuesday and heading north towards the nondescript back of beyond that is Sutton Coldfield and its most famous son: The Belfry, which is where the British Masters is again this year.

The Belfry is of course synonymous with the Ryder Cup, but personally I think that's all the course has in its favour in terms of a golf course because bar the 10th (which as it's strokeplay not that many people go for off the tee) and the iconic 18th, every other hole is on the instantly forgettable side of not very memorable. It's definitely not in my top ten great courses although, to be fair, neither is it in my list of top ten dog tracks. Which says something.

But what I will say is that from what I've seen so far (which is a quick walk round and the back nine in practice), it's in great condition, just minus the normal penal rough you usually get round here as apparently it has hardly rained for nearly two months. All of which makes it already look like another week of (and we've had a few of these recently) flyer-central from the rough to small firm greens, so hindsight might be a useful club to pop into the bag come Thursday morning.

And as for rain, well that appears to be making its first appearance for weeks later in the week, making some wit in the Caddy Lounge's observation that 'we should take this tour to Africa: we'd do a lot of good' look like something worthy of investigation. But we'll see.

Until then at least it's dry. So basically me clutching at small straws of mercy given that this week the players are staying 'on-site', i.e. in a hotel on the golf course, which for us caddies is the worst of all worst possible scenarios. In fact it's a fucking nightmare.

And it's a nightmare because no one has yet invented a tour pro who had a scooby doo about how to usefully fill his time away from a golf course when he's away from home. Never met one yet. And I've been out here more years than I care to remember.

No, all an on-site stay means is more opportunity for your average tour pro to do, or try and do, as much as they possibly can and, yes you guessed it, as often as they possibly can. Which would be fine, only it almost always involves their caddy, i.e. us. So we can forget anything other than a number of quite long days divot-watching or rolling balls back on the putting green. Or worse, calls asking where you are, and can you get here as I fancy playing nine holes tonight: even though he knows that you're not arriving into the UK from Germany until 5pm Monday because that's the last thing we talked about Sunday – a classic case of tour pro in-one-ear-out-the-other-itis.

I suppose it's also not helped by the sense from outside the ropes that, maybe for the first time since the Middle East Swing, this is a REALLY big tournament, which it is of course, and actually the start of a run of really big tournaments stretching right up until The Open in a month's time.

Not something you'd necessarily think from a casual glance at the depth of the field this week, though. Yes Justin Rose is here, but none of the other real star names have come back from the States for this one, and so the field has gone down into Category 18, which is the guys who finished between 118 and 133 on the Race to Dubai last year (i.e. they lost their cards) and the guys who finished between 21 and 30 on the Challenge Tour last year (who didn't get their cards). But don't ever let the category number fool you: these guys are still bloody good players in their own right, and therefore worth watching in their own right. Even if you would have preferred to be watching more of the top 50 players in the world.

And watch, people will. In their thousands. And they'll be proper golf crowds. Because while we certainly get big crowds in a few other countries, nowhere else in Europe, or in fact the world, are they as knowledgeable as UK ones. I know that sounds like a cliche, but it's true. UK crowds are proper crowds: always have been, always will be. Even on the practice days. Oh, and obviously from Monday right through to Sunday there will not be a single helmet shouting 'get in the hole', 'mashed potato', 'babbabooyee' or any other shite like that.

All of which does beg the question why there aren't more tournaments held in the UK: as a sponsor you'd definitely get more spectator bang for your buck. Especially because it's these crowds that give this tournament a real buzz about it: something that filters down to players and caddies alike.

Well and truly buzzing come Sunday afternoon were Daniel Hillier and his caddy as a late eagle–birdie–eagle run turned his Category 14 status (guys who finished 1–20 on the Challenge Tour last year) into a Category 3 one for the next couple of years. Or job security as it's also known.

Not that any of this really bothered me. Mainly because, not for the first time this season, his golf balls refused to float. All of which had us floating off early over to Denmark for the carnival that is Made In HimmerLand.

Another 'can't wait' week on tour.

The Roommate Conundrum

One of the big changes over the years I've been out here has been where we all stay. Back in the day it was always a hotel, generally secured on the Monday of the tournament week by the first few caddies to arrive in the town closest to the golf course.

Over time and the advent of the ETCA there was, most weeks, an official caddy hotel sourced by someone in the ETCA, serviced by official transport to and from the golf course that week so everyone stayed there. That too has now changed, and while there is more often than not a caddy hotel, more and more of us tend to source our own accommodation, mainly through Airbnb. If only because sitting in hotel rooms and hotel bars becomes tedious quite quickly.

But when we do have, or choose, to stay in a hotel, one thing that has not changed over the years is that when you're 'sharing the room', you need to choose your roommate carefully. It's a skill you have to develop early as a tour caddy. And one that borders on a dark art.

Indeed an American colleague (known as much for his intellect as his caddying skills) once claimed to have conducted a two-year experiment in this field. An experiment which in year one simply involved being incredibly organised and booking flights and accommodation as far in advance as sensibly possible; but in year two doing completely the opposite, and making all his arrangements at the last possible minute.

At the end of which time his conclusions were that doing everything in advance did in fact save money, but not nearly enough to make it worthwhile in terms of the effort you have to make, or, and this was perhaps the more interesting one, to compensate you for the fun you'd miss out on with making last-minute arrangements. Because that fun involved making new friends by staying or sharing with people, or discovering

Alsatians

in fact that some people are ****s. Either way, at least in his eyes, this was valuable knowledge.

Personally I favour a more cautious approach. To the point where if I do end up staying in a hotel, I'll get a single room rather than share with anyone and take the chance that I might actually become friends with them, or discover that they fall into the other category so eloquently described by my American colleague.

Except of course the time recently when I did end up sharing a hotel room with a fellow caddy, which like I say isn't something I would ordinarily do and, in fact, hadn't done for years. Not because I like to watch porn each and every evening. And definitely not because I like to get some hookers back. Nor is it because I'm an introvert with no friends, BO, and a liking for sitting staring at the wall. I also don't necessarily hate being around people. I literally just hate 'sharing the room'.

This does beg the question why I'm doing it this week. And the answer to that one is because I'm soft. And because my old mum always said you should help people when they're stuck.

And 'Johnny'[4] was stuck. His player got into the tournament last minute. He didn't have the time to even look for a hotel before dashing for the flight. And anyway, all the hotels are full for miles around here. And we're in an area where the locals' Alsatians have Rottweilers as bodyguards.

So I responded to his plea for help and offered him the spare bed in my room. Had Johnny been Jimmy, however, I would have completely ignored the plea for help. Like everyone else in their right mind. That's because with Jimmy you won't get a wink of sleep all week, because he snores.

---

4 Not his real name in case you're wondering. And in the same vein, neither is Jimmy, Jimmy; Chris, Chris; Davey, Davey; Brian, Brian; Billy, Billy; Stephen, Stephen or Martin, Martin: their names have been changed to protect the guilty.

Incessantly. You'd be forgiven for thinking the council were digging the road up next to your bed. And like all snorers he always drops off to sleep the minute his fat head hits the pillow. You won't. That I can guarantee.

And with Jimmy, like so many snorers, the usual excuse is 'sorry, mate, I only snore after I've had too much to drink ...' That'll be every night then you walloper. Oh, and I'm not your 'mate'. Mate.

Chris is another snorer. One who ironically makes way more noise when he's asleep than when he's awake. As is Brian. He once snored all night, got up at 6am, made his own bed, then stuck Sky News on full blast. His roommate didn't think he should have done this, and this led to what are referred to at football matches as 'angry scenes'.

Jimmy, Chris and Brian may snore, but Stephen has a reputation for pulling back the duvet in the middle of the night – while still asleep – and pissing straight up into the air. So don't share with him either.

Then there's Davey. Davey is prone to random fits of shouting and swearing in the middle of the night. In his sleep. Unnerving and annoying in unequal measure. Another don't share.

Billy falls into the same category. Mainly because he has been known to both snore and have swearing fits. Though not at the same time, thankfully. That, and rumours continue to circulate that he is prone to using every single towel in the bathroom, leaving you without and heading down to reception in search of extra ones. Some might see this behaviour as 'odd'; I couldn't possibly comment.

Another colleague, now sadly no longer with us, once came back in the late evening waking his prone and not very well roommate up with a choice of 'Thai or Indian?' Only he wasn't talking about food.

But worst of all is Martin. How his regular roommate puts up with him is frankly unfathomable. Because Martin, bless him, is a big lad and has big – and by all accounts smelly – poos. It's just that he never 'rakes the bunker properly' afterwards, leaving the toilet and toilet bowl Out of Bounds until housekeeping arrives. Presumably in hazmat suits and full breathing apparatus.

Thankfully Johnny isn't like any of these spanners. Which makes him the exception that proves the rule.

Not because he doesn't snore. Not because his conversation isn't limited to football and beer. And not even because he has opinions. Of his own. Rather than ones significantly to the right of Hitler or a straight rehash of the bile spouted by the UK tabloids.

No, he's the exception because you never hear him get up and get out for the 4.30am bus to the course. Nor do you ever hear Johnny coming in when you've gone to bed at 21.00 because it's your turn to get the 4.30am bus the next day. And I know that Johnny has got my back should the current roles ever be reversed.

But most of all, I know that Johnny will always rake the bunker properly. So it should be a nice week. But next week in Denmark will be better. Because in Denmark I'm definitely not 'sharing the room'.

The Story of the Week of Made in HimmerLand 6–9 July 2023

Theoretically this tournament never looks very inviting. Schedule-wise it's in that awkward spot before the $9,000,000 Scottish Open and The Open, so do you really want to play the week before two such big tournaments?

Location-wise it's a pain to get in and out of as it's 55 minutes from the nearest airport and two hours from the next nearest, which is important if you want to get a Sunday-night flight out to Scotland for next week.

Weather-wise it can be apocalyptic perched at the very northern tip of Denmark, making it uniquely placed to catch whatever wind and rain is around: sometimes lots of it. Thursday this week being a prime example.

And finally, accommodation-wise it's a pain as unless you stay on-site it's a 50-minute each-way journey to Aalborg where the nearest decent hotels are.

But. When you stand on that 16th tee none of this matters one jot. Because this is the world-famous HimmerLand Hill. There's few other places on the golfing planet you'd rather be. Not because of the 96 metres that stand between you and the pin. Or the ridiculously small green with equally ridiculous slopes on which it sits.

No, simply because of the setting which is basically a dead-end mini-valley with a green perched at the end surrounded by natural slopes on three sides. Slopes which are crammed to the rafters with 5,000 people from first group until last group. Every day. And no matter how many times we come here it never gets old and is genuinely the best hole we play on tour each year.

It doesn't even seem to matter that virtually every one of the 5,000-strong congregation is armed with a small plastic squeaking duck which they squeak each and every time someone makes a birdie. Which is kind of funny the first time. But not so much thereafter. Barring the time when one of the Danish players proposed to his girlfriend on the green. The crowd all went nuts. We went all nauseous.

Arguably though it's not this hole that's the most amazing thing about this week. No, that honour goes to the unique connection the Danes have with this tournament. Something which starts with the literally hundreds and hundreds of volunteers, each decked out in their volunteers' apparel. There's a palpable sense that this is THEIR tournament. It belongs to them personally. And they take immense and very obvious pride in it. And it's wonderful to see.

And that's just the volunteers. The same can be said of the thousands who come to watch – despite the course being pretty much in the very north of Denmark and pretty inaccessible except by car.

Hence the fact that there is a glamping site across from the 15th fairway. In previous years this has been huge, and I mean stretching as far as the eye can see huge, but this year it looks pretty miniscule by comparison, due in part, we all suspect, to the fact that this is apparently the last (or if not, then definitely the penultimate) time we'll be playing up here, as from 2024 it seems the tournament is moving to Aarhus. And closer to people, presumably.

But while the glamping site might be smaller, even just having it there all adds to what is a pretty special atmosphere all week long. We don't opt for the glamping option. And thankfully the containers full of bunk houses idea they tried for the caddies a few years ago only lasted one year, so isn't available this time. Thankfully, because although you literally stepped out of bed into the Caddy Lounge where they served us breakfast, lunch and dinner, before letting us loose in the ten-pin bowling alley and the crazy golf course, comfortable it really wasn't.

Instead, after much discussion, we've decided to stay in one of the hotels in Aalborg, and take the official transport up to the golf course each day. Although it takes a minimum of 50 minutes and means a seriously early start if you're first off, at least it offers a greater range of eating options at night and a much greater range of bars to sit outside.

All of which seem remarkably caddy-free at the start of the week given that the majority of guys chose to stay around The Belfry on Sunday night as the Tour put on coaches to ferry everyone down to Stansted to catch the only direct flight to Aalborg from the UK on the Monday lunchtime, which everyone piled on despite it being with everyone's least-favourite budget airline.

Apart of course from those guys who were at The Open Final Qualifying on Monday and Tuesday, meaning their

Aalborg

travel day ended up being either very late Tuesday or first thing Wednesday. All straight on the back of a practice round at whatever venue they were at Monday and then the two rounds on the Tuesday. Yet another example of why you're wrong if you think that we spend the time between you seeing us on TV on Sunday afternoon and when you next see us on TV on Thursday just swanning about. No, this job can, especially on weeks like this, be physically demanding: and you only know how much if you actually do it.

But once everyone did get to the course, they found it in really great condition; in fact perhaps the best it's ever been since we've been coming here. And irrespective of this, it's also a pretty decent track in its own right with enough birdie chances here to keep everyone happy and in with a shout, especially down the last few holes. Happy, though, is not a word used to describe the walk, as there are enough hills out there to keep HimmerLand's reputation as being a **** of a walk for players and caddies alike. And while we might all end up missing the atmosphere, etc., no one's knees and ankles will miss the North Face of the 4th hole, vertical torture of the walk to the 11th tee from the 10th green, or that of its partner in crime, the short lung-busting walk up to that 16th green. Good riddance to them.

Nevertheless, it was a fond farewell to this place come Sunday afternoon. Well, it was for the crowd, who were treated to a six-hole play-off and a Højgaard home win; less so for Nacho Elvira, who airmailed the green on that sixth extra hole. And the Out of Bounds line. So handing the tournament on a plate to the home hero.

All of which proved, yet again, that not having a professional caddy on the bag is fraught with danger, especially at the business end of the tournament. Now there was obviously a good reason for this (Elvira's new caddy couldn't get there in time), but even if he only managed to get there for the play-off, Elvira definitely would not have done what he did on that sixth extra hole. No tour caddy in the world would have let their man do that. Especially not the guy Elvira now has on the bag.

And to make matters worse, he'll have missed his Sunday-night flight too.

Stats Are the New Currency

Looking around the Caddy Lounge this morning it did strike me that times are definitely a-changing out here. Because certainly when I started caddying, and probably as recently as even ten years ago, I'd have been sat here in the midst of a group of exclusively men, the vast majority over 40 years old, most of whom had been caddies since leaving school. And a good few for a lot longer than that, preferring fairways to classrooms. But all eventually making their way on to the European Tour, where they first survived – then thrived.

Today, however, I am not. Because as we reach the mid-point of the 2023 season, I would say that these guys, and I'm very much one of them, are becoming something of an endangered species out here. And they, or rather we, are endangered because our numbers are ever-decreasing. Nothing too obvious, or too dramatic: the odd one here, the odd one there. But reducing nonetheless. Mainly due to the inevitable wear and tear this job puts on your body: it just gets harder to lump a tour bag up those hills as the years roll on. But also because, with half an eye on the dwindling number of jobs open to them, over recent years a fair number have surrendered to the inevitable, and sought sanctuary, and employment, in the caddies' afterlife that is the EU Legends Tour. Where they'll be young once again.

But outside of the Legends Tour, time waits for no man. And in their place we have a new generation of caddies out here. Not that, and I know I've said this a few times already, those of us who are 40 over par or worse have completely disappeared or no longer thrive out here, because, and I'll

179

leave myself out of this one, they do – if for no other reason than at the top of their 'CVs' is experience. And a lifetime of it. Something not even a Mastercard can buy.

These are the guys who answer 'what do we have behind this one?' question almost before it's been asked. And certainly without needing to look in the book: they already know. These are the guys who have seen this shot, in this situation, a thousand times before and know what the best play is, often based on bitter experience.

These are the guys who know to say, 'The day we're having … let's just lay this up.' These are the guys who will sometimes give their player no choice: because if the situation merits it, they'll pull the club for him, hand it over and simply walk off.

And these are the guys who can adapt to an employer (i.e. a player) half their age: so much so that it really doesn't matter that they think the rap music he likes is shit, or that they've never watched *Love Island* when that's all he wants to talk about.

No, it's just that we are increasingly being replaced by younger models as caddying continues to become more of a young man's game. And yes, with a couple of exceptions, it is still basically a male preserve. Something that this morning's cursory glance round the Caddy Lounge confirms.

Yes, there is the occasional dinosaur revelling in how it was much more fun in the old days but just like their prehistoric friends they're dying out year on year. And instead, you see more and more young faces out here. Lots of them in fact. And from all four corners of the earth.

In fact, if they picked the right week, any self-respecting golf pervert would immediately spot a former national amateur champion chatting away to that lad who won a world-ranking amateur tournament the other year. Where his warm-up consisted of a pint of Magners and a club sandwich, rather than anything involving a sand wedge. Then their wandering eye would spot that guy who wins on the Gecko Tour in Spain when he's not helping his man win golf tournaments. And a lot of them, too. Before a final double take when they see those two lads who used to be good enough to be next door in the Players' Lounge, but these days aren't. And so find themselves with us in the Caddy Lounge having come across to the dark side over the last few years.

But most importantly, along with their young faces, what these guys are also bringing is a different mentality and approach to caddying. Leaving aside the fact that they're more likely to head to the gym than the bar after getting back to the hotel, and that they're better suited to deal with the heat and humidity of some of the early-season venues, perhaps the biggest difference is in how they prepare.

Because preparation is now a serious part of the job. And one that takes up quite a bit of your evening. To the extent that nights in the pub have been replaced by nights in front of the computer. Primarily studying your player's stats, and increasingly studying some form of pre-tournament report telling you how your man should play the golf course, which is about as far away from the preparation anyone my age would have done back in the day when we first started out here. And even from say ten years ago when the studious types would spend an hour or so 'doing tomorrow's pins', which was little more than noting where the pins were going to be tomorrow, seeing where the 'smelly ones' were and writing ourselves notes on where the best misses to these were. As well as maybe just checking tomorrow's wind direction to see if any drives or approach shots might need some attention. Something that everyone still does, obviously. It's just that that is where the standard stuff ends. And the appliance of the science begins.

And while it's not necessarily every player who does this, the bedrock of this science is increasingly some form of pre-tournament report, in which is set out every single thing the player needs to know to get them to the 1st tee on Thursday as prepared as they possibly can be. Hence it typically runs to 25-plus pages.

The player gets a copy (obviously). The caddy gets a copy (again, obviously). The coach gets one (fairly obviously). The strength and conditioning guy gets one (less obviously). And the club manufacturer gets one (way less obviously, but we'll see why in a minute).

First off this report sets out what you need to do well to do well this week. And at its highest level this is about what previous winners (and high finishers) round this golf course have done well in the past; for example, they have hit 75 per cent of the fairways, or their strokes gained putting has been off the charts. Because once you have this, then as a player you can look at how this stacks up against how you might have played here in the past, which will show where your performance needs to improve if you too are to do well. This might be as simple as your putting from 25 feet and above was inconsistent last year, when everyone in the top ten was laying these putts stone dead. But can be as 'complex' as highlighting that your club manufacturer needs to build you a specific club for that week. Because they too get a copy of the data for their staff players.

Then there is generally a plan for how the player should play every hole out there – based on previous pin positions, wind direction, temperature and what your tendencies are. With special advisories about which pin positions on which holes have produced high scores in previous editions of the tournament, because again that might alter your strategy on that hole on that day: you play the hole already knowing, and accepting, that bogey isn't a bad score to that flag. And it's certainly better than what could happen if you didn't know, which is perhaps the most important section for the caddy to have read, understood and woven into the game plan for that week.

And finally these type of reports tend to set out a few key thoughts for your preparation. Like, driver is key. Like, you're likely going to have a significant number of putts from over 35ft. Like, the rough is Kikuyu, meaning extra time round the chipping green would be sensible.

But none of this would even be possible without data. And that comes from the numbers that every tour caddy now writes in either their yardage or statistics card, as well as the GPS data recorded in play on the fairways. The latter is there immediately, and has to be because it's used in in-play betting; the former requires the caddy to spend an amount of time transcribing these numbers into special spreadsheets that can be fed into the analysis software that churns out these reports.

And completing this task, if not every day, then certainly every week, is pretty much a prerequisite of the job of a tour caddy. Not doing so is not an option.

It was all groundbreaking when this stuff appeared on the scene a few years ago, but nowadays it's commonplace, with Dodo Molinari's StatisticGolf program (which is apparently driving the set-up of the Ryder Cup course in September to ensure that it suits the games of the European team) being pretty much the gold standard out here. And if you don't use reports and tools like this, then you could argue that as a player you're pretty much giving away strokes to the rest of the field right from the off. And no one out here is good enough to do that anymore.

No, properly interpreted, these statistics will tell you which pins to go at, which to come in 15ft short of and 10ft right of because statistically you will make more birdies from there than going at that back-left pin. And why, despite what you might think, you should go at every tight right pin. They are that powerful. To the point where using them right might make the difference between you keeping your card or keeping going back to the Tour School; or at the other end of the scale, getting your hands on a Green Jacket or getting your hands burnt trying.

Yes, in our world stats are the new language. And the new currency. And to survive and thrive out here in the future, a tour caddy will need to be fluent in both.

The Story of the Week of the Genesis Scottish Open 13–16 July 2023

Forty-odd years ago we studied (or should have: I was more likely to be skiving off at the golf course) the Renaissance in school history lessons. My only memory of it then was that it was long, boring and really rather shit, which just about sums up my view of this Renaissance today.

I mean of all the great golf courses in Scotland, what are we doing here? This is a corporate club for people who can't get into Muirfield next door. It's not fit to wipe its neighbour's arse, nor that of at least 100 other links courses in this country; 99 of which would provide a much better test, and offer much better preparation, for the main event next week: The Open.

Though to be fair there's a perfectly logical reason for this and that is quite simply that the number of clubs willing to give up their course for the tournament is around the same number that would provide this better test and preparation. Having their course closed for the tournament week alone costs them too much revenue in terms of greens fees at the busiest time of year, and that's before you add in the disruption in the weeks (if not months) before and after erecting and taking down all the infrastructure around the tournament itself.

And at the venues where this might not be an issue, then the playing time lost by members most certainly will be, especially at places like Loch Lomond which is basically only open in the summer anyway. So they refuse any approaches to host the tournament, no matter how prestigious it might be – which is a long-winded way of explaining why we have to drive in from Edinburgh casting envious glances at first Gullane, then Muirfield before turning into the Archerfield

Estate and through the pompous gates of the Renaissance Club itself. All the while wishing we were playing at the other two. For the reasons already stated.

Now whether any of the best players in the world share my – and many other people's – views is something we'll never know unless they take to social media after one too many down The Old Clubhouse in Gullane this week, but what we do know is that they're all here. Even the likes of McIlroy and Scheffler: although more likely because someone has probably popped some cash into their bank accounts (allegedly), rather than an endearing love of the layout.

But here's a few things that you might not know. The Scottish Open is now a co-sanctioned event with the PGA Tour, hence the $9,000,000 purse whereas back in the day when it was a European Tour event everyone thought the £3,000,000 one was enormous. That $9,000,000 is just about enough to get the likes of Scheffler, Schauffele, Thomas, etc. to play; although it's a fair question as to whether it would if it wasn't the week before The Open.

These guys make up some of the 75 spots available to those who usually ply their trade on the PGA Tour. And when you read down the list of names in Category 8, it's bloody impressive. Unless of course you're one of the DP World Tour players sitting below the cut-off line of the Entry List which, as I'm typing this, sits at number 79, meaning that around 35 guys who have full status on the DP World Tour don't get to play. In which case it's not impressive at all. And something that does seem vaguely wrong, if completely understandable.

Now obviously it's a long way to come from the USA, and what with virtually every player over there being on the breadline, coupled with the need to actually dust off (or in some cases obtain) a passport and the price of private jets these days, the PGA Tour smooths things over for its more delicate souls by paying their players a 'travel allowance' for the week, rumoured to be in the region of $8,000–$10,000.

No such luck for the DP World Tour guys who have decided to travel in the opposite direction this week to play in the Barbasol Championship, which is effectively the sop to the DP World Tour for giving up 75 spots in what was one of their flagship events. No, they get nothing, zip, nada, rien.

And that goes for next week too when there are a similar number of spots open to DP World Tour players in the Barracuda Championship opposite The Open. So any of my colleagues heading out there for these two are effectively taking a punt that their man does well. Because if he doesn't, then their wages, even with getting 50 per cent of the flight paid by their player, will not cover the cost of their travel, hire car (there are no courtesy cars or caddy buses on the PGA Tour), their accommodation and their food; they'll make a loss for working their asses off for two weeks in stifling heat. Yet again, what other job offers you such an opportunity?

I for one wouldn't like to be a fly on the wall when anyone in this position has that 'I know I've been away for two weeks working, and I've actually lost money, but honestly this job will pay the bills, put food on the table, clothe the kids, etc., just not this week' conversation with their wife/partner. And probably not for the first time this season either.

But for the 80-odd DP World Tour caddies whose players are in the field, this week does offer up an opportunity to make hay while the sun shines with a top-ten finish offering around $15,000 bonus. Except that it appears the sun might not be shining too much, especially Friday through Sunday which, with the Saturday and Sunday finish times being put back to cater for US TV, might not be great. But we'll see.

And see we did. Because Friday was pretty grim to say the least, making it just as well we were all subject to PGA Tour rules and timings rather than the normal DP World Tour ones. Because these allowed us way more time to do the decision-making over the shot than we would ordinarily get: something that made it way less stressful when that wind and weather rolled in.

And with the prospect of thunderstorms for Saturday afternoon, we dripped off the course knowing that it was highly unlikely we'd be finishing top ten to get one of the spots in The Open that are on offer this week; somewhat in awe at how much better the PGA Tour guys are, especially with the wedges and putter; and facing a 7am to 9am U-draw in the morning instead of the much-needed lie-in I was looking forward to.

And if we had thought that was bad, then the forecast of high winds for Sunday afternoon meant we were all up at even sillier o'clock again Sunday for another U-draw. As if it wasn't a tiring enough week already. But on the bright side this 'Scattish weather' might deter a few PGA Tour guys making the journey next year. Unless of course this tournament is moved to a decent venue, which, after another four days round here, I can assure you this one most certainly isn't.

But actually all the weather issues meant was that McIlroy got to hit those two incredible shots (the tee shot at 17 and the 2-iron through that wind at 18), do all his media and get down the road (or more likely into the sky) to Hoylake a bit earlier than he would have done. And in doing so, prove once again what every tour caddy out here knows fine well; and that is that when he's on his game, like in Dubai this year, you just don't beat him.

And as nice as the Scottish Open is; it's not The Open. And that's what's on everyone's mind. Including mine. And I won't even be there.

How Slow is he by the Way?

A few months ago the first round in Delhi finished in the dark. Or at least it would have done had they not put the floodlights on so the groups still on the course could finish the last couple of holes, which they did, avoiding the need for them to come back at silly o'clock the next morning to finish off and then head immediately straight back out for their second rounds.

Something similar also happened in Japan and Korea, where in the Land of the Rising Sun, the sun could frankly have done with actually rising a couple of hours earlier than it did. That way the guys at the back of the field the first two rounds would have finished at a half-sensible time. Meaning they – and their caddies – would have avoided the infernal traffic round both venues, and not had to do the room service then straight to bed thing that everyone hates.

What made it worse for some people was that they were late–early the first two days both weeks, so had to endure this twice. Not surprising then that there ended up being a good few debates in the Caddy Lounge and the various tour caddy chat groups about all this. But the conclusions, certainly of the debates I contributed to, which thankfully excluded any vocal talk-over-you-don't-mind-if-I-do types, were kind of interesting. Although it was probably as well no one felt the need to expose them to the wider social media golf perv world out there, as they certainly didn't toe the party line shall we say. As you'll see.

Anyway, our starting point was: is the pace of play in tournament golf (i.e. the time it takes to get round) really an issue? And if it is, to whom? And then, should we actually be getting worked up about it at all? Because it might be that around five hours for a three-ball or 40 seconds for a second shot is just how long it actually takes. And that trying to change isn't necessary. Or even possible. In which case, what's the point in trying?

And the argument goes something like this: why should a tour pro EVER 'rush' a shot potentially worth thousands of dollars/pounds/euros/riyals? Should they do it for the benefit of Sky Sports or The Golf Channel? Should they do it for the benefit of the galleries? Should they do it for the benefit of their fellow man? Should they do it for the benefit of the TV viewer? Or should they do it for their own benefit?

Because at the end of the day this is professional golf. There's a lot on the line. We're talking about people's livelihoods and, taking it to the extreme, legacies. And at the end of the day (or week) that's actually all that matters: nothing else. So crack on, take as long as it takes.

And to be fair, rarely does a tour caddy come off the course railing about how slow it was out there: we've kind of got used to the fact that it takes about five hours on a Thursday and Friday, whereas Sundays are a bit quicker because everyone wants to get the flight at 5pm. It never FEELS slow.

Sure, so-and-so and so-and-so might be snails. And something should be done about them. But even without so-and-so in the group it doesn't take that much less time. The point being that we don't really notice. Or care that much. And we're the ones closest to the action.

The reality could be that the pace of play is what it is. And always will be. And why that is is something that often gets overlooked. Which is surprising, because it's so obvious. It's simply that tricky shots take time. Like when it's super-windy. Like the line of a 45-footer on greens that are way slopier – and therefore more difficult to read – than most you play on on a Saturday morning. And way, way faster.

And definitely like those shots around the types of greens you see on tour. For example, get tempted to rush a chip from one of the run-off areas at DLF in Delhi and there is a high probability of you either degreening it completely straight into the water or leaving your chip at the back end of three-putt territory at the other side of the green.

And perhaps the greatest-ever example of this was Tiger's famous chip-in at 16 in the 2005 Masters. No one can convince us that it took 40 seconds or less to play that shot. It's 13 seconds alone from the start of any of the TV highlight clips to him hitting the ball, which doesn't leave much time to actually see the shot in the first place, work out where it needed to land, consider the alternatives and then actually commit to it. We wouldn't mind betting the total time taken would have been well in excess of a minute, probably nearer two to three.

What no one wants, or needs, at that stage of a tournament (or actually any round) is a rules official pointing at their watch or stepping in with a polite 'you're in danger of getting a bad time Mr Woods'. Shots like that are hard enough. And thank whoever your god is that no one officious did step in on that occasion. Otherwise we might have missed one of the iconic shots in all of golf.

But anyway, going back to the time taken by Tiger. Did that really put people off getting into golf? Or whoever Sky Sports dared to call out for being slow the other week? Get tae fuck did it or a more polite 'quite the opposite' seemed to be the general consensus.

And it's the same across tournament golf in general. Where is the evidence that people are put off playing our game because of the time it takes pro golfers to do their job to the best of their ability? Because frankly we've not seen any empirical evidence or data to back this up. Nor do we suspect we ever will.

And here's one other interesting thing. At the Scottish Open last week the tournament was basically run under PGA Tour rules, not the DP World Tour ones. So, amongst other things, it meant that the time allowed for each shot was significantly more generous. And aside from being welcome in that wind, it meant that no one even came close to getting monitored, timed or penalty shots. Yet we all took almost exactly the same time to get round in the first two rounds as we do at any other event: about five hours.

No. The only person who should be getting worked up about the time it takes for a three-ball is actually the wife of Billy at our golf club. Because she still thinks it takes nine hours.

The Story of the Week of the 151st Open Championship 20–23 July 2023

The Open is the greatest tournament in the world. Period. It's been my favourite tournament since I used to run home from school as a kid to watch it on the Thursday and Friday before being glued to every minute of the BBC coverage at the weekend, and one that I've been lucky enough to caddy in a good few times since.

Now there might be better tournaments out there – many swear by The Masters being the best – but not one comes close to giving you the goosebumps that the walk up the amphitheatre of the 18th hole at The Open does. It is quite simply the best walk in golf.

And one every single tour caddy wants to make every year. But not everyone can. And this year I was one of the ones whose player didn't make the 1st tee, so I had to make do with watching it from afar. Although afar wasn't as afar as it might have been had he decided to make the brutal commute to the west coast of America to play in the Barracuda Championship like he could have done. But thankfully didn't. And with there also being no tournament next week, neither did I have to travel to the next week's venue early to ensure I got to see the final afternoon's play – which I'd have done in a bar, with a whole bunch of colleagues doing exactly the same as me – which in itself tells you how we all view The Open.

Forgetting of course the hassles that come with actually caddying in the thing. First of which is the perennial problem of where to stay. It's never been easy, and is getting worse if we're honest, with most hotels and B&Bs in the immediate area being booked up months, if not years, in advance. Not too much of an issue if you're lucky enough to be playing as, unless you are clinically tight, you generally rent a house reasonably close to the course for the week, although you'll fork out a fair few thousand pounds for the privilege. Even less of an issue if your management company has rented a house for all their players, complete with private chef, and in the case of the IMG house at Muirfield a few years ago, a back gate on to the course itself. And absolutely no issue whatsoever if you're one of the very best players in the world when you'll be staying somewhere like the Old Course Hotel (for St Andrews) or the Marine Hotel (for Royal Troon); only this time for free.

And all the manufacturers are at it as well. They all rent houses or take over small B&Bs for the week, fully staff the place, fly all the top brass from the US in for the week, and add £13.34 on to the cost of that driver you'll buy after seeing the winner using one to pay for it.

Practice rounds at The Open are always interesting too. Not least because you can end up playing a few holes with some legends of the game: it's not been unheard of for Open champions just to stick their name down with basically unknown amateurs, or jump in for a few holes as you're finishing your practice round. That, and obviously there's way more people watching you practise than actually watch some normal DP World Tour events which, if we're honest, makes them way, way more enjoyable than normal practice rounds.

And because, fairly obviously, there's no pro-am at The Open (or any of the other majors), as a player there's less pressure to get yours in before Wednesday when you can. And instead, if you're sensible, you end up playing maybe one 18 holes and two sets of nine holes, with the rest of the time being filled up with lots of chipping and putting. And, crucially, rest.

But when to actually play these practice rounds is something of an art form. Ideally you want to play in or around the times you're likely to be playing the first two days; and if you don't, then at least time your practice to ensure that your caddy can walk the course at these times. Subtleties like the difference in the wind that come with the tide changes are best felt from actually being on the course itself. It's definitely up to the caddy to be up at 4am each of the tournament days at places like St Andrews to actually go see where the pins actually are on the greens: yes, you get a pin sheet but there's nothing like actually doing the hard yards (literally) and going out to The Loop to see precisely where they are in relation to the slopes on the greens. All of which can make it an absolutely exhausting week. Especially if the weather is rubbish.

Because that is another perennial problem of The Open; or at least it can be as, aside from the obvious vagaries of the British weather, The Open is one of the few tournaments in the year where everyone starts from the 1st tee, unlike in regular tour events where you start from the 1st tee one day and the 10th tee the next day, or vice versa: once in the morning wave, once in the afternoon wave. And obviously there is zero guarantee of the weather being the same all day; or the wind staying in the same direction. Meaning that some groups can theoretically play both nines at places like St Andrews downwind; while other groups end up playing both nines into the wind. To that extent it really is the luck of the draw. Although cynics used to suggest that if you were off an hour either side of Tiger Woods in the first two rounds, then you'd be okay. Personally I couldn't comment.

Although this year there wasn't a huge difference across the first two days, although maybe late/early might have been slightly better but only because it was marginally less windy, less cold and less wet. While on Sunday everyone looked like they just got soaked wet through.

Unlike me who was on the settee dry as a bone watching on TV, which did give me the opportunity to keep half an eye on the scores in the Barracuda Championship over in the States. Mainly on the back of last week when a good few of the Europeans in the field had very decent weeks. And it was the same again this week, with a couple of guys vaulting up the Race to Dubai rankings without actually winning the thing.

Or to put it in golf terms, they reaped the reward of risking going for the carry over the water to the States. Something that their caddies might have been suggesting (we always like the opportunity to play against a weakened field for lots of cash), but if they hadn't been are now claiming they did, because they will have made some serious cash: way more than they would have likely done in the two events in Europe the last two weeks. And looking at some of the guys who have benefitted, I'm pretty happy they did. While at the same time still being glad we hadn't bothered.

But going back to The Open, I turned the TV off just as the Champion Golfer of the Year walked out to pick up the best trophy in golf with a lingering feeling that the whole thing had been somehow thoroughly lacklustre this year. And not just because I was in front of my TV rather than in front of those crowds. No, because from speaking to a few guys whose player's score I was following, they too were all pretty much in agreement that there was something 'missing' this year. Yes, the field was pretty stellar, but whether it was the weather, those in the crowd who thought and acted like they were at a football match not a golf tournament, the excessive mindless shouting on every tee you get every time The Open is at this venue, the set-up or even the course itself, there wasn't that spark that there can be in some Opens. And it didn't really help that Harman made it a procession for much of Sunday. Although interestingly he didn't get, and doesn't seem to be getting since, the same amount of fawning and adulation that Tiger got for his supposed dominant performance in 2006. When he won by just two rather than six. Odd that.

That said, and having been there, I know none of this will apply when we go to 'The One True Test' that is the 152nd Open at Royal Troon in 51 weeks' time: the first three of which I'll be spending on holiday as for the first time in living memory the DP World Tour now takes a three-week summer hiatus.

Every cloud.

The 2024 Schedule Let-Down

I don't know Keith Pelley personally. But that doesn't stop me instinctively liking him. He has a vision. He's a leader. He has presence. He has personality. And is, I think, the right man for the job.

But while he's the captain of the good ship DP World Tour, and his hands might be on the rudder, he's forced to sail it in shark-infested waters where unfortunately, such are the size of the sharks, it is they who determine when and where he can sail his ship, not him, which is not ideal.

But worse still, these aren't your ordinary sharks. These are ruthless ones. With distinctive PGA Tour markings on them. And for starters they love nothing better than to eat your best crew members, or at least swallow them whole but then release them unharmed into the private PGA Tour waters. From which they rarely return.

Then there's that a few years ago the sharks started effectively determining when Captain Pelley could sail his ship at all: as in, it would be better if you didn't stray into our waters during the late springtime to the summer as this is 'our time', our feeding grounds are full to overflowing and we've ensured that all our friends are coming to feed, so don't try tempting them with your meagre captain's table offerings. But if you want to arrange something for after this time, then we're just about okay with this. But keep a good few berths free for our friends because they might want to come out to feed again. And yes, I know that means some of your friends will have to be removed from the guest list, but that's the way it is. Remember, these are effectively our waters you're sailing in. Oh, and by the way, we've made it up with that other big ship who we swore would never even be allowed near our waters. So you're not our best friend anymore: they are. Sorry we didn't tell you. But you know how it is.

That in a nutshell is why the DP World Tour schedule for 2024 which was released last week looks like it does. Yes, there's some catchy new labels for the various sets of events: there's an Opening Swing (in November and December), an International Swing (in January through to March), an Asian Swing (in April and May), a European Swing (thankfully, in late May through to the start of July), a Closing Swing (which isn't really, in July and August), the Back 9 Swing (in September and October), before the new DP World Tour Play-Offs (of which there's only two, in mid-November). But when you really look closely, this is kind of style over substance.

Because the real headlines are that this tour caddy will basically be spending the first five months of 2024 east of Dubai; Abu Dhabi (always one of the early-year highlights) has been moved to the end of the year to disguise the fact that the Nedbank has disappeared, there are no new standout tournaments, and the big European tournaments are basically crammed into the late summer when the reduced daylight means reduced playing opportunities anyway, and that's before the 'big names' enter because the main PGA Tour season has finished.

Including obviously the ten guys who get their PGA Tour cards from the Race to Dubai rankings come the end of this season – who incidentally slot in in positions 128–137 on the PGA Tour's Category List for next year, so will get to play basically every event bar the limited field events that form part of the new Signature Events on the PGA Tour.

And while that might be good news for their caddies, if you're going to be caddying for the guys who remain on the DP World Tour next year, there's not a whole lot to get excited about and not much to shout about if we're honest.

Well, nothing positive anyway. Because in 2024 we're going to be spending more time away from home: not a positive. Doing a lot more international travel: not a positive. Staying in a lot more hotels: not a positive. And spending a lot more money doing so: definitely not a positive. Even if the overall prize funds might be up.

But if you think the latter is the definition of progress and growth, then I'm not sure that necessarily holds up to closer scrutiny. Because yes, the prize money for a tournament like Ras Al Khaimah might well have increased to $2.5m, with a corresponding rise of an extra 250 Race to Dubai points on offer; but effectively what that means is $5,000 more for (say) finishing 30th, which in turn equates to an extra $375 in bonus should your player finish in 30th position. Now I know it's not all (in fact, not at all) about us, but this is the financial reality of increased prize funds for the majority of tour caddies. The difference is negligible.

Nor is the promise of jam tomorrow a measure of growth, i.e. the 'it'll be even better next year' line that gets bandied around. Because next year, next year becomes next year. All of which has led to some noise about how Keith Pelley can seriously remain in post. Not a view I subscribe to, or give any credence to, though. Because like I say, when you look at it critically, there's sod all he, or anyone else at the DP World Tour, can do. They simply don't have leverage. Either in the form of the world's top players playing on their tour, or the type of mega prize funds that would turn their heads to come play it. So the schedule they deliver each and every year is always the best they can possibly squeeze out given the circumstances.

That said, the cynics, albeit with the benefit of (tour caddy-like) hindsight, have a point when they say that not 'getting into bed' with the Saudis a few years ago now looks like a poor decision. Certainly from the financial perspective of a fair percentage of the members of the DP World Tour. Because even if that hadn't turned any heads, for the majority it would have delivered prize funds that would have turned paying off your credit card after a good week into paying off your mortgage after a good week. And likewise for tour caddies.

So no, overall the 2024 schedule hasn't exactly set my pulse racing. To the extent that, and not for the first time this season, I'm left thinking, 'Do I really need this hassle?'

Chapter 8

Hi Ho, Hi Ho ...

The Story of the Week of the ISPS World Invitational 17–20 August 2023

Now you would think that after the first mid-season three-week break that I can remember in all my time out here, I, and everyone else, would be raring to get going again. And to some extent that's true. It's just that if there is such an expression as 'before the Lord Mayor's Show', then you can safely apply it to this week.

Because in the same way that the Scottish Open is simply the week before the main event that is The Open, this week is simply the week before we all go to Prague for off-course nirvana. Although it's only really us caddies (and maybe the players) who regard it as this: no one outside the DP World Tour bubble in which we all exist has even an inkling that everyone's eyes are on next week and not the huge shiny trophy that Modest Golf put up for the winner come Sunday night.

In fact, with three-quarters of the field having booked on the 17.15 out of Belfast to Prague via Amsterdam, many caddies might be secretly hoping their man's hands never actually get anywhere near it at all. Because if they aren't, then even allowing for getting bags off and the 30-minute taxi journey into Prague itself, we're looking at a midnight arrival at the hotel, so by half-past midnight everyone can be out in Prague where the night will still be young. And there for the taking.

Anyway, that's next week. Before that there's the slight matter of this week's tournament in Northern Ireland, which is an odd one on a number of counts. First off, we're playing alongside the Ladies European Tour, on the same courses, for the same prize money, but in our own tournaments: one for the men and one for the women.

Then there's the fact that our tournament is a 'dual points' one with the Challenge Tour. Something that happens a few times a year when the Tour knows that they will struggle to fill the field of 156: which is the number of players who play in a normal tour event. In these weeks, the KLM Open and the Porsche European Open being two such examples this year, the field is opened up to Challenge Tour players who are then able to play for proper money, while still gaining points on the Race to Mallorca ranking, albeit weighted downwards to be fair to the other Challenge Tour guys who choose to play; in this case, the Finnish Challenge. Where, by the way, someone shot 59.

On the downside, though, because both the men and women play at Galgorm on the Sunday, only 60 made the cut on Friday night, and that was thinned down to 35 on Saturday night when there was a second cut. Thank God we don't do that every week.

And thank God we don't have extended breaks from playing tournaments too often, because with most of the stars of the show this week not getting into The Open, effectively they haven't played for a month, and so are all itching to get back out playing again. So much so that they appear to be turning up en masse on Monday morning, rather than a Monday afternoon or Monday evening like they would for a normal week. And as we're the stars of the show's caddies, that means we have to travel out on the Sunday too.

I say 'stars of the show', but if you define these as anyone inside the top 75 in the world, then you're going to be sadly disappointed, because unsurprisingly with this one being concurrent with the second week of the FedEx Playoffs in the States, none of them are here. Nor are they likely to be seen across this side of the pond until the big-money autumn tournaments start in early September.

But even if they were here we'd still be faced with one of the other quirks of this week: there's two courses. The first, Galgorm Castle, is where we've played in the previous editions of this tournament, and which every year gets a little better; the second is a new venue because, rather than using Massereene GC which is a decent-enough club but not really up to the standard required for a tour event, we're playing at Castlerock GC, which definitely is up to the standard required for a tour event. In fact it is an absolute gem. The only issue for us is that they're a 45-minute drive away from each other. And while the really wise thing to do might be to send your caddy round the one you don't fancy driving to, and just trust what he tells you in Lucas Herbert Japan style when it comes to playing it, it seems that not many people seem to be feeling that 'brave' this week.

And that means there's zero chance of what could have been a few nice easy days easing my body back into the swing of lugging a fully laden tour bag again after having a blissful month off said torture. Which was actually also how the missus described having me round the house all this time because in a 'normal year' I'm safely away somewhere in Europe, the kids are farmed out to their grandparents, and she's out with her friends every night. Or something like that.

And in a way she's right as it does seem utter madness not to be having tournaments at this time of year, when the weather's decent, courses are generally in their best condition, kids are off school so can come to watch, etc. And there's certainly been no sign of this happening on the other tours across the world: the PGA Tour has finished its regular season and is deep into their Playoffs; Bryson has been shooting 58 at the Greenbrier in one of the LIV events; and even the Asian Tour's International Series has landed on UK soil for two weeks.

In fact the only real sign of activity from the DP World Tour was to release next year's initial schedule last week, which, I think it's fair to say, wasn't exactly met with universal praise, especially by the golfing fourth estate. Not that it was ever going to be anything radical, or even too different, given that nowadays it effectively has to fit around the PGA Tour's schedule.

And speaking of the PGA Tour, interestingly it seems not many players ended up going to the last Players' meeting with Jay Monahan the other week – which to me says they're either pretty apathetic, or resigned to the fact that the rich will get richer. Because with the new Signature Events in 2024 looking suspiciously like the first step to the 'world golf series' we've long predicted, it doesn't take a clairvoyant to work out that one of the categories that will ultimately make up the field (the top 50 on the FedEx in 2023 will form the first 50 spots on the Entry List) will at some stage magically become the way back in for the best of the LIV Golf guys. And that would give you the 14 tournaments with all the top players in the world guaranteed to show up that every armchair golf fan wants to see. Whether they're ready to admit it yet or not.

But like I've said before, this tournament is pretty much as far removed from all this as you can get. But it's an opportunity for someone to win. And change their season. And possibly their golfing life. Especially as the Entry List has again gone all the way down into Category 21, which is for current Challenge Tour players.

And that is sort of what happened after four days of decidedly varied weather. Dan Brown changed a very decent first season on tour, where he'd only played 13 times but made all 13 cuts, into a bloody good one by leading by six into Sunday and getting over the line by five in the end for his first win.

But even better was that there was no play-off, or any need for anyone to wait around to see if there was one. Because that meant that even if your man's hands had been the ones on the trophy, you'd have still made the 17.15 BFS-PRG Express with the rest of us.

Shut the Fuck Up

Imagine one morning at work saying to your boss, 'I think …', only for them to cut you off with a terse, 'I don't give a fuck what you think.' Imagine one morning being at work trying to give your boss advice. Only for them to say to you, 'Shut the fuck up. Stop trying to get involved.' Imagine one morning at work saying 'morning' to your boss. Only for them to completely and utterly ignore you for the next six hours.

Or a morning at work when your boss puts his cigarette out on your arm. Or a morning at work when your boss openly and loudly ridicules you in front of your colleagues simply for not wearing a belt. Or a morning at work when your boss tells you 'you're fucking fired' in earshot of 1,000 strangers. Or a morning at work when your boss has a tantrum during which they smash your expensive watch to smithereens. Or even one when your boss decides to have a physical altercation with you in full view of some TV cameras?

No. You probably can't. And that's because you work in a world in which your boss can't do things like this in that it's a world in which there is HR, in which there are rules, and in which there are consequences when you break those rules. Tour caddies, however, do not inhabit this world.

Ours is a parallel one where this stuff does actually happen. Not every week. But every single one of those things has happened in the time I've been out here. None of it is made up. And yet no one was hauled in front of HR, or anyone for that matter. No one was disciplined. No one went to jail for ABH. Why?

Well, the best and, in fact, only way I can explain this away is by saying that you know how in a boxing match two guys (or girls) knock seven bells out of each other for ten rounds, but then embrace afterwards and are seemingly best of friends? Well that's how the relationship between players and tour caddies is sometimes.

We can stand on the 1st tee with our players seemingly the best of mates, exit the 1st green the worst of enemies, then be at each other's throats for the rest of the round, but then can seemingly be back to being best mates by the time the day is over, just as if nothing untoward happened.

I heard a story once of a caddy whose player had etched their name followed by 'is a ****' on to the scorecard after driving into a fairway bunker they'd been assured was out of range that day. Another whose player reputedly had two moods on the course, 'annoyed' and 'very annoyed', every single day for the five years they worked together. And another who was basically subjected to a minor assault – by his player – in full view of TV. And every single one of us has heard a variation of the 'it's my fault for fucking listening to anything you say' or 'it's my fault for employing you in the first place' sarcastic chastisement at one time or other in our caddy careers.

Most players and their caddies are, however, past masters at ignoring any such elephants in the room. Because once hands are shaken on the 18th green, whatever was said on the course wasn't really said. What happened on the course didn't really happen.

Only a select few acknowledge it, resolve it and move on. And that's because at the end of the day professional golf and professional caddying is a pressure cooker of an environment. Things do go wrong. There are bad bounces. There is bad luck. Mistakes are made. All of which have negative consequences on the day or the week.

And when it's one of those days when these things happen, or one of those days when he's chopping it, these things have a tendency to build up to a point where something has to give. And in my experience that's usually his temper. Cue the caddy getting it in the neck: if only because we're the one closest to him. And therefore are in the firing line. But always in front of the other two or four people in the group – which is kind of embarrassing the first time it happens.

Things not to say in such situations, though, are: 'We're on the same side, remember'; 'You hit the shot, not me'; 'I didn't think it was that club'; or the ultimate no-no: 'I did tell you ...' Because while they might be fair points well made, they tend just to make matters worse still.

Much better is to adopt an 'in one ear, out the other' approach, safe in the knowledge that you know he's only venting, it's not personal (well, most of the time it's not), and 'taking shit' is part of the job of a tour caddy. And you either sharp get used to it, or you sharp get out.

Because at the end of the day us tour caddies put up with any shit we get because we all know it's a small price to pay for caddying for a player whose talent, nurtured in part by us, will hopefully end up earning us a small fortune. And for that reason we can ignore the things that in a normal world would see us heading along the corridor to HR.

And I'm certainly not blameless on this one. I've been on the receiving end of a fair amount of shit in my time out here: some of it entirely justified; some of it definitely not. It's just that I'm smart enough to know when he doesn't mean it, but also smart enough to know that when he does mean it, it's time to look for another player.

But of all the things I know, one thing I do know is that, TV cameras or no TV cameras, if my player ever put a cigarette out on my arm he wouldn't be using his right arm to play golf for a while. Because it would be in a plaster cast.

The Story of the Week of the D+D Real Czech Masters 24–27 August 2023

All animals are equal, but some are more equal than others. The same applies to weeks on tour. And the week of the Czech Open is definitely one of the more equal weeks out here. If not the most equal.

So definitely not one for bringing the family out: that's reserved for Crans Montana next week. If Crans Montana, or even having the family out, is your thing – which for me it isn't. On either count.

No, this week is officially the week where the golf gets in the way of a bit of R&R in the beautiful city of Prague. Where the food is fantastic. And cheap. Where the beer is fantastic. And cheap. Where the women are beautiful. And, well, let's just say that Prague just does its own thing, which in this day and age is unusual, refreshing and very welcome.

Anyway, we arrive late Sunday night but not late enough that we can't get to this week's hotel, dump the bags, freshen up and get out to sample the first two of that list, both of which you can still get sat in the warm (very) early morning air. Because basically this town doesn't sleep. And unless you're disciplined this week, you might not either. Well, certainly not at a sensible time, which wouldn't be very professional. Especially given that, yet again, the field isn't the strongest this year, and so there's another good opportunity to get a W on your career record. And that's despite the likes of Lowry and Francesco Molinari playing this week. Neither of whom I guess have ever played this tournament in the past, but with the Ryder Cup on the horizon, one is here to keep playing, and the other is here to keep an eye on those who are, given that he's just been announced as the final vice-captain for Team Europe and this is the second-to-last counting event before the team is announced at the end of next week's tournament.

Not that this means this one isn't an important one in its own right for everyone else. Because aside from the guys vying for the last automatic Ryder Cup spot, there's those guys who need a good week because they're below 117 on the Race to Dubai rankings[5] and for some there's the added pressure that they won't get into the bigger tournaments coming up in September, so need that good week sooner rather than later.

There's those guys who are already okay for next year, but know that a weak field is an opportunity to win and suddenly be okay for the top 50 for the Race to Dubai Final in November. And maybe even exemption into the likes of The Open next year.

And then there's those guys vying for one of the ten PGA Tour cards on offer for the 2024 season to seize the opportunity to earn those points that will tie up their passage away from the DP World Tour. Because like all sensible organisations at the end of each year, the DP World Tour now gives away its ten best employees (i.e. players) to its biggest rival. For free. And that is quite frankly fantastic for the ten guys who make it, but, some might say, another self-inflicted wound for this tour.

Even if that is just for a year. As when you look at the current list of guys with the PGA Tour symbol against their names on the Race to Dubai rankings, we know that really only a couple would have a realistic chance of keeping that card against the best in the world. Obviously that's not because they're not good players: it's just that for a few it's not their type of golf. Or at least that's what we're predicting. But for one or two, a win or even a top-five finish here might just do the job.

Aside from that, though, what we're also predicting this week is that we'll be paying a lot of attention, especially in the practice round, to those holes at the Albatross Golf Resort (like the unreachable 9th for example) that might end up

---

5   At the moment only the top 117 players on the final Race to Dubai rankings keep their playing rights for the 2024 season.

leaving us the most difficult shot faced by any tournament pro: the easy lay-up.

Now to even the most trained of tour caddy's eyes, this 178-yard lay-up to the 90 spot that will leave him his favourite gap-wedge distance to the flag looks easy. It's only a 7- or an 8-iron to get there. There's no wind to speak of. There's no change in elevation to take into consideration. The target line is obvious. And the target area really wide. Hence the term 'easy lay-up'.

Except we're not hitting the shot. And sometimes for the person hitting the shot the complete lack of anything to worry about leads to a complete lack of concentration. And suddenly that bunker or rough left that neither you nor your player had even thought about is in play. In fact you're in the middle of it. Because that's where the ball has somehow ended up.

The trick, and it's something you only learn with experience out here, is spotting when your man might fall victim to 'easy lay-up syndrome', and really take inordinate care to ensure he's focused on the shot in hand in these situations. And not the easy wedge to an open pin that ought to follow. Because that can sharp become a wedge from a tricky lie under the lip of that bunker over water to a front pin. And when that happens, believe me our shoes are something you don't want to be in, because we're in the firing line and have been known to get it in the neck. Like it was our fault. Which of course it wasn't.

And the likelihood of that happening always increases round here as typically they keep the fairways soft for the first two days, then stop watering them, making them fast and fiery for the weekend, at which point those lay-ups demand even more attention. Thankfully we managed to avoid any such issues this week, especially on the par-fives, which you have to take advantage of round here if you want to finish high up. And so have a decent-enough week.

But speaking of decent and weeks, I've also had a decent-enough amount to say this week about the new statistics collection system that appears to be about to be foisted upon us all in the weeks when IMG Media[6] aren't there to collect shot-by-shot data on the fairways.

Starting with pointing out how smart the Tour was when it first introduced the current incarnation of requiring statistics to be collected. Because they placed responsibility for collecting the data they need on to the players, knowing fine well that they would simply devolve responsibility to their faithful caddy. Or put another way, they placed responsibility on the people they can control (the players) rather than the people who they can't (us).

That and they also knew fine well that the players are the acquiescent sort, and wouldn't ask any awkward questions about how much money the Tour makes out of these stats, which, as they're used for the datasets that sit behind in-play betting, is quite a lot. In fact it's a right little golf gold mine.

And if you pay your data collectors who help populate this little gold mine as little as possible, then that means your net profit will be that much higher than if you paid them the true value of the data they collect for you. It's something we all spotted years ago; but somehow ended up settling for £12.50 a round when these new stats first started to be collected, with the promise of jam tomorrow.

Except that we didn't actually 'settle' at all. This rate was agreed sometime around 2016 by whoever 'represented' the ETCA at the discussions with the Tour. But only if you define 'represented' as having your arse in the air while having your belly stroked at the same time until you scream (not for the first time), 'Yes Sir, yes Sir, whatever you like, Sir.' Which I don't. I call it being deferential bordering on acquiescence.

---

6   These are the guys responsible for the shot-by-shot graphics on the DP World Tour app: it's just that this data is also used for in-play betting.

And now it turns out that 'jam tomorrow' is actually going to be a paltry £2.50 extra. So really the ETCA ought to be banging on the door and asking for a proper sit down with the Tour to thrash this whole thing out once and for all. And be taking the consensus view of its members to that sit down, not just going it alone and reporting back later. And I'd hope that that consensus, not that anyone has bothered asking me, would be, 'If we collect these stats at x per cent of tournaments, how about you pay x per cent of the money you make? We can negotiate about what x per cent actually is, but the principle of you paying us what your input is worth is not. Because that is fair. Paying us £15 is not.' And take it from there. With of course the last resort being that every ETCA member will refuse to fill them in, we'll pay their fines out of the ETCA's cash reserves, and in the meantime be all over social media exposing what you're doing.

And that's before your currently acquiescent players wake up to the fact that it's them who are being played, and decide they want a fair slice of the pie too. Or someone asks questions about whether, because you're paying me £12.50 or £15 or whatever, that makes me technically an employee, and if it does, then how about I get the things like minimum wage, holiday pay, pension, national insurance, etc. It's called leverage.

And while we're at it, that £7,500 goodwill payment you intend making to the ETCA to smooth things over needs to be withdrawn pronto, while you go away and have a real careful think about how you compensate every caddy, not just those who still choose to be members of the ETCA.

But sound off as much as I like, and I've certainly been guilty of doing that this week so apologies if you were in earshot and had to listen, short of getting involved in the running of the ETCA there's very little I, or anyone else, can really do to influence what's going to happen. And that's because any discussions with the Tour about this appear to be going on behind very closed doors, from which no sounds or soundbites have been emerging. It's all very cloak and dagger. And not very transparent. Making me yearn for the time when the ETCA was led by some guys who'd do all the door and head banging required to get what we deserve.

And to continue the theme of banging heads, I'm inclined to think that Todd Clements might have one in the morning. Because if you're going to shoot nine under final round and win when you've never even had a top 20 before on tour, then Prague is a pretty good place to do it. And, more importantly, to celebrate it.

And for once on a Sunday, there was time. Mainly because those considerate people at Eurowings had, admittedly completely unwittingly, scheduled a 6.30am flight on Monday morning to Geneva (it's Crans next week), so Clements, and everyone else for that matter, could have one more night out in off-course nirvana. And at the time some of those ended, there wasn't exactly time for sleep before heading to the airport for a 5am check-in.

Proof that indeed all good things must come to an end.

You're Fired!

After another poor week at the Czech Masters my mate Jimmy[7] got 'fired' by his player. 'Fired' being tour caddy speak for 'got sacked'. Not that this was a surprise to anyone, least of all Jimmy. Because from what he'd been saying the last few weeks, his now ex-player had started 'bitching about everything' on the course, which is never a good sign. And something he certainly wasn't doing when he'd been playing half decent at the start of the season. Odd that.

So when Jimmy's player pulled him aside after another missed cut on the Friday, that was that. But not before Jimmy had to listen to the full 'Sorry mate, this is very difficult

---

7 Not his real name.

[dramatic pause] because you've not done anything wrong; it's just that I need a change. I need to do something' spiel, which he knew was pretty much bollocks. As did the guy saying it.

But at least Jimmy's player had the balls to say it to him face to face. Some guys find out that they're fired via the player's manager, or worse still by text, which I always think is on the cowardly side of spineless.

It seems, though, that the final straw for Jimmy was being right on the 18th when they needed par to make the cut, and he advised chipping the ball out to lob-wedge distance rather than trying to get it over the water from that lie. Advice which, if taken, might have led to par, followed by a ten-under weekend, and his player going on to keep his card. While going for it, which wasn't his advice, categorically didn't, as the ball came up a yard short in the water, meaning a bogey five for his player, and a P45 for Jimmy.

But at least Jimmy made it to the end of the tournament, or at least the end of their tournament, before getting fired. Because over the years other guys haven't been so lucky. Which is why, when you occasionally come off 18 at the end of the first round and one of your colleagues is sat outside the Caddy Lounge or scoring tent with his loop strap and waterproofs in hand, you don't like to ask. Of course you hope it's because his player has pulled out injured, or even been DQd, but you never ask him directly. Just in case. No, it's far better to hear confirmed on the caddy grapevine what you suspected all along, and that is that he's got fired halfway through the tournament. Personally I wouldn't wish that on anyone.

Worse still, though, must be being fired mid-round: a fate that has also befallen a few caddies over the years. Usually, it has to be said, to the surprise, and delight, of the random spectator who then gets asked to carry the bag the rest of the way round. Or at least until a recently fired caddy turns up on hearing the news in the hope of benefitting from someone else's misfortune.

All of this is of course absolutely fine when it's the player dispensing with the caddy's services. But woe betide if it's the other way round. Players have been known to act somewhere between incredulous, outraged and offended that the guy whose life they have made miserable for weeks puts the bag down at the end of a tournament and says, 'Thanks, but we're done,' before walking off into a happier future. After all, what did they do wrong? Apart from making their caddy's life miserable, obviously.

Real genuine player incredulity, however, is reserved for the very rare occasions where a caddy fires their player midway through a round. Or 'putting the bag down on someone' as we call it. Like the player whose caddy was last seen disappearing down the hill at the back of the old 12th hole at HimmerLand midway through the second round a few years back; or the original exponent of this art who, back in the 1990s, waited until him and his player were at the farthest point from the clubhouse before doing the same. Although apparently he was then nearly killed in the stampede of caddies running to pick the bag up when news filtered through. But to be fair, I think the general consensus remains that both caddies' conduct was unprofessional. Funny, but unprofessional.

Thankfully though I've never been sacked midway through a tournament or midway through a round. Because I'd find that pretty damn humiliating. And that's even with classing my ego as one of the smaller ones out here.

But it's worth noting here that whether you're fired after five years in the job, at the end of a tournament, midway through a tournament or midway through a round, what you can't do is head down the corridor to HR, take your (former) employer to a tribunal, make a claim for compensation or anything else for that matter. Like we've said before, this is not the real world. And basically when you're fired you're fired. That is that.

And no matter what anyone might tell you, no matter how long you've been out here, and no matter who you are, it's not nice being fired. Even if your player has been a twat to work for. But however you take it, what's actually important is not how you feel: what's important is how you get yourself another bag.

And late into the season that can be quite tricky, especially with the late-summer schedule on the DP World Tour now being heavy with big events with limited fields due to the ever-reducing daylight. There may well be plenty of opportunities in the 'smaller' events after the Ryder Cup this year, but before that, well, that could be very tricky.

So you basically put the word out amongst colleagues and any player managers you know that you're magically now looking for a new bag because you've 'finished with' so-and-so. 'Finished with' being the other phrase we use if we've been fired; if for no other reason than it just sounds better.

And then you sit back and wait to get a call from someone either offering you a bag, or alerting you to the fact that so-and-so is looking. Which in either case probably means that another colleague has suffered the same fate as you. And introduces a whole new realm of potential awkwardness if you then take their old bag. Especially if they're a mate. Or it would do if this were the real world. But it's not. And we all accept that at some stage this is bound to happen, which is why it's always courteous to exchange texts with the now-former caddy if it happens to you. Especially if it's them who have actually recommended you for the job in the first place: something that happens way more often than you'd think, which in itself tells you something about the generosity of spirit of your average tour caddy.

Not that getting fired by a player means you'll never work for him again. In fact there are occasions when you know that it's only a matter of time before you get a call asking you to come back. Looking back, I think my personal record is probably in the range of seven years between the 'Sorry, mate …' and 'Hi there, mate, listen, I don't suppose you fancy …' conversations. For some it might be as little as seven weeks.

And, generally, whenever it is you get the call, it's because once the initial irritation that caused you to get fired in the first place dissipates (which is very different from disappears by the way), your ex-player might well discover that your chosen replacement irritates him way more than you ever did or, quite simply, isn't as good as you. Because we've all been in the Caddy Lounge when whatshisname is showing everyone the text they've just got from their former player complaining that their new caddy (who is sat on the next table) keeps saying the wind is in off the right when 'at least you knew to always say "two o'clock into"'; that their Eau de Cerveza aftershave hums, or about all manner of things that you used to do, but 'he' doesn't. And that basically he's made a big mistake in dispensing with your services.

Get a text like this, and you know at some stage you're definitely getting the call to come back on the bag – which gives you plenty of time to think how much more he's going to have to pay you to make you say yes.

The Story of the Week of the Omega European Masters 31 August–3 September 2023

This week we're high up in the mountains in Switzerland for the annual trip to Crap Montana. Or Crans Montana to give it its proper name.

Now for some of my colleagues, not to mention many of the players and all of the TV people, this appears to be more a holy pilgrimage than a trip to a golf tournament, such is the reverence in which people hold this place. But for me, every day here is just one day less until we can jump in a courtesy car or a bus, head down the mountain to Sierre/Sidiers and get the flock out of here. Because I can't stand this place.

I hated it the first time I ever came here; I hated it the second time; and third; and the fourth; and every year since. And having to put up with everyone saying how wonderful it is every bloody year just makes it worse. And me more miserable. I know the scenery is pretty good, especially the view from the 7th tee with mountain peaks as far as the eye can see, but for me, frankly that's about it.

And it starts with just getting there. The train journey from Geneva to Sierre/Sidiers might be quite pretty (although not this year as the clouds were down and it was raining hard), but one, it seems to take forever to get not very far, and two, it's eye-wateringly expensive. And the players and their families waving at us from their paid-for-by-the-promoters first-class seats on the same train frankly doesn't help. But once we get to Sierre/Sidiers we're not done: we either have to get the public bus up to Crans itself or, if we're lucky, jump in a courtesy car if a player happens to have space and a generous spirit. And when you get there, it's always uphill to wherever you're staying, or downhill to wherever you're staying but then uphill to the course. Either of which by the end of the week is just a pain.

It also doesn't help that the course is a bit Mickey Mouse, mainly because for a few months of the year it's a ski piste apparently. Not that many in this Caddy Lounge could actually afford to ski here. And while we're at it, and this is going to sound sacrilegious, don't let anyone tell you that Seve did anything other than butcher this course when he did a 're-design' all those years ago. Because that's what he did. Saving his worst for turning perfectly good greens into upturned saucers that no one could keep the ball on. Except him, of course.

Thankfully, however, the golf club appears to be engaged in a 'let's put it right' programme and are redesigning/ revamping a few holes a year. And of note this year is the change to the 5th green, which now is sensible with a few sensible pin positions; instead of not very sensible with very few pin positions like it was post-Ballesteros-butchering. And with them also sorting out the 1st and 4th greens since last year, even I have to admit that the course is actually getting better, and I may have to put my 'Mickey Mouse' line to rest one year soon.

But one line I'll never have to put to rest up here is 'How much …?!!!' – which I find myself asking every time I try to buy anything; whether it's in the local bakery, the supermarket or, God forbid, a restaurant. Because the prices here are as high as the place itself. And why most of my 'How muchs' are uttered in the supermarket because it's years since I've ventured into an overpriced restaurant here, where that 'How much …?!!!' would be prefaced by a few other choice words. And this would also be the case were I ever tempted to go out for a few drinks up here (which I'm not), because beer is the price of champagne and champagne the price of gold. All of which means it's always a quiet week for me. Trying not to sulk. Count the days. Or look miserable. But like I say, I am definitely in the minority. And for everyone else it's a great week.

Especially this year as Monday's snow just above the village had disappeared by Thursday morning and everyone could play golf without two jumpers on like they had done on the practice and pro-am days. While all the while pretending that the greens weren't the consistency of puddings after all the rain, and in the kind of condition that would incite a riot at your local muni. But on the bright side, the vagaries of the usually rock-hard fairways and unexpected run-out distances were no longer an issue like they usually are up here.

So this made it kind of a level playing field (on not a level course obviously) for the three guys vying for the last automatic spot off the European List for Ryder Cup qualification: Bob MacIntyre, Yannik Paul and Adrian Meronk. And come Sunday night it was MacIntyre who came out on top of this mini-tournament despite finishing near the bottom and only making the cut due to a lucky ricochet off the Out of Bounds fence at his 14th on Friday, which left Paul and Meronk having to wait to see if they get a pick on Monday afternoon when the European team is finally announced. Along obviously with the rest of us.

And at that point we'll finally know exactly who will be lining up against the US team that was announced this week. A team that includes Koepka despite him playing on LIV Golf. And fair play to Zach Johnson for picking him, and not being petty. I mean, why would you not pick one of the best and most competitive players on the planet, no matter where he plays his golf? It'll be interesting to see if Europe adopts such a pragmatic and, dare I say, mature approach. My guess is not.

Although to be fair there's not actually any of the Europeans who chose to play on LIV Golf who have produced the string of eye-catching performances that would cause Donald a selection dilemma so he's dodged a bullet on that one. That and he can always pull the 'my hands were tied' card when it comes to explaining why Sergio won't be in the team.

Weirdly, though, this might not matter anyway, as seeing the US team on paper it somehow doesn't look as intimidating as the 2021 team, which looked like it had the nucleus of one that had flipped the balance of Ryder Cup power into American hands for a generation. But the proof of the pudding will be in the eating, and that's served up in three weeks' time.

This week, however, it was Ludvig Aberg who served up the goods by pulling away from the field with four birdies in the last five to win his first pro event, along with a two-year DP World Tour exemption and, in all likelihood, a Ryder Cup pick. None of which will stop the usual tedious suspects dissecting and criticising Donald whoever he picks. Which is sad really.

But as for me, no sadness here because we're off out of here for another year without so much as a fond farewell or longing backward glance; just the vague disappointment that in 12 months I'll probably be back to renew my feud with Crans, although by then another three holes might be better than this year, and that on the horizon will still be snow-covered mountains. So all is not lost.

And speaking of horizons, next week's horizon is actually the Horizon Irish Open.

I've Got Your Back

One of the things I love about coming to work every day is that I can wander into the Caddy Lounge and basically sit next to any of my colleagues knowing that there's a fair chance they, or someone else at the table, is going to make me laugh. Mainly because there is no humour like tour caddy humour.

That said, though, it's also a fair point that every single one of us likes a moan from time to time. Obviously, usually about things that would be filed under 'First-World Problems' for the rest of mankind, but from time to time these are about things that, unless you're a tour caddy, you might not immediately understand. Like, for example, someone bemoaning, 'I'll be getting 18 pins today.'

This refers to those weeks when the two other caddies in the group are not professional tour caddies, and have no idea about some of the intricacies of caddy etiquette. In this case meaning that the one proper tour caddy in the group will end up putting the pin back in every hole: something that he wouldn't normally do.

Because fairly obviously the pin has to go back in the hole after everyone in the group has putted out, but which caddy actually ends up doing this depends on the order in which the players end up retrieving their balls from the hole. Which is why, and you'll have seen this if you've watched golf on TV or even been to a tournament, you see caddies passing the flag to each other on the green. It might look random, but like a fair few things in our world, random it is not.

It starts when all three balls are on a green, and clearly it's the player furthest away who putts first. Now at this stage, it's likely that the caddy whose player is closest to the hole will already have asked whether the player about to putt wants the flag out or left in. And remember, in your first tournament out here caddying, this could actually, if the stars align, be the world number one: at best, you'll have a tremor in your voice; at worst, well far worse than that. Another reason not to give up that day job.

Anyway, in this instance the flag is out, and is being held by the caddy whose player is closest to the hole. The player who is 'away' putts, and the ball comes up a few feet short of the hole. The flag would then generally be passed to that player's caddy on the basis that it's still possible that the other two putts to come will result in tap-ins, so his man will be last to putt out.

The second guy to putt also misses, but ends up closer to the hole than the first, meaning that the flag gets passed to his caddy: again on the expectation that his player will be last to putt.

Along comes the third player in the group. He also misses, but says, 'I'll wait,' at which the flag would end up being passed to his caddy. Any subsequent hockey round the hole might result in the flag changing hands again, but let's not go there.

Things do, however, get slightly more complicated if, for example, one of the caddies in the group is raking the greenside bunker his man has just splashed out of. Because in this situation one of the other caddies in the group (if it's a three-ball) effectively takes their place, and holds the pin when it's their turn, while they do what they need to do. Likewise if a caddy needs a toilet break and has legged it while the group putts out.

It's a similar story when it comes down to cleaning the golf ball on the green, which all tour players do before putting, as any speck of mud, sand or whatever on the ball can make it deviate from its intended line. Again this is all very straightforward when everyone is actually on the green. But when a caddy is raking a bunker or not on the green yet, then absolutely it's caddy etiquette to offer to clean that player's ball in addition to your own player's. Not doing so is a pretty heinous break of this etiquette, and has on occasion resulted in some pretty 'frank exchange of views' after the round.

Likewise back down the fairway when one of the group ends up in a fairway trap, and their shot out means they'll be playing their next one before your player's next one. Because here, as far as is practically possible (you might be 100 yards away), you would offer to rake the bunker for that caddy as they disappear up the fairway to get the yardage, etc. for their man's next shot. It takes a little experience to work out when to offer, and when you don't need to, but out here we all help each other out.

This also goes for little things like throwing divots back to your colleagues saving them a few steps, (very, very rarely) raking over footprints that a colleague in front might have missed in a bunker, or even down to saying very audibly to your player, 'We're off the forward tee today,' when you realise a colleague hasn't spotted it in the hope he'll hear you in time to knock 25 yards off the yardage he's just given his player. All of which is just part of generally having each other's backs out here. Even in some tricky situations.

Like a good few years ago now when one of our colleagues suddenly disappeared off the second tee on the first day of the tournament into the trees next to the tee with the bag still on his shoulder. Eyebrows were raised in the group, mainly because they thought the guy might have been ill, but when the guy then emerged ashen-faced admitting he'd done something really stupid, eyes ended up being narrowed.

Because in fact what he'd done was to ditch the extra club he'd found in the bag on the 1st green (they'd had an extra wedge in the bag in practice and forgotten to take it out): something which, kind of to his credit, he was now openly admitting. But ultimately that's cheating, and the Tour really had no option but to sanction him, basically ending his caddying career right there and then.

But not before the-then ETCA chairman (a giant of a man with a presence to match) had sat the guy down and asked whether he really did this off his own bat, or whether he'd actually been told to do it by his player. Because if it was the latter, he and the ETCA would have gone into battle for him. However, the guy continued to maintain it was him and no one else, so there was nothing anyone could do, other than to lament such a stupid decision, and accept the lifetime ban handed out. Well, that and occasionally continue to wonder whether this was a case of admirable honesty after doing something highly unadmirable, or whether he just took one for the team. But to this day this is the only instance in all my years out here that one of us has been caught cheating. And long may it remain so.

Because while the phrase 'honour amongst thieves' might be a fallacy, there absolutely is honour amongst tour caddies. And a big part of that is having respect for your colleagues when you're out there working. So it's best not to stand back and watch a colleague get a fine (later rescinded) for not raking a bunker rather than doing it for him like he assumed you would; or wrap the flag tight around the flagstick so the group behind can't see which way the wind at the green is blowing; and definitely don't have a watch that gets stuck at four minutes 50 seconds (this was in the early 2000s) until your player eventually does find his ball. Because these would be exceptions that prove the rule.

And out here, we've all got each other's backs.

Chapter 9

Autumn is the Best Month

The Story of the Week of the Horizon Irish Open 7–10 September 2023

Not for the first time in my caddying career, the first day of the new week reminded me of what a mad life we all lead. We woke up in the ski resort, but a train, a plane and an automobile later, by the end of the day we'd walked a golf course 1,677km to the west. And not just any old course, this one was the K Club around 35 minutes west of Dublin, the venue of the 2006 Ryder Cup, and home of this week's tournament: the $6m Horizon Irish Open.

While all the while, 1,677km further east, someone else was dismantling the infrastructure at last week's venue as if we'd never been there at all. And it'll be the same next Monday, and the one after that, as the mad circus we perform in moves into the final two months of the season. Mind-boggling when you think about it.

But at least this week the circus has some star performers for the crowds to marvel at, notably McIlroy and Lowry, along with a small sprinkling of PGA Tour players who don't think $6m isn't worth getting out of bed for. Not that any of them had to get out of bed at the time those who'd chosen to stay in Crans Montana an extra night and catch the Monday morning flight options from either Geneva or Zurich straight into DUB had had to. Because that might have swayed their decision as to whether to bother coming or not.

But if our life and travel days seem amazing, believe me they are not; well, not compared to the news that it's going to be completely dry all week with not a single drop of rain forecast. In Ireland! Which makes it officially a drought around these parts. Unlike the last time we came here in 2015 when the weather was truly horrific the first day and not much better the second: which was when our involvement in that particular tournament ended. Although that was good news for the trench foot I had acquired over those first two days.

No such issues this year, but that doesn't mean it's been dry here all through the summer. Because it hasn't. In fact according to the Tour's agronomists it's been the wettest summer here since, well, last year. And that means the rough is up: severely up. In fact it's some of the thickest and most penal stuff we've had to hack out of all year.

Whereas the rest of the course is actually playing fast and firm, mainly due to the new(ish) owners raising, at significant cost, every fairway by six inches over the past few years to aid the drainage. To the point where the course is in stupendous condition. And as you know it's not that often we say that.

Also absolutely stupendous is that this week everyone in the field gets to play in the pro-am as it's split across two days, with every player playing just nine holes and being free to play the other nine as a practice round before or after the pro-am itself finishes. For a tour caddy this is as close to Tuesday and Wednesday nirvana as you can get: i.e., there's no chance of your man getting bored (and therefore inattentive) in either the practice round or the pro-am, and no chance of us getting tired in either.

While for the amateurs it really is nirvana: they get to play with two different tour pros in the same round. Assuming of course that one or both actually engage with them. Because whereas most do, and pride themselves in making sure the amateurs, who after all have generally paid for the privilege of being there, actually have a good time, there is the odd one, particularly where there is a language barrier, who still feels compelled to virtually ignore their unfortunate partners – which is as rude as it is excruciatingly embarrassing for us tour caddies. Thankfully my man falls very much into the former category, which makes every pro-am we play in that bit more tolerable.

Like this one for example, where, mirroring what we've all been talking about off the course, all the pro-am guys want to know is what me and him think of the final six picks that made up the European Ryder Cup team. And I think, to a man, we'd already guessed that Aberg would get one, not just because he won last week, but because he was already on everyone's radar after such eye-catching results towards the end of the PGA Tour season. Fleetwood and Straka were always getting in, while Rose and Lowry bring a second backbone and presence to the team. I guess the 'surprise' pick, though, was Nicolai Højgaard, but only because he was below Meronk on the ranking, not because of his golf. Because if you've ever seen him play, well, then you just know. That and he'll have had Bjorn 'on his side'. Allegedly.

But looking at the team there are some obvious hungry-looking partnerships in there, especially for the four-balls, and with the US team (at least on paper) not looking quite so invincible as we might have thought, suddenly my colleagues and I are more optimistic about Europe's prospects in two weeks' time. Or at least a bit more optimistic than we were a few months ago.

Now while there might not be a drop of the wet stuff forecast this week, the same doesn't go for drops of the black stuff, which tastes better here than anywhere else in the world. In fact this is the only place in the world where I'm ever tempted to drink any. But I don't, mainly on account

THE SECRET TOUR CADDY

of the fact that it's just not fair on my arse or the toilet in whichever hotel or Airbnb I'm staying, let alone whoever I might be sharing with this week.

But in a week of pro-am nirvanas, sponsor nirvana then showed up on Saturday. Because as McIlroy only just made the cut, he was off early, and that meant the crowds were out in force early too. His 66 meant they then had something to celebrate, and so a fair number no doubt retired to the hospitality pavilions and public village to do just that. By which time Ireland's opening game in the Rugby World Cup was just kicking off. And Ireland winning meant that no one then left the golf course, or the hospitality, or the public village until they'd finished celebrating that too. Which was by then quite late. And the golf had long since finished. Horizon didn't see that on the horizon, but were no doubt pretty damn glad when it heaved into view.

All of which was pretty much the icing on the cake of probably the best Irish Open I've ever caddied at. And over the last few years there have been some pretty special ones, starting I think with the 2019 version at Lahinch where McGinley persuaded the authorities to close all the roads in the town for the week, creating a very special party atmosphere that the tournament has kept to this day. It was a stroke of genius. So God knows what it will be like the next time there's an Irish winner at this tournament. And with there not having been one since Shane Lowry in 2009, when he was still an amateur, it's long overdue. Something that hasn't gone unnoticed in the tour caddy grandma community.

The other 66 of note this week came from Bjorn in the opening round. But not before one very funny colleague had suggested he only shot this because he'd walked off after 15, which was around about the same point he'd already had 66 shots the next day. At which point he may as well have walked off.

It also wasn't too surprising that the promise of no rain turned out to be a false one, with everyone scrambling for shelter on Sunday when play was suspended due to lightning being a little too close for comfort. Not that it bothered Vincent Norrman, whose win vaulted him to seventh on the Race to Dubai rankings after basically only five days on European soil this year, i.e. this week, showing you the value of the two co-sanctioned events with the PGA Tour in July, one of which he won, because now he plays in the Race to Dubai Final, is exempt for the next few years in Europe (should he need it), in prime position for a hefty payout from the Race to Dubai Bonus Pool, and exempt into The Open next year.

But if Norrman chose a good week to have a good week, then so did Hurly Long. Starting the week in 150th on the rankings and way outside the top 117 for next year having not finished higher than 30th all year, by Sunday evening he was suddenly in 37th on the Race to Dubai. All thanks to finishing second on his own. So that means he too will now likely be playing in the Race to Dubai Final in November.

And just like the other week in Czechia, if you ever wanted somewhere decent to celebrate your latest win or just keeping your card, then (just outside) Dublin would be probably quite high up on that list. And even if Norrman or Long didn't (and I've no idea whether they or any of their 'teams' did), then from what I saw in Dublin on Sunday night a large percentage of the spectatorate were more than happy to do it on their behalf. To the point where it was probably just as well none of them were off to the next venue the next day like we were.

But whether you left on Sunday night or Monday morning, you left knowing that next week is the 'big one': the BMW Championship at Wentworth. The DP World Tour's flagship event.

The First Reserve

Now this one isn't strictly about tour caddies, but last week one of the lads' player ended up being first reserve, and we all got talking about it. Me especially, as the way the first reserve is treated is still one of the things on tour I've never been able to get my head around.

First reserve is the guy one spot below the cut-off line on the tournament entry list each week. So it follows that someone is first reserve each week. It just varies who that person is. Obviously there is also a second, third, fourth, fifth and so on reserve each week too, but bollocks to them.

First off, what the first and all other reserves have is a choice to make – basically, do they bother coming to the tournament in the hope that someone pulls out before their Thursday tee time? Or not? Not that it's much of a choice in reality. Because obviously if I'm first reserve and I decide not to come and someone then pulls out, I've potentially missed out on an opportunity to earn what might be very important and valuable Race to Dubai points, i.e. money. And generally if you're in first reserve territory, your ranking is such that you probably need to come.

The only real debate is if the tournament happens to be on a continent where you currently aren't because travelling as a reserve costs money. And if you're on the other side of the world and get the 'by the way, you're now first reserve this week, are you coming?' call from the Tour, quite a lot of money. Especially if it's on the Monday of the tournament.

But no matter where you come from in the world, there's obviously absolutely no guarantee someone will actually withdraw, promoting you from first reserve to Last Man In. But you still need to prepare like someone will. So you play the practice rounds. You do your practice. You do your drills. You do your gym work. You pay for a hotel. You pay your caddy. Just like you do any other week when you're actually in the field.

It's just this week you do all that, and then have to turn up at the golf course on Thursday morning like you're in the first group out. Because someone in that group might pull a muscle in their warm-up and pull out, so you have to be there near the 1st or 10th tees to take their place.

But you don't want to warm up too much, as potentially you have two hours of morning tee times to wait to see if someone does pull out. Beat balls for two hours, especially if we're in a hot country, then you'll be too tired to actually play should the opportunity arise. Too little and you won't be warmed up enough.

Anyway, once the last group of the morning wave has teed off intact, as first reserve you then have to sit around for another couple of hours until it's time to warm up again in case someone in the first group in the afternoon wave pulls their muscle in their warm-up and pulls out.

Best case, someone does and you get to play. Worst case, no one does and come the last group teeing off in the afternoon wave, you smash one final driver of frustration down the range and trudge off to the locker room, potentially to pack the bag and head straight home, which might be on the other side of the world.

Actually that's not the worst case. That is something different. That is when someone isn't 100 per cent fit but tries to play anyway. Only to discover after three holes what they knew all along: they can't get round. So they withdraw. And then avoid you like the plague. Unless they're a decent human being; in which case they search you out and apologise profusely.

Why do guys pull out last-minute? Well, the number one and most obvious reason is they pull their back or neck or whatever in the warm-up, and not even instant treatment from the DP World Tour physios who are on-site from two hours before the 1st tee time (however early that may be) can patch them up. Other reasons include, 'Sorry, I'm currently

THE SECRET TOUR CADDY

shitting through the eye of a needle' (usually in India); the wife gave birth two hours ago (what the fuck was he doing there in the first place?); and a good few 'I slipped in the shower this morning' (code for I had a late night last night that may or may not still be going on).

But ultimately it's kind of pot luck whether someone does pull out. And if you've been out here long enough, there will have been weeks when your man got in as first reserve sometime on Thursday, and weeks when your man (and you) were on the range all day Thursday and didn't.

In terms of the ideal scenario for getting to Thursday morning and your man still being first reserve, I'd say that either you want that Thursday to be at the end of a discrete 'stretch' of tournaments as there's theoretically more chance of guys carrying injuries, or you want to wake up that Thursday morning, open the curtains to find that it's pissing down as again theoretically anyone in any doubt about playing might have their mind made up for them. Or you want serial withdrawee Victor Dubuisson to be in the field. Preferably all three. So that is kind of how it all works.

But what doesn't work for me, and never has, is why the first reserve isn't paid, or at least have his expenses paid by the Tour. Now I totally get that it might be in their financial and career interests to travel as first reserve, but if no one did, that would leave the tournament field short by one, or maybe more. And no tournament wants to be in that position. Perhaps it's just another example of how professional golf isn't like the real world.

My friends who have real-world jobs all shake their heads whenever I pop on to my high horse and get them to imagine what they'd say if their real-world employer were to ring them next Monday morning and say, 'Jimmy, it looks like we might need you in work this week on Thursday, but we won't know definitely until 2.30 Thursday afternoon. Is that okay?' And before you've had a chance to tell them to stick this where the sun don't shine, they quickly add, 'Oh, and while we're on, it's just that if we don't end up needing you, you won't get paid. And yes, yes, I know you're in Asia at the minute and the office is in Sweden this week, and that getting here will be super-expensive last minute, but you'd be doing us – and possibly yourself if we do end up needing you – a real favour. How about it?'

Strangely they all think this (a) isn't a very good offer, and (b) they wouldn't still be on the call after the first sentence. They also think I'm right in saying that if LIV Golf can pay their reserves' expenses, then so too can the DP World Tour.

The Story of the Week of the BMW PGA Championship 14–17 September 2023

Of all the events we play each year, certainly for every British tour caddy, I think this is the one everyone looks forward to the most. Which is why nearly everyone opts for one of the Sunday night DUB-LHR flight options, enabling everyone to get to wherever they're staying in good time and good order on Sunday night, because at Wentworth Monday is always a work day.

And 'Wentworth' is actually what we all call this tournament, rather than its official rather longer name: as in it's always 'have you got a bag for Wentworth?' rather than 'have you got a bag for the BMW PGA Championship?' It just sounds better.

But let's be clear, the reason everyone looks forward to this week has everything to do with the tournament itself, and not the golf course, which to me has always been a lot of very average holes in the middle of some very average but very expensive houses. But, years ago now, those average holes often made for a fascinating finish for the tournament as guys could easily finish bogey, eagle, eagle. And often did. But then along came some new we-know-nothing-about-golf owners and commissioned a butchering of this once-good finale with a daft green at 16, can't run the ball on at 17 anymore, and usually a lay-up last. So neatly removing the 'fascinating' from 'fascinating finish'. At least that's the way I see it.

But the tournament itself is great. I'd even go so far as to say it's unparalleled apart from The Open. I mean where else are there huge crowds on the Monday and Tuesday of a tournament week? Crowds that would be the envy of the Sunday at some of the early-season tournaments.

And they come because it's a chance to see a lot of the very best players in the world, lured to a degree by the $9,000,000 prize fund. Like the six major winners in the field. Like Hovland, who's probably playing the best golf in the world at the minute. And like the likes of Hatton and Rai before they go back to the PGA Tour. All good news if you're a spectator.

But less good news if you're a player in Category 14, which is the category for those guys who finished 1–20 on the Challenge Tour last year – which, by the way, is an utterly rotten name for that tour. Because with the tournament now being in September rather than it's 'traditional' (or at least until a few years ago) slot in May, the reduced daylight means that whereas the tee times used to run from 7am to 3.40pm, they now run from 6.45am with the last three-ball going off at 2.30pm, meaning five less groups and 15 less opportunities to play in the biggest event of the year.

But at least gone are the ten spots that used to be given for 'National Spots', which were effectively club pros who'd qualified for their own championship: hence the tournament's official title of the BMW PGA Championship, as it was effectively run by the PGA when it first started out. Instead now there is only one spot. And this year it's filled by a guy who used to play on tour, so actually has a realistic chance of making the cut.

But. There's a bit of me that thinks, once again, the DP World Tour has missed a trick here. Because if you really want to elevate this tournament, and remember it's now held when there is really no tournament anywhere in the world this week in which any of the very best in the world would play, you'd have opened the entry list up to the likes of Cam Smith, DJ, DeChambeau, Oosthuizen, Westwood and even Poulter. Because that would have turned the tournament into an 'autumn major'. And when all the PGA Tour v LIV Golf settles, that's what the Tour will end up doing anyway. So why not do it now? Because that would have been better than good news if you are a spectator. Not to mention a loyal sponsor like BMW has been. And although that would have been even worse news for the Category 14 guys, who ever said golf was meant to be fair?

But whether you've come to watch one of the stars of world golf or just your favourite player, the one place you won't see them over the first few days is the range. Not because they won't be there beating balls like you'd expect them to be: they will be. It's just your view of them will be totally obscured by the legion of hangers-on (as we call them) who descend on Wentworth this week. Mostly it's 'the coach', i.e. the one from home who never comes to any other tournament all year but this one. Because he wants, and likes, to be 'seen'. There's frankly no other reason or explanation for them being there.

For these special people tour caddies generally harbour, at best, contempt. As all they end up doing is getting in the way. Or worse, they feel inclined to start tinkering with a swing that you've seen become pretty damn consistent over the last weeks on tour when, fairly obviously, said coach hasn't been there. Nor has he ever asked you, who sees it every day, what you think.

In fact it's always fascinated me that guys who are at the very top of their sport don't get coached virtually every day, like footballers, athletes, even tennis players. Although, to be fair, the smart players out here use one of the coaches who are out on tour every week. There's not many of them, but each and every one of them is a top, top coach. They're visible. They're there when things are going well, and they're there when things are going badly. They're not afraid to 'say it like it is'. Or for everyone and anyone to know they're part of so-and-so's team, no matter how badly they might be doing. Because they're not in it for their reputation: they're out here to make players better. And no matter who you are, you can always get better. And for these guys, tour caddies harbour total respect. They are proper coaches.

But it's not just the hanger-on coaches who get in the way this week – there's a whole host of other manufacturers' head honchos, equipment hawkers, etc. who descend and stand there on the range between the crowd and the players. Quite why the Tour issues so many range passes to these people is beyond me. They don't need to be there. And if you're trying to catch a glimpse of your favourite player, or on Wednesday your favourite celebrity, you don't need them to be there either.

In fact Wednesday is maybe worse for this than even the Monday or Tuesday, as although the Tournament Director walks along and politely requests that any players not playing in the Celebrity pro-am vacate the range one hour before that starts, they never ask the hangers-on to do the same. And boy, do they love being there when all the celebs start arriving to warm up their various lunges, swings and shanks before adoring celeb-spotters. But the pro-am itself is always fun, because a lot of the celebs are basically show-offs, and they interact really well with the huge crowds so making their day. And making our six-hour day, because that's about how long it takes to get round, fly by.

Certainly, not the case in the tournament itself with rounds taking well over five hours, despite a few of the par-five tees being moved up 50-odd yards to try and stop rounds taking well over five hours. And that's pretty much all down to the West Course having quite a few obvious narrow pinch points, where it just takes time to get players and spectators through, adding to the time it takes to get round. And while the Tour does everything they can to get the field round, the reality is that this isn't the best course in the world for modern-day tournament golf. But on the bright side, the narrowness allows the spectators to get really close to the tees and fairways, so from a fan-experience point of view it's actually one of the best tournaments to come and watch. Especially as they now have a whole range of live music after play finishes every night, so people really do come and make a day of it.

And while these pinch points and bottlenecks were not an issue in terms of daylight when this tournament used to have a May date, in September they are. Especially on the back of a fairly lengthy fog delay, which there was on Friday morning. Because that meant the whole golfing world was witness to a whole bunch of guys finishing literally in the dark come Friday night. A bit of an own goal in so much as it just adds fuel to the fire of the slow play debate. As well as why no one had started making 18 a call-up hole long before they did. Not that we had to come back to finish our rounds on either Friday or Saturday mornings. But with the first round taking five hours and 42 minutes it was close. And we didn't exactly fly round on the Friday either.

But in the end it was Ryan Fox who flew by everyone else on Sunday, scooping up €1,435,857 and 57p for his troubles, and giving his long-time caddy his second win in this event. More importantly, though, with seven of the Ryder Cup team finishing in the top ten and two more inside the top 20, the final result gave everyone watching at Wentworth and at home some hope that if these guys continue this type of form the week after next, Europe may indeed keep their unbeaten record on European soil that stretches back to The Belfry in 1993. And right now we've only a week to wait before we find out.

But first, there's a hop across the Channel to the best golf course on mainland Europe: Paris National. And the Open de France.

What You Hear on TV – the PhD Version

If you were at Wentworth last week, one of the things that you might not necessarily have noticed is how narrow a lot of the holes actually are: holes like 15, 16 and 17 for example are not much more than slivers of grass between the trees, which harks back to when the course was first designed in 1922. Because back then it was built for the residents of the new Wentworth Estate to play golf in what was effectively their backyards. Away from prying eyes. It certainly wasn't built to stage a golf tournament on the scale of the BMW Championship.

And while that causes all kinds of issues around pace of play today, what it does do is allow the spectators to get much closer to the fairways, and therefore the players and caddies, than they will any other week of the year.

And so they get to hear first-hand, and really close up, a lot of the player–caddy conversations that TV loves to listen in on.

But if you were one of the people who heard him ask me, 'What have we got?', and then listened intently to our debate about the second shot into 17 from the right rough on Friday, you might be forgiven for thinking as we walked off up the fairway that 'caddying seems pretty straightforward, I could do that'. But if that was you, then it's probably worth remembering that we were at sea level at the time; the hole was basically pan flat; the temperature was at or around 20 degrees; there was no humidity to speak of; and the gentle breeze that was blowing was neither too warm nor too cold. In other words there was nothing untoward in terms of what could affect the imminent flight of his golf ball, or how far it was likely to go.

And also that it's not always as simple as this. Although obviously every tour caddy would prefer that it was. Because that way we wouldn't get as stressed as we sometimes do. And that's because at the last count – well, this was according to a veteran caddy who still gives masterclasses to up-and-coming golfers from one of the European Golf Federations – there are over 50 things that can affect the flight of the ball and the distance it might end up going.

Fifty. Yes, 50.

A fair few of which we're going to have to consider in the real world of a tournament round. So here's the PhD version of a tour caddy's answer to the 'What have we got?' question, and why it's rarely as simple as it seems when you see or hear it on TV.

We'll start with the really obvious thing that can affect a golf ball, followed by some less obvious ones. And if you really do want to know the 45-odd ones I miss out, then just hire this guy for a morning. His rates are very reasonable. He, however, sometimes isn't.

And this really obvious thing is, of course, altitude. Because, and admittedly this isn't the most scientifically presented explanation, at altitude the air is thinner, and therefore the ball encounters less resistance in that air, meaning it travels further.

Now it just so happens that when we play at altitude in places like Kenya, Joburg, Crans Montana and Sun City, that 'further' equals around ten per cent further than at sea level. It's definitely not a hard-and-fast rule, though: it's just a rule of thumb. And so, like a lot of other things in our world, it's never quite that simple.

Because 'further' might actually be more than ten per cent or less than ten per cent depending on what time of the day you happen to be playing. For example, the date of the Omega European Masters high up in the Swiss Alps in Crans Montana is generally around the start of September each year, and in the middle of the day absolutely the ball goes ten per cent further so you need to take ten per cent off the yardage you come up with. But in the early morning it can actually be pretty chilly, so at this time of the day the ball will actually go closer to the distance it would at sea level. The trick here is obviously to recognise when to start taking the ten per cent off the yardage you're giving him: too early and the ball is short; too late and it's through the green into the trees, or worse.

So remember that 'Four off red. 178. Up three. That's 181 front. 13 on. 191 flag.'? Well, that just became 'Four off red. 178. Up three. 181. Minus the ten per cent is 163. 13 on. 176 flag.'

But if Crans is bad, then the absolute worst course ever for altitude has to be Chapultepec in Mexico where they used to play the WGC event. Here the ball could go anything between ten and 15 per cent further. Oh, and that depended on what clubs you were hitting. So the short irons weren't that affected because they spent less time in the air; whereas the longer irons were. Not that that stopped the occasional flushed 3-iron coming up 20 yards short. Still it was a free money event, so unless you were right up there, no one really cared.

But don't be thinking that it's just in the mountains that caddies need to worry about things like this. Because watching the BMW in June in Munich you'd be forgiven for thinking that altitude is in any way a factor that week, only Munich is actually at an altitude of 520m or 1,710ft above sea level, so you bet your life it is. Joburg is the same, although again you wouldn't think that watching on TV.

How do we calculate out ten per cent, etc? Well, for us guys that caddy for players who use yards (rather than metres) it's pretty straightforward: we use a 'metres book' that week. Because – give or take – the numbers in the metres yardage books are ten per cent less than the ones in the yards yardage book. Simple enough. The guys who use metres need to be a bit more mathematically agile that week. Whereas in Mexico everyone carried what amounted to a spreadsheet in the back of their yardage book with columns for 12.5 per cent, 15 per cent and 17.5 per cent off every number starting at 50 yards in five-yard increments. Thank fuck we don't play there anymore.

But if altitude is the most obvious of the 50 things that can affect the flight of a golf ball, then one of the less obvious things is grass.

Yes, believe it or not, the grass you're hitting off can massively affect a shot. For example, on courses that have very grainy turf (because it's the only stuff that will grow in that climate), you have to be really quite careful. If the grass is growing into you, the club is probably going to get momentarily stuck at impact, causing the ball to pop up more off the face, which in turn alters the flight. And those numbers we discussed before? Again, the trick is to spot this. And as ever that comes with experience. Bitter experience in a few cases. Usually involving water short of where you thought the ball would pitch.

So in this case, assuming we're still at altitude, that 'Four off red. 178. Up three. 181. Minus the ten per cent is 163. 13 on. 176 flag' I talked about previously could well become 'Four off red. 178. Up three. 181. Minus the ten per cent is 163. 13 on. 176 flag. But it looks to me like that's sat against the grain there so I think it's coming out high so we should probably play 168 front, 181 flag.' With me so far?

And while we're talking about grass, how the grass is mown on the fairways definitely affects how far the ball goes. So if the fairway is mowed away from you, and you can tell this generally by looking at what colour it is, on landing, the ball may run a significant distance. A bit like it does on a links course, which is perhaps the best example. You need to factor this in on, for example, a tee shot, as a bunker or water that is 30 yards further than your carry distance might actually be in play. Conversely if the ball is landing into the grain/grass, then it's not going to run far so there may be occasions where you can be more aggressive off a tee than you ordinarily would, for example.

The same goes for grain on the greens. Again, pitching into the grain on a green will mean the ball will stop quicker because it's meeting resistance from the grass; but if it's pitching on a part of the green that is downgrain, then it's likely going to release out rather than necessarily spin. Yes, another thing to factor into your view of where the ball should ideally pitch.

So again going back to our original PhD version, that could just as easily become 'Four off red. 178. Up three. 181. Minus the ten per cent is 163. 13 on. 176 flag. And we need to pitch this on the down grain, so pitch 168, yeah?'

And finally, one you regularly hear commentators speak about, although usually after they've heard the player shout, 'Fuck, flyer.' Yes, the flyer. A flyer is where grass gets trapped between the ball and the clubface at impact, causing the ball to jump off the clubface and go further than you were expecting. Sometimes ridiculously further. And here it's the same old dilemma: there's no finite way of telling whether the lie you have is a flying lie, or a normal lie. Being able to predict what is a flying lie comes with experience. And again this might often be bitter experience. It's a brave caddy that calls a flying lie when there's water short. Because if you play for a flyer and it comes out soft, it's in the water. And you're in the bad books. Or the dole office. Thankfully we're not going to go into a caddy–player conversation about a possible flying lie, over water, to a green with water behind: we just don't have enough time. Or ink.

Yes, caddying might look easy on TV, but on the course, at altitude, in a hot country, with Bermuda grass on the fairways, believe me it isn't.

The Story of the Week of the Cazoo French Open 21–24 September 2023

Take one Monday morning red-eye from LHR to CDG, then simply add an Uber across Paris, and voilà you have Monday lunchtime at the finest golf course on mainland Europe: Golf National just outside Paris. Perennial home of the Open de France, but perhaps more famously, venue of the 2018 Ryder Cup.

Or at least that's what should have happened. But in another classic example of 'the best-laid plans of mice and tour caddies, gang aft agley', what should have been a simple stress-free hop across the Channel from London to Paris proved to be anything but simple or stress-free.

So much so that in fact the guys who had opted for the 19.45 Sunday LGW-ORY flight that was first delayed by three hours, then diverted while it was actually in the air to CDG because of a mid-shift strike at Paris Orly, requiring everyone to then take the hugely expensive taxi ride across Paris to Versailles or Paris National itself because public transport had long since finished when they eventually landed, actually got off lightly. Because at least they got off the plane in the right country, unlike the guys who'd opted for LHR-CDG that ended up in Amsterdam (because of the same strike) requiring them to sleep on the floor in the airport before being put on an AMS-CDG early Monday morning. And then of course there were the guys who ended up giving up trying to fly altogether, requiring them to bin their flight tickets and instead get last-minute tickets, at last-minute prices, on the Eurostar. But on the bright side all of this travel chaos gave virtually everyone the excuse they needed to have a day off on Monday, do some much-needed laundry or simply sleep, before going up to the course on Tuesday morning, I wouldn't say refreshed, but as close to it as anyone gets at this stage of the season.

And this was a shame as a Monday at Paris National is never a Monday wasted. Because it is without doubt my favourite course on the main DP World Tour schedule. Mainly because on probably 17 of the 18 holes, you stand on the tee saying, 'Wow, this is a good hole,' which is the mark of a great golf course in my book. And I say 17 only because there's probably only the 17th hole that doesn't have that wow factor: it's not a bad hole, it's just that it's not as visually great a hole as the 16 that come before it or the one that follows it.

Several of those holes could actually be lifted and put on any links course in the world without looking out of place – in itself remarkable given that the course is built on the site of an old rubbish tip, and is 170km away from the nearest stretch of links land. The 10th hole for example could easily have the Firth of Forth sat below the back of the green; the 12th could be dropped on to Royal Birkdale without looking out of place; the par-five 14th could run along the shoreline of any course on The Open rota; while holes like 15, 16 and 18 would grace the very best stadium courses in the world. It's a masterpiece.

All it needs, and to be fair it's not actually part of the course, is the current hotel sitting behind the 16th and 18th greens demolishing, and being replaced by one that is as spectacular to look at as the last few holes which it overlooks. The French are very good at architectural statements, and this place is crying out for one.

Maybe they'll do it if ever the Ryder Cup returns here. Which hopefully it will. And sooner rather than later. Because there has been no finer Ryder Cup course golf-wise, and no finer Ryder Cup course spectator-wise, certainly this century. If ever. We can but hope.

Anyway, we're not staying here, and have instead gone for the Versailles option, which we never used to take when the French Open was played at the start of July. Mainly because Versailles at that time of year was always ridiculously hot, rammed with tourists, and none of the hotels had air conditioning, which meant you never slept a wink all week.

But this week we have not exactly got Versailles to ourselves, but at least we can go out to eat without having to queue or reserve the night before. And the temperature is obviously a bit cooler too, making things much more tour caddy-friendly after a good few weeks in a row.

However, while the standard of golf course is definitely up from last week, that's about the only thing that is actually up: for starters, the prize fund is down from the Rolex $9m level to the 'normal' level of $3.25m, and the Entry List has gone down a long way: mainly due to the fact that, fairly obviously, no one who is playing in the Ryder Cup next week is here. Well, except the guy who has obviously been told to play to try and recapture some form.

But what one lost another gained, and that means said Entry List has gone right down into Category 20, which is for guys who made the 72-hole cut but finished lower than 28th place at last year's Q School. A huge opportunity for them (or any of the categories immediately above theirs) to have that ridiculous week that suddenly gets them their card for next year, but a far cry from the 'old days' when the French Open was one of the biggest tournaments of the year, commanded that early July slot in the schedule, and so attracted quite a few guys from the PGA Tour as part of a French Open, Scottish Open, The Open road trip.

And instead, while the likes of Tom Kim and Billy Horschel are here, the field is perhaps more eye-catching in terms of guys playing their final-ever DP World Tour events. Like Raphael Jacquelin playing his 681st and final tournament; like Grégory Havret playing his 558th and final tournament; and like, thanks to a special invite from the Tour back to the tournament he won in 2007, Graeme Storm playing his 500th and final tournament. A fitting swansong for all three: proper players and gentlemen alike.

And speaking of swansongs, this course has sometimes been the swansong for a few caddies' employment: a course playing firm and fast with water in play on ten of the 18 holes was occasionally a recipe for a parting of ways come Friday evening. But with some heavy rain as everyone was trying to get here on Sunday night, topped up by a real downpour on Monday night when finally everyone was actually here, means this year things are much softer and the number of wave partings should theoretically also be down. Although ask any tour caddy and they'll tell you the same thing: round here, until that ball is safely on the green at 18 on Sunday, you cannot relax or switch off for a second. This is definitely not a stress-free end-of-season type week for any of us.

Especially when the rain and wind that had been forecast all week for Thursday duly arrived, making conditions for the morning starters on the desperate side of brutal, with that lashing rain and wind. Brutal but playable, as the course had been set up superbly to cater for the conditions, with some of the tees being brought forward on a good few of the real danger holes: another week where the TD really earned their money. And universal praise.

Unless of course you'd gone, or were watching at home, hoping to enjoy seeing a load of top tour players struggle around a really hard golf course. In which case you'd have been a bit disappointed. But able to count amongst your numbers some of my colleagues, who also enjoy seeing pros struggle: a number that doesn't include me though. I like it flat: a palm-flat golf course, flat calm conditions, and a flat calm player. But not necessarily in that order.

I also now really like what the tournament lays on for us, and how much that has continually improved over the last few years. Granted the locker rooms are still down in the bowels of the hotel with a bag store that opens at 6am, and not a minute before even if there are 25 caddies waiting to get their man's bag out ready for the day ahead, but at least now we get to eat in the main restaurant where we eat really very well, rather than queuing up to order from a choice of an overpriced and under-flavoured cheese and ham baguette or an overpriced and under-flavoured ham and cheese one like we used to. In fact we eat sensationally well.

What I didn't like though, and to be fair I only caught it on the TV coverage as I was having something to eat before heading off to the airport (so it's not like it spoilt my week or anything), was hearing one of the old boys' brigade of failed 1990s players who still commentate on Sky (Radar excluded of course as he definitely could never be described as that) having a pop at one of the more experienced caddies out here. His 'crime'? Not retrieving his man's divot after a shot into the 13th hole, which, had that divot not been floating away towards the middle of the lake at the front of the green at the time, might have indeed been one. Something he declined, or chose not, to point out.

And this isn't the first time he's made these kind of seemingly random (which they're not by the way) derogatory comments about some of our number. Now we can all take criticism out here; I mean we get enough of it from our players when things aren't going well, but when it's unjustified it just makes us all the more certain that it's high time that Sky recognised that this kind of commentary, and some of the other thinly veiled prejudices and jealousy of the modern player that gets spouted every week, has passed its sell-by date. And did something about it.

And this is precisely what at least one colleague did a year or so ago when he was on the receiving end of some nonsense about him taking too long over his club selection in the final round, and how that could cost his player the chance of winning. The caddy in question wasn't having this, sought this individual out face to face and pointed out that maybe if he'd had a caddy who cared as much about him, then he'd have done a lot better in his own career. Which was a fair point. And if he'd also been better at checking he had the right card in his hand at The Open one year, then that also would have been better too.

No, I think it's fair to say that in addition to the likes of Ewen Murray and TJ on the main commentary, we much prefer listening to the guys who have only recently stopped playing, because, and Anthony Wall is by far the best here, they actually understand what the 'modern game' is like and what it entails. They get it, and they appreciate it. And so their commentary from the fairways, like Radar's, is insightful, educational, and about as close to how me or any of my currently fuming colleagues would describe our man's upcoming shot. Which is why they have our respect. And why the failed 90s brigade don't.

That aside, all in all it was a fine week, topped off by everyone being offered tickets to the Ireland v South Africa rugby on the Saturday evening, Europe retaining the Solheim Cup the next day, Hisatsune flying the flag for Japan and everyone else in Category 17 and winning by two, and a few guys' grannies then relieving Ladbrokes of a good few quid as those grannies in the know had had an eye on this guy for a couple of months now. Allegedly.

Although what they didn't know was that this had been due to be Hisatsune's last week in Europe: at the start of the week he'd informed his caddy that this would be their last week as he was giving up on Europe and returning to Japan to play there instead, where his wife would be on the bag. But no throwing in the towel or doing a half-hearted job from the caddy, and six days later both their immediate futures suddenly looked a little different. One has the chance to now play in the end-of-season wheelbarrow of cash no-cut tournaments and maybe even get his PGA Tour card rather than scratching around on the Japan Golf Tour; while the caddy has another W in his résumé, and can go on holiday for four weeks rather than having to look for a job before meeting up with his man in Sun City and Dubai.

If ever there was such a thing as a win–win, this was it.

But let's just hope next week's winner isn't in doubt until the last game on the last hole on Sunday. Although, having said that, if that's what it takes for Europe to win, then right now I think we'd all settle for that.

The Art of the Possible

The 3rd hole on the West Course at Wentworth measures 459 yards, or 420 metres. There are two bunkers up the right from 260 to 310 yards, and one up the left at 320 yards, making it a very tricky driving hole.

The last time we played this hole a few weeks ago in the BMW PGA Championship, my man hit a perfect tee shot up the left half of the fairway, we wandered up to the ball, I got the yardage from the red spot conveniently situated seven yards in front of where his ball had finished, remembered to add the seven yards rather than taking them off, came up with the front number, added on the pin to give the total yardage, and made a mental note of the number to the back edge and the carry past the right greenside bunker in case he asked. I then conveyed the front number and the total yardage to him, who by now was rushing back from having a pee in the trees (or at least I think that's what he was doing), along with the necessity of staying left of this pin. He listened, pulled out the 7-iron like I knew he would, and two practice swings and a waggle later his ball was dispatched greenward. The fact that we did stay left but meant we ended up on a hideous downslope with the green running away from us is another matter but hey … we really only found that out when we got to the ball.

But fast-forward to 2030. And things are very different. For a start I've retired. While my current player has gone on to do great things since that 7-iron landed up by the green, including six more wins, one of which was a major; although admittedly the majority of these were with his new caddy.

But what's really different in 2030 is caddying itself. Because if I was still on the bag and we were on the 3rd tee on the West Course in 2030, I'd no longer be looking at the book for the run-outs on those bunkers. And neither would any of the other caddies working that week. Because no one carries them any more. And hasn't for years.

Instead I have a small next-generation tablet device in the pocket of the caddy bib, which we all still have to wear. And before I even step off the tee, this device is already telling me how far the tee shot has gone, how far we have to the front, back, flag, over that slope, and a myriad of other reference points.

This technology that enables this has actually been around for years: it's just an extension of the Trackman software that is still the staple diet of TV coverage. It's just that over the last two or three years it's been rolled out into something called TCEB, or the Tour Caddy Electronic Book to give it its full name. And it's this that is hosted on our individual tablets: every tour caddy has their own, and the players have their own.

Each number is 100 per cent accurate 100 per cent of the time. Keeping the device dry in the rain isn't an issue like it was with the old paper yardage books. And it's adjustable to cater for even the most short-sighted tour caddy so no one needs those +5.5 reading glasses round their necks like they used to.

Although as you can imagine, its introduction didn't come without some resistance – mainly it has to be said from people from my generation based on the vague notion that this was somehow devaluing their job. But thanks to the younger generation of tour caddies who were quicker to see its potential, the migration to this new technology wasn't too problematic, and we are where we are in 2030.

And where we are is 178 yards from the 3rd hole, front edge 162, back edge 189; 166 carries the small ridge you need to get over to get on to the right tier for this tight right pin. One click and we get to see what we've hit into this hole in practice and rounds 1, 2 and 3. Another and we can see what we hit at this hole last year, and the year before that should we need those numbers too.

In the practice rounds I had also been able to overlay the likely finish position of his second shot based on the club he'd selected based on his real-time dispersion stats, either in that round, the last month or indeed his whole career. Such is the power of these things. And also why this function remains disabled for the tournament days.

And gone too is, unless you really feel the need to do it, the need to 'walk the course', because even before travelling to a tournament tour caddies can download a full topographical version of the course on to their laptops, map on to it the likely pin positions, and lay on top how their player's stats indicate that they are likely to play the hole. There's a clear interactive 4D view of where the trouble is round the greens so again everyone knows, without walking round, where you're 'dead' to a certain pin position, where you are 'marginally fucked', and where's 'not too bad there'. All of which means that a tour caddy Sunday, be it on a plane, in an airport or simply at home on the settee, now involves studying the course pretty much as closely as you ever could by walking round on a Monday.

And because there's generally no need to walk round on a Monday, most guys either travel Monday night or Tuesday morning, saving themselves time, money and marital grief in the process. While in some cases, players have started choosing to only arrive on Wednesday afternoon if they're not in the pro-am, because they've basically done their practice round on a computer screen. The technology has really opened up a world of possibilities.

And we're not the only ones benefitting. A version of the software we use has been made available to the viewing public (for a hefty fee obviously) via their smart TV. And when this is paired with the enhanced TV coverage Sky have championed, you can follow any player shot by shot, lie by lie and option by option throughout their entire round; and see and hear what the caddy and player do over the ball. It feels like you are out there with your favourite player; or ex-boss in my case. All from the comfort of your home.

But best of all this new technology, and its embracing by the caddies and players on the DP World Tour, is recognised as being the main reason why play has speeded up like never before. Five years before our imaginary shot, it was taking over five hours for a three-ball on Thursdays and Fridays, but in 2030 that is down to a much more tolerable four hours and 20 minutes.

Mainly due to tour caddies having better data, faster. So making our advice better and more timely. As well as eliminating any risk of giving the dreaded 'mystery'. And if nothing else, that's got to be a good thing.

Chapter 10

Here Come the Gladiators

The Story of the Ryder Cup Week, September 2023

As a tour caddy, if there's one thing you can absolutely guarantee, it's that if it doesn't matter if there's a travel delay, there absolutely won't be one. But when you absolutely are in a hurry to get somewhere so it absolutely matters if there is one, then there absolutely will be one – which is what happened the last two weeks when we were all trying to get from Dublin to London, and then from London to Paris.

And so for this reason on Sunday night I manage to saunter through Paris CDG, board a plane that actually takes off on time and lands where it's meant to at the time it's meant to, get straight through immigration, arrive in the baggage hall in LHR to find my luggage is first off the belt, get an Uber within three minutes of ordering one, arrive home, pop my washing in the washer, and remind the missus who I am again: all with zero hassle and all before 22.30.

Meaning that all that remains is to come up with a plan as to how to get everything I need to get done this week done before Friday morning. Because from 6.30am Friday onwards this ass won't be moving from the settee, other than to, hopefully, punch the air when Europe wins. Or make inane gestures if those tedious shouts of 'YOU S A' get too audible. We all do it: so don't worry, it's not just you.

Because for this one week it doesn't matter how much you like America (and I do), how much you like Americans (and I do), or how much you like the American players and caddies (and I do); it's quite all right to, as Paul Casey once might have intimated, 'hate' them for a week. Well, for three days really. And only when they're winning if we're honest.

And really only in some Ryder Cups: because last Ryder Cup their team was at such a level that every one of us was simply in awe at the level of golf they produced that week. To a man they produced nothing short of phenomenal golf, to the point where all you could do was sit back, applaud, and start to get pretty nervous that the balance of Ryder Cup power had switched to the US for maybe a generation. Such was the strength of that team.

In 2023, though, their team, at least on paper, doesn't look quite as formidable for some reason. Maybe it's because despite the nucleus of the team being pretty much the same, a US team, certainly without DeChambeau, is absolutely not their best team.

And this should give Europe some cause for optimism that their unbeaten record in Europe going back to The Belfry in 1993 might just remain intact come Sunday night. Although, arguably, the way the points system is used for automatic qualification might need looking at again for next time, as whether it's served its purpose of actually enabling the 'top' DP World Tour guys to make the team is up for debate. Key witnesses for the prosecution being Adrian Meronk and Yannik Paul, one of whom would definitely have got in on the rankings, with the other having a pretty fair claim on a pick. The issue being, and we all know this so why not just say it, that MacIntyre effectively got in the team by birdieing 18 on Sunday at the Renaissance: a par and the points being so frontloaded, he doesn't. Although an unbeaten MacIntyre come Sunday night effectively nullifies that argument.

And while there's been a lot said about the effect of LIV Golf on the US team, it's certainly not the case for Europe. Because when you look at it critically there's perhaps only Garcia who might have merited a captain's pick: the Ryder Cup stalwarts like Poulter, Westwood, Stenson and Casey simply wouldn't have got in the team even if they had still been members of the DP World Tour. Their performances in the majors, and on LIV itself, have been slightly less than eye-catching if we're honest. The guard has well and truly changed.

That said, to not even consider them for the captaincy at any stage in the future still looks mean and small-minded to me. Even hinting that no one who 'defected' to LIV Golf will be a future Ryder Cup captain looks like another knee-jerk reaction by the DP World Tour, which will require another climbdown at some stage in the future. Especially now all the anti-LIV emotion seems to have dissipated a good bit, mainly on the back of a good few of the more vocal golf journalists having their soapbox rug whipped from underneath them by June's announcement that the world's golf tours would come together in association with the PIF of Saudi Arabia. Because like it or not, a lot of the animosity was stirred up by them too.

But captains are really only judged by whether they win or not. Or, at least, in recent years: it's worth remembering that Tony Jacklin, who really first made Europe a consistent competitive force rather than Ryder Cup whipping boys, didn't win in his first outings as captain. But everyone knew he'd started something.

This year's captain might come across as a bit beige on the outside, but 'inside' he's been one of those captains, a bit like McGinley in 2014, who's thought of everything, and done a lot of the 'little things' that create the type of togetherness and passion within the team that wins these things. Nothing appears to have been left to chance, especially the way he and the backroom staff have worked to try and negate some of the advantages the Americans may have in terms of World Rankings by setting up the course to favour the Europeans as much as possible. So, like Paris National in 2019, the rough is up; the speed of the greens is down; and as far as possible, there are no drive-wedge holes out there this week by all accounts.

Or at least that's the word from a few of the 12 caddies who are there, and not on their settees like I am. And for them it's a tremendous week. The togetherness and the intensity of weeks like these never leave you. And that's just for the caddies. For the players it must be a thousand times more intense.

But win, lose or draw, as well as the memories, what each caddy takes away with them is the full set of team outfits. Because everyone gets a set of clothes to wear for each day of the week, including the practice days. As well as, not that they'll need them this week by the looks of things, a set of waterproofs, hats, gloves, etc. Not that any of these are really any good to anyone after this week given that I think every caddy on this team is obligated to wear the same branded apparel as their players in any other tournament. But they certainly look good on the clothes rail in the wardrobe at home. Or they are donated, fully signed by the team, to friends or charities. Unlike the pretty substantial fee each caddy receives for caddying anyway.

And for any tour caddy not there, and who likes the authentic team gear, then it pays to be on good terms with the caddy who has the CaddyMaster role in Rome. Because every Ryder Cup a few extra shirts seem to find their way into his suitcase across the week, and he gives them away if you specifically ask for one. Though to his credit, he never ever sells them.

In the end I managed to watch pretty much all the action from Rome, spent a fair amount of time punching the air, and very little making stupid gestures – which was just as well as most of the three days I was fending off texts from friends reminding me that pretty much all year I'd been predicting that Europe would get thumped. Shows how much I know.

But I only managed to watch so much because the kids were at school all day Friday and my amazing missus had secretly arranged for them to spend the weekend with the outlaws so we could watch the golf in peace. God knows why she looks after me so well after all these years, but she does. And I for one am forever grateful.

So grateful in fact that I'm whisking her away on holiday next week. Admittedly, though, it is to St Andrews. And it is the week of the Dunhill Links Championship. In which I'm caddying.

But that still makes her a lucky lady, right?

Speeding up What's Slowing us Down

Hot topics on tour vary from month to month. And this year has been no exception. At the start of the year it was all about LIV Golf (every tour caddy I know generally thought it was a good thing; a lot of the players and the world's pre-eminent golf tours didn't); around the middle of the year it was the merging of the tours under the umbrella of PIF (every tour caddy I know generally thought it was a good thing; a lot of the players didn't); and towards the end of the year where we are now, it's been about slow play (where for once everyone is on the same page). Except obviously the snails.

But there are signs that the nearly six-hour rounds at Wentworth the other week might be the straw that finally broke the snail's back. Because behind the scenes there appears to have been a lot of players doing a lot of whingeing to the Tour about it, to the point where something positive might come out of it all.

We know this because one particularly enlightened referee collared a couple of us in the airport the other week and asked what we, as caddies, thought, and what we would do about it. Me and the other two guys I was with homed in on two things that contribute to play being slower than it might be and, crucially, two things that could be relatively easily fixed. Although in the case of the second one, it might take money. Which is probably the death knell for that one. But anyway.

First up we talked about what for a good few us ranks as probably our biggest bugbear at the minute: these bloody reusable water bottles we all have to use these days, and how these have single-handedly made things a bit slower out here than they used to be. And all because the Tour wants to engage in a spot of virtue signalling about how green they are.

The fact is that for a few years it all used to be so easy. On every tee, or on every other tee, there was a bin or a fridge with bottles of water. All plastic. All recyclable. It took two seconds to pick however many you needed out, and a similar amount of time to pop any used ones in the recycle bin. All good.

Only now we all get issued with these metal bottles for the week, usually with the sponsor's or tournament's logo on them. The idea being that we just refill these from a cold-water tap where the water bin used to be. Sounds fine. No evil plastic in sight anywhere.

Only it takes me, and I'm going to be generous here, 15 seconds to fill my bottle up. I then have to screw the lid back on. I then do the same and take the same amount of time to fill his bottle. All of which takes around, in case you haven't worked it out, half a minute.

Only then the second and third caddies in the group might have to do the same. So if you think about it, the third caddy in the group has to wait over a minute before he can even start filling his up, and by the time he's done so he's 90 seconds behind his player.

Who, unless he's the world's slowest walker, is not that far away from his ball. So what used to take virtually no time at all – most caddies grabbed enough bottles for the other guys in the group – now takes a lot longer, and in hot countries where you're needing to refill virtually every hole, well, just do the maths and you'll see why rounds are suddenly taking longer!

Oh, and by the way, we end up throwing these metal bottles away at the end of every tournament as (a) they weigh a bit and that bit extra in the travel bag might result in excess baggage fees, (b) we know we'll likely get a new one next week anyway, and (c) after a few days God knows what bacteria are brewing in the bottom of them. So far, though, it's Virtue Signalling Rovers 1 Commonsense City 0. And there's no sign of that changing any time soon. But I for one will keep chanting about it.

The other thing we homed in on were the snails themselves: the slow players. And how everyone knows who they are, yet no one seems to do anything about it. Even to the extent where one week a few years ago someone decided it would be a really great idea to 'draw' three of the slowest players on tour together. And even more remarkably, that it would be even better if they were put out first rather than at the back of the field where they would get on people's tits less. That little experiment didn't end well as I recall. We were out there forever. Patience was lost. Words were exchanged. And – believe it or not – the snails didn't actually get any faster the next week.

Each week you can guess who they have been drawn with by listening out for the audible 'sighs' when the draw is posted on a Tuesday afternoon. If you're unfortunate enough to be in their group the first two days, you already know you'll be seeing a fair amount of the referee that week as you fall further and further behind the group in front. And even though it has nothing to do with you (or rather your man), there's nothing you, or anyone else by the looks of things so far, can do about it.

We, however, had a cunning plan – which went something like this:

Start by targeting the three slowest players on tour. And instead of waiting for them to fall behind the group in front, stick them on the clock from the 1st tee shot. Half the time you'll only be saving yourself a few holes anyway. So why postpone the inevitable?

And to do this you just need one more referee. But not one walking with the group. This referee needs to be out of sight walking in the trees or out of sight in the crowd. That way the old 'speed up when the ref appears, and slow back down to your normal snail's pace when they're gone' routine won't work. All the referee has to do is wander across the minute they're out of position, administer one warning, then vanish back into the trees. Next time the snail sees them it'll be to advise him that they are being penalised shots. Fines don't work. Especially for the well-off snails.

We'd even go so far as this referee videoing them as part of educating them as to where and when they can speed up. In fact you could label the whole thing a 'Pace of Play Education Programme'. But whatever you call it you need to do something. Because whereas five hours for a three-ball never feels slow, anything longer than that shouldn't be acceptable. And unless the Tour tries something new, that may well become the new norm based on the last couple of weeks.

And at the end of the day, if just one snail gets the message and speeds up, then it's a step in the right direction. Only then you have to replace this snail with the fourth-worst snail on tour. And so on. Because one thing is guaranteed, the other 153 other players that week will thank you.

And at that point we were thanked for our views and we left for the flight fairly confident that we'd been heard even if we'd not really been listened to. But 100 per cent confident that we'd be more than happy to eat our words if in fact we had been.

The Story of the Week of the Dunhill Links Championship 5–8 October 2023

At least with the Ryder Cup being on mainland Europe rather than say on the west coast of America, I was able to get a sensible amount of sleep on Sunday night before the drive up to St Andrews. Whether this was technically enough to be fully compos mentis behind the wheel at 4am is another matter, but 434 miles and two stops later, me and the missus are parking up outside the New Course clubhouse in St Andrews safe and sound.

We dodge the autograph hunters who are already gathered by the entrance to the clubhouse area and behind the range ready to collar any of the celebs who've turned up to make a full week of it, and head inside to pick up all the yardage books for the week.

All, because obviously there is one for each of the three courses we play this week: the Old Course here at St Andrews, Kingsbarns and Carnoustie.

And because he is flying in mid-morning into Edinburgh, it's the St Andrews one I'll be using first, albeit we'll probably only play nine holes, as it'll be pretty chilly by the time he's got here, had something to eat, chatted to a few celebs he knows, and hit a few balls to loosen up, leaving Tuesday and Wednesday for practice rounds at Carnoustie and Kingsbarns.

The day, or early morning to be precise, that we picked for a practice round at Carnoustie was also the day the wind decided to kick up, making the practice ground there quite possibly the coldest place if not on earth, then certainly in Scotland. So cold that after just a few shots we sacked that off, and headed straight out to play, all the while acknowledging that Korea might have been cold, but it will never ever be as cold as here. But at least we managed to get all 18 done in the dry, as well as the drive back down to Dundee, across the Tay Bridge and along to St Andrews. Where, especially in the late afternoon, the first sight you get of the Auld Grey Toon is still as magnificent as ever.

Freezing my nuts off on the range at Carnoustie aside, along with many of my colleagues, I love this tournament, but with a good few of the star South African players like Grace and Schwartzel not being here this week as they play on LIV, then I do fear for its future. Basically because it, like the Dunhill Championship down at Leopard Creek, is bankrolled by Johann Rupert, and him not being able to have guys he's supported for years, and who are his friends, playing in 'his' tournaments on the Tour he's supported for years, doesn't feel like a sensible, or sustainable, position for the DP World Tour to take. They risk losing a huge supporter of golf, and with him two fantastic tournaments. So we'd better enjoy this one while we can.

And in Tuesday's draw my man gets a pretty nice amateur partner for the week.[8] We've played with them before. And it's always a pleasure. For a start, they are a very decent player in their own right: so if nothing else, we'll not be in the heather half the time. That and they know when to pick up, and when you kind of stay out of the way when 'their pro' needs them to. And they definitely aren't one of those guys who have to wear their sunglasses when they're being interviewed by Sky Sports before their round due to it being before the round the morning after the night before, if you get my drift. We also get drawn at Carnoustie on what looks like it might be the calmest day of the four (not that it actually went to four days in the end). So, at that stage it was so far, so good.

---

8 Each pro is drawn with an amateur partner and there is a team competition across the week: best net score wins.

Our partners also look pretty good too. Because you also get to know them on the Tuesday. Basically, and obviously, my guy plays with his amateur the first three days, but we have a separate pro/am team as partners on all three. While on Sunday it's a little different in that only the top 60 pros qualify for the final round at St Andrews, making it actually the hardest cut to make all year. And if their team makes the cut in the amateur competition (again, quite hard to do), then they play alongside them again. But spare a thought for the pros who miss the cut, but their team somehow makes the cut, because they have to play Sunday for nothing. Not ideal when, if you're a UK-based guy, frankly you could be at home.

Anyway, for us all goes pretty well despite the idyllic flat calm of Thursday not lasting very long. And if we thought it was pretty iffy on the Friday, then Saturday was frankly apocalyptic. In fact, the minute I looked out of the window when I woke up, I already pretty much knew that there was absolutely no way we were going to play, especially with a couple of holes at Carnoustie actually being below sea level, meaning they get very wet very quickly. And so it panned out, as after a couple of hours' delay play was called for the day on all three courses without anyone actually hitting a shot. And it was exactly the same on Sunday, too: play was abandoned for the day around 9am, also without a shot being hit.

It was just as well as a lot of players, caddies and amateurs had effectively played rain-delay roulette come Saturday lunchtime, and decided if the locals were saying there was absolutely no way we'd play on Sunday, then that meant we wouldn't be, no matter how much hope the Tour were holding out; and so descended en masse into St Andrews for a Saturday afternoon's 'relaxation', mainly in and around The Dunvegan Hotel. And a long old afternoon it turned out to be by all accounts. So maybe it was just as well I had the missus up with me, as I avoided what would have been an inevitable hangover, and the waste of Sunday that would have brought with it.

Play being washed out on Saturday and Sunday obviously also meant that we were going to the dreaded Monday finish, necessitating the usual scramble to extend hire car reservations, re-book flights, and generally deal with the nightmare of any tournament 'going into Monday'.

And the thing about playing in conditions like we did late on Friday afternoon, nearly did on Saturday, and thankfully never even got close to doing on Sunday is that most of the amateurs I've seen in this event over the years clearly aren't used to playing in them: I mean, why would you? But thankfully the St Andrews caddies they tend to use for the week are, and can guide them round without them losing more balls than they started with. Which, looking at some of the swings on show, is nothing short of miraculous, and shows you how good these caddies are in their own right. And also why a fair few tour caddies started their caddying careers on these very links: they're just very good. It's just a shame that occasionally the odd amateur doesn't necessarily reward them accordingly come Saturday or Sunday night.

They who also had a good week were the two first reserves. Although whether 'good' is the right word is debatable. Because at the Dunhill there are two first reserves: one is at St Andrews on the basis that even if someone pulls out virtually at the last minute at Kingsbarns, it's no problem as it's only ten minutes up the road; while the other first reserve is at Carnoustie, and on the basis that it's not just up the road someone having to pull out at the last minute definitely would be a problem.

However, although the first reserves are technically only first reserves for less than two and a half hours on the Thursday morning as there are only 56 players at each venue starting off two tees, they have to remain on-site for the

Friday and the Saturday too in case someone has to pull out during the first three rounds, leaving their amateur partner without a pro. So it can be a pretty strange week for them, although unlike in any other DP World Tour tournament they actually get a few thousand pounds for being on-site as a reserve. This year, though, all the reserves actually ended up playing thanks to a few withdrawals early on Thursday morning, so in the end things went well for them I suppose.

Things appear to have gone less well at the ETCA's AGM. This is always held the week of the Dunhill Links, mainly because for years the Jigger Inn at the side of the Old Course Hotel hosted the post-ETCA AGM party, and spoilt everyone rotten afterwards. I chose not to go, instead preferring the delights of our annual trip up to the Strathkinness Tavern just outside St Andrews, where I suspect we had a rather better time than anyone who attended. Not that many people did by all accounts.

But even allowing for some guys not being at the Dunhill, the draw of the Strathkinness, and general apathy, when only around 20 people turn up for what should be a pretty important evening, then something isn't right. And the danger is now I think that the ETCA risks becoming a bit of an irrelevance, undoing much of the good work of the last 30-odd years, which would be a real shame. Because at times out here our voice needs to be heard. And listened to.

I think what's actually needed, and maybe this would make me want to engage a bit more, is someone much younger leading the association, someone more representative of the average age out here now, someone who focuses on driving a hard bargain with the Tour on the things that matter, and someone who doesn't bad-mouth my colleagues, who have chosen not to be members, at every opportunity. Because the latter just reminds me of one of our esteemed and much-loved Zulu colleagues out here who wisely observed that 'a pig squeals its loudest as it's about to be put on the fire'.

But at least by early afternoon Monday we actually had a winner: something which certainly didn't look possible even on Sunday night with Carnoustie completely flooded, and only possible because of, I guess, an overnighter by the greenkeepers at all three courses. Quite simply, if you didn't see the pictures or watch any of the coverage, what they did was nothing short of miraculous.

And while Fitzpatrick was looking forward no doubt to a few weeks off after his win, our 'next week' started with a long drive home, feeling about eight stone heavier after a week eating those vanilla-filled buns from the Balgrove Larder after every nine holes for six days, and talking about nothing other than the magic that is the Dunhill Links Championship. Even in that weather.

Let's just hope it's not the last one.

Coping with Caddying

Being a tour caddy is not all plain sailing. Far from it. Which is why resilience is our trademark, and the 15th club we carry around each week.

But there are times when not even this is enough. And that's pretty much the situation one of 'our crowd' found themselves in recently. We knew something was up – after all, it's pretty difficult to hide anything from your friends out here when we basically all travel, work and socialise together for 30-odd weeks a year – to the point where a couple of us were concerned enough to invent some pretext, sit in a quiet corner somewhere and ask him whether everything was all right, which obviously we knew it wasn't.

In the end, though, I think it was only the 'we're only asking because we care' that did the trick, because after that he started to open up a bit on what was indeed wrong. Proving that even the most experienced and brilliant tour caddies' stores of resilience can occasionally drop to danger levels. Which his had.

And at the heart of everything was worry. He was worried because his player is in a precarious position with just a few tournaments left. In fact it transpired he'd been worried for a few months now, and as long ago as the early summer had thought the writing was on the wall. There had been a lot of 'it's definitely getting better' weeks; but a lot of them had been MCs nonetheless. There had been a lot of decent weeks; but only decent enough for a top-30 finish, such is the standard out here. There had been a whole lot of expense; but not a whole lot of income. And now they'd run out of time.

He also knew. He knew logically he should just put the feelers out and find a new player; but being the old-school loyal type he didn't want anyone to find out he was 'looking' or 'available': that would be being disloyal. He knew that the second payment to the tax people was due next month (his once-dependable player had won nearly €1m last season), and that he only just had the spare cash to pay it. He knew that the 'twinge' in his back was getting worse not better, and that Whatshisname had had the same thing a few years back and it had finished his caddying career. He knew that the answer was a month or so's complete rest followed by a month or so's physio and gym work; neither of which would be cheap. He knew that the income protection thing he had needed to get round to investing in a few years ago was something that he now needed but obviously didn't have. And he knew that it was basically too late to do anything about making provision for his retirement in a few years' time. All of which was royally doing his head in. And why he was basically a shadow of his former positive bubbly self.

Not that there was a lot any of us could do to help other than listen; so that's what we did. And even just doing that seems to have helped: his answer to our 'all right?' greeting is now (when no one else is listening) 'better, thanks'. So that's good.

But it did strike me afterwards that our friend was probably not the only caddy out here going through something similar. And that if we are affected by this stuff, then there's a fair chance that a few of our employers will be too – at least we're getting paid when things are going badly. They aren't. And if there are people going through tough times out here, is there something practical the Tour, us as caddies or anyone for that matter could do to prevent some of this? Because prevention is better than cure. But this brought me straight to the one thing that has always amazed me out here.

And that's why don't the DP World Tour players have someone, employed by them, to deliver the things that would make their lives out here easier? Yes, they have their Players' Committee and that's allegedly their line of communication into the DP World Tour; and yes, there have been Player Liaison roles for a good few years now, both of which should help make their lives on tour easier. But committees never work, and what on earth makes you think that someone appointed and employed by the DP World Tour is really going to fight your corner against the DP World Tour when push comes to shove is beyond me. Because ultimately the Player Liaison guy's loyalty will always lie with the person who's paying his annual salary. All six figures of it allegedly. And that's the DP World Tour. Astonishing nepotism really. And all hidden in plain sight.

Instead, what they need, and have needed for years, is a Head of Player Experience role. Filled by one of their own. Paid for out of their own pockets. Completely independent of the DP World Tour, but recognised and engaged by the DP World Tour. And responsible for one thing and one thing only: delivering their agenda. In fact it makes me suspicious why they haven't been crying out for a role like this, especially given what they see being provided on the likes of the PGA Tour and especially LIV Golf.

But first they need an agenda. And as you can't play professional golf without travelling, you start with that. It's things like why don't DP World Tour players have access to preferred airlines offering free changes to any ticket bought with that airline? An instant saving of potentially thousands of pounds a year, and absolutely ending the practice of buying one ticket for Friday night and one ticket for Sunday night.

And why are there no charter flights to the next venue for those weeks where everyone will be making the same journey to the next venue? Again, it would just make economic and practical sense to do so. So you need someone to stand up and demand this for you.

Then there's accommodation. I know a few ex-pros who now lament being lazy and shelling out hundreds of thousands of pounds or euros on the 'official hotels', which they booked knowing fine well that the rates they were paying included a healthy profit margin, first for the promoter and secondly for the Tour's for-profit travel service, when there were cheaper options available. I have never understood why the players tolerated being ripped off like this: I mean, just imagine how much money a player would save in say a ten-year career during which time they circumnavigate the globe 20 times.

Off the course, what if there was 'someone to talk to' about things like cost-effective loss of income protection, access to specialist financial advisors and specialist financial advice, access to inexpensive private health insurance that helped them rather than line someone's pockets, and you'd also have someone to fight your corner when the Tour decides to fine you for something but denies you the chance to even put your side of things.

It's about having a package of 'stuff' that would just make the players' lives easier, allowing them to focus 100 per cent on the job in hand. One that their talent and profile bloody well deserves. And while it might take a few years to deliver, during which time priorities may inevitably change, then at least the Head of Player Experience is on the case. And accountable.

After which there would be nothing to stop these benefits also being made available to the players' caddies. Or any other member of a player's 'team' – meaning we might never have to have another sit down like that with another of our friends in the future.

Chapter 11

The Last Chance Saloon

The Story of the Week of the Acciona Open de Espana 12–15 October 2023

Welcome to week one of the DP World Tour's Last Chance Saloon Swing. Not its official title obviously, but that's effectively what the next three weeks are.

It's the last chance to save your season. Whether that's by making it into the top 70 to get into at least the first of the two Final Series events; by getting that win that was on your list of goals for the year; by finally wrapping up that PGA Tour card for next year; or simply just retaining your playing rights for next season. Which is where the real drama, and if we're honest interest, is these three weeks.

And as of now there are, as usual at this time of year, a number of guys whose names the average golf fan at home can't believe are below the cut-off point for retaining their playing rights for next year, a line which currently sits at 116 on the Race to Dubai rankings: one place lower than it was last week because someone has declined to take up their DP World Tour membership, and so has come off the rankings list.

But as someone once said about football, the league table never lies. And if you're down near the bottom, it's not because of last week, or the week before that: it's because of the entire season. A season in which, by definition, a lot of guys have played a lot better than you.

And there's absolutely no sentiment involved. Well, certainly not amongst the players. In fact players have been known to avoid players who are 'down the bottom' in case any of their bad play somehow jumps into their body and they start struggling too. Even wives and girlfriends, once keen to be all chatty and chummy when things were going well, seem to be distinctly more distant, despite knowing the worry that their 'friends' might be feeling inside.

Thankfully there's none of this shite within our ranks. Because I think we've all been there at one stage in our caddying careers, hoping that our man is the one guy who each year seems to find the result (or results) right at the very end of the season to keep his card. And if we haven't been, then it might be next year. So it's definitely best not to tempt the golfing gods by wishing ill on others.

Getting in the way of those trying to keep their cards, though, is the issue of daylight this late in the season, meaning that this week and next in Spain are reduced field events, as is the week after in Qatar, where the regular season will finally end. And so this week the Entry List has only gone halfway down Category 17, which essentially is for those guys who got their cards through the 2022 Qualifying School, meaning a few guys who need a good finish won't even get to start. Right when they really need to.

Again, there is zero sentiment out here at this time of the season.

But while there might not be a huge amount of daylight this week, there will be a huge amount of sunshine. After last week at the Dunhill that will come as a welcome change. As will not having to wear waterproofs and beanies, and carry two spare towels in the bag.

Especially as, and maybe, just maybe, it was due to caddying in that weather last week at the Dunhill, I have picked up the mother of all colds that seems to have got me in a death-like grip.

I had started to feel a bit ropey on the way home on Monday, but by the end of Tuesday when, instead of staying in bed feeling sorry for myself which I could and should have done, I'd flown down to Spain on my hastily rearranged (and expensive) flight, I was in full snot mode, complete with a hacking cough. Not something you really want on a plane in the post-COVID world; unless you like getting filthy looks from every other passenger.

And so I already know that it's going to be a long week. But as a tour caddy you can't, or actually don't, ever ring in sick and say hope to be back by the end of the week or early next week like you might in a normal job. Out here life must go on. Even if the next few days of that life include waking up on Wednesday morning feeling terrible knowing that ahead of you is a day when just lifting the bag is going to be a supreme effort, especially in that heat, although hopefully the first round the day after won't be as bad, but absolutely will still be a struggle. The only consolation is that Club de Campo is pan flat. Except that it isn't. At all.

So I'm there trying to make light of exactly how rubbish I'm feeling, while hoping that I don't end up passing even half of this on to him. Especially as this place really suits his game, and it's a chance to end the season with a W. Because he's already said that if he does win, we're not going next week and possibly the week after that, although Qatar would be an easy hop down to Joburg and on to Sun City.

But to win we're going to have to beat Jon Rahm on home soil first, not to mention Justin Rose. However, at the end of the day it was actually Matthieu Pavon we should have been worried about, as he went one better than his second-place finish here last year, easing to a four-shot win, and leaving the likes of Rahm and Rose well down the field. And a few of us being forced to admit that maybe finishing with his long-term caddy after a disappointing week at Wentworth and taking a really experienced older caddy had indeed been the right thing to do. No matter how much we sympathised with the guy who got fired.

Leaving this aside, though, the real drama was always going to be in or around the 116 position on the Race to Dubai rankings. And so it proved. Because from nowhere Fabrizio Zanotti found four decent rounds and vaulted up 38 places to the safety of 89th on the Race to Dubai rankings. With the other two big movers being Mike Lorenzo-Vera and Alfredo Garcia-Heredia, who also managed to clamber out of the mire and into the top 116. And while neither are by any means 100 per cent safe with two tournaments to go, they have certainly given themselves some breathing space and, perhaps more importantly, a bit of confidence going into those events. At least for now. But for some other notable names, their best form remained elusive; as did the really good week they need to guarantee their playing rights for 2024. To the extent where they actually dropped down a few more spots below that all-important 116 position. And so for them the season will go right down to the wire. And that's stressful for them. And their caddies. Even if they don't admit it.

Thankfully my man had his playing rights secured a good few months ago now, so we're not in this boat. But with Pavon winning, we definitely didn't get the W we were after either.

And so next week it's San Roque and Sotogrande for us, rather than San Miguel and the seaside for me.

Breaking the Law

There is a conversation we probably need to have. Because tour caddies work hard. Bloody hard.

I mean you already know from these pages that on a typical Monday our working week often starts with an early flight to a different country, after which we find our way to whatever course we're playing that week, and then walk that course, ready for his arrival should he be taking a flight at a more sensible time than we do. And if he has done, or actually arrived on the Sunday night, then this usually ends up with some practice followed by nine holes.

Tour caddy Tuesdays are typically the main practice day, consisting of, though not necessarily in this order, a full-scale putting session (which involves technical drills, pace drills and generally getting a feel for that week's greens), some time on the range, a nine- or eighteen-hole practice round, finishing up with, 'I'll just hit a few more balls.' Not to be confused with a short day.

On Wednesday it's 'divot-watching' (every tour caddy's least-favourite activity) if your man is not in the pro-am; or 18 holes pro-am if he is. And these pro-ams can take a long, long time, believe me.

Thursday is Round 1, when we meet our players an hour or so before we play, caddy for five hours, then watch them hit a few balls afterwards.

Friday is Round 2: same routine, just late if you were early yesterday, or early if you were late yesterday.

Saturday is either the same routine as Thursday and Friday if he's made the cut; or if he hasn't, either another mammoth divot-watching session on 'Misery Hill' (caddy shorthand for spending Saturday and Sunday watching him beat balls on the range) or kicking your heels if he's headed home in on MC huff.

Sunday? Well Sunday is pretty much the same as Saturday.

And on top of this lot, I also spent some of my evenings preparing for the tournament day the next day, as well as recording and analysing his stats. All of which adds up to, at a conservative estimate, around a 53-hour week. For which, and remember we are all pretty much specialists in our chosen field, we are generally paid around £1,000 a week in wages, which is fine.

Or is it? Because out of that £1,000 the vast majority of tour caddies pay their own travel to get to the tournament, their own accommodation for the week, their own food and anything they may care to drink. So if travel averages (and these figures err on the side of 'charitable') around £150 a week, accommodation say £300 a week, and food at night costing around £25 a night, then suddenly that £1,000 wage magically becomes £400.

And that means tour caddies, certainly in Europe, work around 53 hours for £400, or just under £8 an hour. And in the UK this is borderline illegal. Actually, no. It is illegal as the current 'minimum wage' in the UK is, as I write this, set at £10.42 if you are over 23. And I for one certainly am. If you were a director of a UK company caught paying this little, somewhere along the line you'd be parting with a £20,000 fine and being barred from being a company director for 15 years.

So maybe it's time to have a rational, informed debate about tour caddy wages. And start that debate by looking at the root causes of the 'problem'. And that's the ability to pay. Because when players first come out on tour they incur lots of new expenses: the caddy being one of them.

Now I know that the Tour introduced their Earnings Assurance Programme in 2022 to 'help' players at a time when the cost of playing on tour was rising at a far higher rate than the prize funds, such that anyone playing 15 or more tournaments in a year would, from 2023, be guaranteed $150,000 in earnings that year. And very laudable that was, even if you suspect that they only did that because of LIV Golf being fairly public about how much the guy finishing last in their rankings would be earning.

But for me laudable doesn't really cut it. Or not when you look carefully, and see that if this had been applied in 2022, then only around 13 players in the top 200 of the final Race to Dubai rankings would have benefitted, and only a further seven within the top 250.

So for me the real solution should take as its starting point Keith Pelley's own words that 'it is an incredible accomplishment for any professional golfer to simply gain their playing rights on the DP World Tour', because that is generally the starting point of every tour pro's journey. Whether that's ultimately a journey to stardom, being a 'journeyman', or realising that just being very good is not good enough.

And so wouldn't it be better to say that when you get your card through the Qualifying School, or even say in your first two or three years on tour, the Tour will help you out financially? Or at least until you reach a threshold in career earnings where money is no longer an issue. And set that level of financial help at the level that allows players to get themselves to tournaments, allows them to stay in decent 'stay better play better' accommodation, pay their bills at home and, of course, pay their caddy a rate that properly reflects their outgoings on tour and at home. Not to mention their expertise.

A reasonable parallel would be the way Student Loans was in the UK. The player would repay the financial help given over a number of years should he still remain on tour, or in full once they reached a threshold of career earnings. For those guys who don't quite make it on tour, the debt would simply be written off.

The spin-off for us tour caddies might then be a long-overdue move away from players setting their caddy's wages on the back of a 'I pay mine £1,000 a week' conversation with a guy who's been out here a while; and instead enabling them to be set at a rate based on a caddy's actual outgoings, work and experience.

And that rate would likely be much closer to £1,500 a week. Yes, you can pay more; but no, you can't pay less. Because that is – if absolutely nothing else – culturally unacceptable. Not to mention probably illegal.

But before anyone points out that tour caddies are pretty privileged and pretty lucky people anyway, or that being a tour caddy is effectively more a lifestyle than a job so we really ought not to be bemoaning our lot, just be aware that we all know this too. Just as we also know that being a tour caddy is a choice.

But so is paying us a decent wage.

The Story of the Week of the Estrella Damm NA Andalucia Masters 19–22 October 2023

The longer you've been caddying out here, the more likely it is that you'll find yourself caddying for someone who is coming into the last couple of tournaments of the year needing, frankly, a miracle to keep their card. It might be because your man has struggled all year. Or it might be because you have been parachuted in on the bag right at the death in the hope that your experience might be the thing that delivers said miracle. Either way the pressure is on.

But as a tour caddy all you can do is to treat it like any other week. Or at least certainly try and act like it's any other week. Because what your man certainly doesn't need if he's 'in trouble' this season is for his caddy to be looking nervous, tense, anxious or stressed. Or any combination of these four Deadly Horsemen. Especially not if you're the guy who's been parachuted in. Easier said than done. No matter how many times you might have been in this position.

Now thankfully for me, neither my player nor I find ourselves in this position this year. But a few guys I know very definitely are. And each one of them is hoping, even praying, that this is the week their player finally wakes up. Because every year there's one or two guys who seemingly suddenly realise that the shit they're in is now above shoulder height, and rising, and so finally, getting a really nasty great whiff of it, they start to flush every shot rather than whiff every shot. It's like they've been inside the top 16 all season, rather than outside the top 116 all season. And so they somehow manage to drag themselves out of the mess they've got themselves into. Some even do it multiple years in a row. So you never know.

But the trouble is that if they do, that means someone else doesn't. And so from a position of being basically safe all year, some players can suddenly find themselves, at best, looking over their shoulders, and at worst taking their now shit-free colleague's place in the shit.

And this is how the caddies of the likes of Scott Jamieson, Ross Fisher, Jeunghun Wang and Marc Warren (all winners on tour in the past) may also be feeling at the start this week. What state they're in at the end of it remains to be seen.

But if you ever wanted a course to try and find something on, then the Real Club de Golf Sotogrande, on the south side of the A7 highway from Valderrama, is probably not one of those you'd immediately pick. Mainly because it is not a million miles away from being as difficult as its more illustrious neighbour.

However, at least getting here wasn't very difficult. You either opted for the hour or so's flight down to Malaga, or you did what a fair few guys did, which was to pile on the bullet train down that takes three hours but saved the hassle of checking bags in at the airport. And any possibility of them going missing.

Either way, if you left Sunday night, that got you into Malaga and along the coast at a half-sensible hour, meaning that come Monday morning everyone was out walking the course as it's the first time we've had a tournament here for a long, long time. In fact I actually can't remember ever coming here. And thankfully when I do walk the course, I find that in fact all 18 holes are not 400 yards or 366 metres as the Tour's website was showing the other week when I last looked.

And coming off after a leisurely walk round, the consensus seems to be that if you're struggling to keep your card, or even just struggling with your game, then the chances are you'll be struggling round here too. The fairways aren't exactly wide, which is bad news if your lowly position in the Race to Dubai ranking is due to you not hitting many this year. And if it's your short game that's been letting you down, then probably the last thing you want are grainy greens and some very tight lies for chipping off should you miss them.

But at least I'm feeling human again after last week's end-of-flu health struggles. And at the moment it's also forecast to be nice and warm down here, apart from Thursday. Which is just as well as this is our last chance this season to have dinner sitting outside watching the sun go down over the sea, reminding ourselves that you just can't do this in England at this time of year, and maybe that's why so many expats choose to spend their winters here.

Apart from Thursday, obviously, when the weather was on a par with the winds from UK storm Babet by all accounts. And when spectators are asked to leave the course, like they were on Thursday afternoon, but you have to keep on playing, that's when you know you are really on the wrong side of the draw.

Fortunately, though, we manage to avoid the worst of it, and again do all right this week, but it's Meronk who wins. For the third time this season. And maybe another little reminder that he's not just the guy who didn't get a pick for the Ryder Cup.

But if we're being honest, who wins this week and next week isn't where the real interest is. That is all about who out of the guys who start the week inside the lower reaches of the top 116 manage to stay there; who out of the guys who start inside the lower reaches of the top 116 end up dropping out of it; and who out of the guys who start outside the top 116 manage to push (or more likely edge) their way into it.

And by Friday night we know an MC means the likes of Wang and Levy aren't doing any of these three; MCs for Jamieson and Van Tonder mean they have a nervous weekend ahead as they are suddenly vulnerable; while at least the likes of Knappe, Fisher, Garcia-Heredia and Warren all have a chance of making some progress towards safety by Sunday night as they'll be playing all four rounds.

And they may well have done so had it not been for a Sunday that served up a few curve balls, not least of which was an early U-draw as, in complete contrast to the initial forecast for the week, bad weather was apparently coming in in the late afternoon. Which it duly did, but only as the last groups were finishing on both sides of the course. So that was another good call by the Tournament Director, and not for the first time this season either. More kudos to them.

Because by then it was enter Matti Schmid, who had lost his PGA Tour card at the end of their regular season last Sunday, and had rushed back to try and secure his DP World Tour future in one of only two tournaments left open for him, which he duly did with a solo second, vaulting him up 84 places in the Race to Dubai and guaranteeing his playing rights for next year.[9] All with a stand-in caddy, who had actually lost his own job the previous Sunday too.

And then there was Chase Hanna, who hadn't finished higher than 36th anywhere since last December but, with his old caddy back on the bag, ended up finishing T4, which duly also moved him well inside the top 116 and safety.

But not to be outdone, Jeong weon Ko, now with a caddy with two wins this season on the bag, also made it to the relative safety of 113th in the rankings after a T7 this week. Not bad for someone who hadn't finished inside the top 50 in any tournament since June.

And it was a similar story for Richard Mansell, who left Sotogrande with a spot in the Nedbank in two weeks' time,

---

9 He then subsequently went back to the PGA Tour and did exactly the same over there in their Fall Series, which was altogether pretty amazing stuff.

when just a few weeks ago it looked odds-on he wouldn't have a job next year at all: sometimes a new caddy can make all the difference.

But what one gained, another lost. Because them pushing their way into the top 116 meant the likes of Jamieson, Van Tonder and Garcia-Heredia, who were all inside the top 116 at the start of the week, finished the week outside of it. And with their MCs, other former winners on tour such as Levy and Wang both sank further outside the 116, and now really do need something special to survive. While the likes of Lorenzo-Vera, Knappe and Fisher, who all managed to start and finish the week just inside the top 116, will now very much still be looking over their shoulders. Leaving John Axelsen as the guy in 116 going into the last chance saloon that is the final tournament of the year next week.

And that last chance saloon is around 7,600km east of here in Doha, Qatar. Where ironically there aren't actually any real saloons.

The Early–late Debate

PGA Tour Featured Groups is a staple of our Thursday and Friday afternoons, especially on weeks off. And aside from being a sneak preview of what TV coverage of golf will be like in the future, i.e. yes, at some stage in the TV future you will be able to watch every shot of your favourite player(s) and see how they plot their way round the course – for the observant it's a window into how a tournament actually works.

First up you'll see that around the 1st tee most weeks there aren't that many spectators, mainly because they're all still in bed given that it's around 7.30am, and often quite chilly, which is why the keen-eyed amongst you will also spot the dew on the ground in the early weeks of the season, and a lot of the players wearing jumpers. And that goes for us caddies, too: only we're also daft enough to wear shorts rather than long trousers or waterproofs.

You'll also notice that there's maybe three or four groups of the best players drawn together, with the commentators plugging that so-and-so and so-and-so is playing in the afternoon. These groups are what are referred to as the 'marquee groups'. God knows why.

But anyway, on the first two days of a regular tournament these marquee groups, and every other group, play one round in the morning one day and one round in the afternoon the other day. So if you play your first round on Thursday morning, you play your second round on Friday afternoon, and vice versa. The former is referred to as 'early–late'; the latter as 'late–early'. Which is better is an existential debate.

The late–early lobby in the Caddy Lounge would have us believe that late–early is better mainly because if you're playing well, it feels almost like you're straight back out there after the first round finishes. Albeit with a night's sleep in between. And the magic and momentum are more likely to still be there.

The early–late lobby counters this with the view that if your man has had an afternoon tee time first round and played shite (described in the Caddy Lounge as 'shot millions' or 'no good'), then there's precious little time to retire to the range and find whatever was missing. And the answer to that is to turn up a bit earlier on the Friday morning because by that time it'll be back, confidence will have returned, and the six under he needs to make the cut is on.

Yeah, but how often does that happen, counters the late–early lobby? Who, inconveniently, have statistics on their side here. Because although it does happen (my personal 'record' was seven under second round to make the cut on the number), it's not that often.

But then the late–early trump card of the Friday night flight home gets played. Now there are tour pros who book two flights every week, especially when we're in Europe. One for the Sunday night after the tournament ends; and one for as late on Friday night as they can. The thought process here being fairly obvious: if you make the cut, you can easily bin off the Friday-night flight as you'll win way more than that even if you finish last come Sunday night. And if you MC, then at least you can get out of there on Friday night and be home for the weekend. Presumably to see the wife and kids. Or more likely, the coach.

What you'll never see, though, is a caddy trying to dissuade their man from going home on a Friday night if they MC. No: make no mistake about it, we actively encourage it. Anything to avoid two days on Misery Hill.

It has even been known for us caddies to get up at 4am on a Saturday to drive our players to the airport for the Saturday morning red-eye just to ensure that they really do Foxtrot Oscar for the weekend. That way the weekend is our own. And no, we won't be heading off for a game ourselves.

The early–late lobby doesn't really have a counter-argument to this one, because they're looking at their start time and secretly thinking, yeah, if we MC then there's just enough time for me to get the bag packed, him to get back to the hotel, check out and get a car to the airport in time for the last flight back. That way they too have a weekend to themselves.

Neither do they have a counter-argument to the other so-called late–early benefit of being able to stand on the range on a Friday afternoon knowing you've made the cut, and feel quite safe, secure and slightly smug. Or is that just me? Because if I'm totally honest, I still do. Even after all these years. Because missed cuts still hurt. And the minute they don't, I'm out of here.

But in reality, ultimately whether early–late is actually better than late–early or late–early is actually better than early–late is entirely dependent on the weather and whether you've been 'screwed by the draw'. Screwed by the draw refers to those weeks where it's been fine for the morning starters but shite for the afternoon starters, or vice versa. Because, fairly obviously, there are days when it can be flat calm in the morning (= low scores) whereas by the time the afternoon starters get to the tee it's blowing a hoolie and/or raining (= high scores). Some weeks you win; some weeks you lose. Like last week for example, where if you played on the Thursday afternoon, you weren't screwed by the draw, so much as royally rodgered by it. Which made it a lose week.

But even if you were on the right side of the draw at Sotogrande, every single one of us can reel off a much longer list of a whole host of other occasions when we were screwed by the draw. I remember one year in Ireland when the weather was that bad in the morning into the early afternoon that only one guy broke par, everyone walked straight off the course and straight back to the hotel as there was no point in going to the putting green, never mind the range, only for the weather to change completely. And everyone who'd started their afternoon naps secure in the knowledge that they'd made it through to the weekend woke up to a seemingly parallel universe, and a rush to try and get the last flight on the Friday night. Of all the times I've personally been 'screwed by the draw' that was definitely the worst.

Although technically being 'screwed by the draw' implies that there is actually a draw. Only there isn't really. Not in the truest sense of the word, anyway. Instead what actually happens is that, like we touched on earlier, the Tour creates marquee groups for TV and, to be frank, shuffles everyone else around these. With the only restrictions allegedly being that you can't be last off more than three weeks in a row.

Or those weeks earlier in the year when the naughty boys from the scumbag LIV school weren't allowed to play with the nice boys from the proper DP World Tour School – which at the time a lot of us looked upon, and still do, as being about as petty as you can get. And definitely not the DP World Tour's finest hour.

Anyway, my guy has been on the fringes of the marquee groups and hasn't been naughty, so actually we seem to have had pretty decent tee times this year. And if the Thursday one is in the morning, then so much the better.

The Story of the Week of the Commercial Bank Qatar Masters 26–29 October 2023

If these last three weeks have been the Last Chance Saloon Swing, then this week is the last chance saloon itself. Where for some guys the only important thing is where they are at kicking-out time. Because for these guys, just being in the saloon at kicking-out time, even if they're out on their feet and on their last legs propping up the entire bar, is just perfect. And just what the doctor ordered. Because tomorrow they will at least get up knowing they have kept their card, have a proper job for next year, have avoided a trip to Tour School, and their various club, apparel and sponsor deals will probably all still be renewed. So they can head home and spend the next several weeks heaving the mother of all sighs of relief, while getting back to work on their games before next teeing it up on tour.

But for others, come kicking-out time, where they next tee it up is a moot point. Because effectively they'll have been summarily kicked off tour. They'll no longer have a full card on the DP World Tour. The week before they were very much part of the elite of European golf; this week they aren't. Just like that. There is no right of appeal. No sentiment. No immediate way back. Other than by regaining your card at the upcoming Tour School, or after a year on the Challenge Tour: very much the second division of European golf.

But unlike at many a kicking-out time, here there will be no histrionics, fights or acrimony. Not even when you might see the guy (or guys) who might have leapfrogged you right at the death securing their playing rights and, by doing so, taking yours away. Just a philosophical acceptance that these things do happen in the life of a tour pro.

And it will be the same in our ranks too. Because a good few colleagues are coming here hoping it's their man that does a spot of leapfrogging this week. Mainly because their immediate futures also depend on it, or certainly their immediate job security. As come Sunday night they too want to be heading home knowing that their man is safely inside the top 116, and that it's likely that their loyalty, not to mention help in securing his playing rights for next year, will be rewarded, if not in a year-end bonus, then continued employment on the bag for next season.

But at least since the World Cup we don't have to shell out a few more euros to buy a 'visa on arrival', which we used to have to do even before getting to baggage reclaim. First there was the small matter of getting here from southern Spain, which was neither cheap nor quick. For example, the AGP-MAD-DOH overnight express (or expresses) at 17.40 on Sunday was coming in at about €1,000 one way.

Fortunately, this year no one manages to get themselves arrested and thrown in jail for a night for shouting at the locals who think they have a divine right to get off a plane before anyone else, and a cheap taxi ride later it's a safe arrival at the hotel on the Pearl where we're all staying this week.

And quite magnificent it is too. As is everything else in this part of Doha, as opposed to the old city where we used to stay when this tournament was the third one in the now-long-gone Abu Dhabi, Dubai and Qatar early-season Desert Swing. That literally was a hotel next to a few restaurants in the middle of basically nowhere. But even now you never see groups of women walking on the streets alone like you would anywhere else in the world: in the malls maybe, but outside on the street, never.

Our hotel is also an oasis of late-season value in the desert of late-season expenses, and entirely due to one of our colleagues putting a lot of effort into sorting it, and a very, very decent rate, through one of his contacts out here. I for one am always grateful for his efforts, as is everyone bar the seriously small-minded minority who continue to moan about him getting a free room for his troubles. I say, 'Good on you, mate,' and thank you.

Another oasis of value this week is that the Tour announced a few weeks back that, just like last week, the prize fund would be increased by €500,000, which makes this a pretty decent tournament in its own right, and doing well here would be a very nice end-of-season earner for player and caddy alike. Especially if you are in the last chance saloon.

And further kudos to the Tour here for ensuring a level playing field around the 116 position by giving both Alfredo Garcia-Heredia and Jayden Schaper invites in this week, meaning that everyone ten spots either side of the 116 is in the field. Because without these invites neither would have been. And although Schaper currently sits at 109 in the rankings so might already be safe, he'd still have had one nervous week at home; while Garcia-Heredia, who dropped from 116 to 118 last week despite making the cut last week after two top tens in the three weeks before that, wouldn't have even been allowed into the last chance saloon. Which arguably wouldn't have been fair.

So all that is between them and finally knowing their fate for next year is the 7,466 yards (or 6,828 metres) of the Doha Golf Club. But stepping off the new Metro line from the Pearl to Lusail on Monday morning (we'd decided to try it just for the sake of it rather than getting the bus) we stepped into a bit of a problem in that the yardage books were not ready. Now normally they are. And to be fair they have been every week this year. But not this week. And instead it's going to be Tuesday morning before we get our hands on them. Not an issue if you'd decided to fly over on Monday or weren't planning on going on the course anyway, but if you were, like us, and wanted to walk it, or you'd MCd in Sotogrande and changed your flights to come across early, then it most certainly was an issue. Especially if your name is John Axelsen. You're 116 on the rankings. And you've arrived early for three full days' preparation. Not exactly what he was expecting, or needing, in what is obviously a very important week for him.

It seems the reason for the delay is that there have been a few subtle but important changes to the course since the last time we played here, all under the watchful eye of the new greenkeeper who's come in from the Abu Dhabi Golf Club. And what a difference he has made. The place is absolutely immaculate. You'd never even know that the greens have been relaid and not down that long. But that does mean that we need to do some work early in the week to really get to know them again. And this can be done, at a pinch, without a yardage book. But you definitely need the yardage book for the other changes where lines off tees have changed ever so subtly, at least certainly to the eye.

And my eyes seem to spot new buildings every year here. Four or five years ago there were no big buildings between the 15th tee and the coast, now there are a whole host of them. But despite this, and the World Cup infrastructure that's also new, there's still something authentic about seeing all the acres of sand around the course and remembering that when we first came here, none of the buildings that are the backdrop to the first few holes were there.

Not that you could see any of them on the Thursday afternoon when the forecast shamal blew in, causing play to be suspended just as the afternoon wave had all started. But not before it had derailed a few guys' chances before they'd really even begun, as well as playing havoc with the later finishers from the morning wave. For anyone affected it was scant consolation that Thursday, 26 October was the first day it had rained in Qatar in 2023. Proving two things: firstly, they really ought to take the DP World Tour to drought-affected regions of the world, and secondly, that early–late is in fact sometimes better than late–early.

Especially if you double the par-five first as the shamal hit, when earlier in the day most guys were birdieing it. And then look at the forecast after the second suspension, which this time was for the day, and realise that you'll be finishing your first round and playing your second in similarly strong winds on Friday; whereas the morning wave will now only have to play about nine holes in it, before finishing their second rounds on flat calm Saturday morning.

Although at least that meant they got to play either the par-five 9th or the par-five 18th downwind, making both of them easily reachable, when normally they might not be. Which is another thing I quite like about this place: each of the two nines start and end with par fives, if only because it offers the chance to get off to a great start, and pick up a shot right at the end if you haven't or are having a bad day. This would be my signature design if I had ever ventured into that field.

And come Saturday morning, when the second round finally finished, it was the par-five last hole that was kind to some, and unkind to others. Because even with a birdie, John Axelsen, who was in 116th spot at the start of Thursday, missed the cut, and with it any chance of staying there. And gone too were the likes of Alex Levy and Marc Warren, both serial winners in their day, whose birdies also weren't enough to make the cut, or save themselves. While not birdieing the par-five 9th (his last hole of the day) meant that Garcia-Heredia, in 118 before the week, also missed the cut, and with that went any chance he had of creeping back inside the top 116. Gut-wrenching for them. And their caddies.

But the real drama was saved for Sunday. Or would have been if there had been any. There were nerves, of course. And there were of course guys needing not to make any mistakes over the last few holes. But in the end not much else. Because even before he birdied 18, Ross Fisher was already safe, albeit in 116; Alexander Knappe also scraped home in 114, although he eagled 18 just to make absolutely sure; while Jeong weon Ko only dropped one place to 115 despite his missed cut on Saturday. In fact the only drama was really around whether Scott Jamieson, who started the week at 119 on the back of missing seven of the last ten cuts, and without a top ten since Korea in April, could actually win rather than finish better than the tie for 53rd he needed to keep his card. And while in the end he didn't win, by the time he parred 18 he already knew he had a job for next year, as did one no doubt very relieved long-term caddy alongside him.

But with him being the only guy to climb inside the top 116 at the death, that meant that one guy fell out. On the last day. Of the last tournament of the year. An unimaginably sickening way to end his season. And one that consigned him to the Tour School in November or the Challenge Tour next year, and his caddy to starting their search for a new player for 2024. I think I speak for every single one of us watching on when I say we wish them both well.

While this was playing out though, at the other end of the last chance saloon in the VIP Lounge open to those who are vying for those ten PGA Tour cards on offer at the end of the season, there were two unexpected changes. Because as Samir Valimaki lifted the famous pearl trophy aloft on Sunday after beating Jorge Campillo in the play-off, they both moved into the reckoning for one of the ten PGA Tour cards with only two tournaments in that race to go. And with both these having limited fields, it means that as of tonight there are now only 70 guys who can get one of those cards. And that will drop to 50 after Sun City in two weeks' time. So effectively it's a two tournament shoot-out. And because the points are so frontloaded that those who have consistently had that PGA icon next to their names all season could yet be bumped out by the last player in the field having the week of his life and holding off the likes of Rahm and McIlroy in Dubai – which again doesn't really feel right.

The same, at least on first glance, could also be said on Monday's slow news day announcement of changes to the membership criteria for next year. Because the headline seemed to be that this was another example of the strategic alliance between the DP World Tour and the PGA Tour delivering more opportunities for PGA Tour members to get into events on this tour, and ultimately qualify for the Race to Dubai bonus pool, etc. And that definitely wouldn't have felt right. But once the initial noise subsided, a slightly more sanguine analysis might be something along the lines of 'not much to worry about really', as 'we've sent you ten of our best, and in return you're sending a maximum of five of your not so best', which isn't so bad after all.

But whether your man was still in the saloon at kicking-out time, or had been freshly kicked out, for us tour caddies the Sunday night of the last regular tournament of the year was, as ever, a bit of a weird one. Because as you leave the golf club or head for your gate in DOH, you know everyone is basically scattering to the four winds and the four corners of the earth once again. And you won't see some of your friends and colleagues until January or February next year, and that actually, in some cases, you might never see them again, such is the attrition rate in our tour caddy world.

But for the lucky few it's, 'See you in Sun City in a fortnight.' For the first of the two wheelbarrow of cash events that make up the DP World Tour Final Swing: the Nedbank Golf Challenge.

The End of the Line

If the end of the regular DP World Tour season yesterday brought with it its fair share of emotions, it also brought with it the most poignant contrast in the relative fortunes of our band of brothers and sisters this year, and what lies in store for them next.

Some, as we've already said, are already enjoying their week off before the first event of the Final Series down in Sun City where there is no cut, and therefore guaranteed money. And no matter how much of it you end up picking up, that always feels nice. But they are the lucky ones.

Because for everyone else, and remember that's effectively half of all full-time tour caddies out here, the next time they will work may well be next season, or at the Q School in November. They certainly won't be hiring a caddy to 'shag' (caddy) for them like guys who are working at Sun City. Some may already even just be settling for finding a player who will provide them with an opportunity to caddy again next year out here.

Every single one of us knows someone in all of these camps. And every single one of us knows that next year it might be us in the latter one. So there is no excuse or room for gloating, bragging or acting generally superior. Because that would be tempting fate, and the caddying gods have a nasty habit of coming back to haunt you if you do.

I've certainly been in the camp where your player has lost his card, and has had to make the trip to the DP World Tour Qualifying School to try and regain his playing rights for next season. Or Tour School as we all call it, which for some players over the years has become a fairly regular, and even annual, pilgrimage, and just another part of their golfing career. Some even appear to enjoy the whole thing. To the point where there may have been occasions where bookmakers have been relieved of substantial sums of cash, because while they didn't know this, a few of our grannies did.

As a caddy, though, if your player is having to go back to Tour School, then you're really hoping that he was inside the top 150 in the Race to Dubai rankings at whatever the cut-off date was earlier in the summer/autumn. Because that means he's exempt into the Final Stage, held at Infinitum Golf in southern Spain in late November. Otherwise he'll have to play in Stage 2 first, where he'll have to finish reasonably high up in order to progress to the Final Stage: the exact number of guys who will make it through is only determined once all players have teed off on day one at each of the four venues used. And because you've played on the main tour this year, it gives you no divine right to progress, because Stage 2 is where those guys with some form of ranking start their journey, along with the guys who have made it through Stage 1. And if you don't, then suddenly you don't really have a status anywhere, meaning your 2024 is suddenly looking pretty bleak unfortunately.

But even if you are exempt into the Final Stage, it's not plain sailing as the field for that stage can often resemble, or even rival, that of a half-decent tour event in its own right. And that's because you have the next best guys from the Challenge Tour playing, guys who've lost their DP World Tour cards, and a smattering of up-and-coming stars and amateurs, while tournament winners from the last three DP World Tour seasons are also exempt. Some years there are even guys who have played Ryder Cups in the past in the field. So again, getting your card back is more possible than probable.

All of which makes for an interesting week from the outside; and a pressure-filled one if you're on the inside. No matter who you are. So interesting and pressure-filled in fact that it really ought to be shown live on Sky Sports every year. Especially the last round. In fact it's always surprised me that they have never done so, because however macabre it might be, watching someone stumble their way into the clubhouse at the end of six rounds, look like they're just about going to do it, but then hit one bad shot, or get one bad break, just at the wrong time that shatters their dreams for another year would make great TV. And so much the better if they're in tears. In fact the more gut-wrenching the better. Because that would really show, probably for the first time, the reality of professional golf. The margins between can be so fine; and the differences so great.

And as Final Stage this year finishes just a week before the 2024 season actually starts, there will likely be guys who caddy full-time on tour working that week: either for their usual player trying to regain his playing rights, or for another hopeful trying to get theirs in the first place. Either way, at least it's eight days' work at a time when you wouldn't otherwise have any. So very welcome financially, if not physically.

It's eight days because Final Stage is six rounds, preceded by one practice round on each of the two courses. More than one if your man is so inclined, which, as one of the courses is called The Hills, you really, really hope he isn't.

And at the end of the 108-hole marathon, 'all' you have to do is finish in the top 25. That gets you your playing rights (or 'a card' as it's known) for the next season. But even though that alone is an unbelievable achievement in its own right, what it doesn't entitle you to do is to play in every tournament next season. In fact far from it. Because while you should get into the tournaments in South Africa or Australia before Christmas, you won't play again until the end of January when the prize funds drop, and after that it could be May time in Belgium before you hit another DP World Tour tee shot in anger.

Not that it puts anyone off. This year, for example, around 850 people entered Stage 1, even though history shows that the odds of any of them getting through that stage, then Stage 2 and then Final Stage are frankly negligible. In fact, it's pretty much headline news if anyone does. Which does beg the question of why have Stage 1 in the first place? And the answer to that is, unsurprisingly, money. Because 850 people each paying £2,500 nets the DP World Tour over £2m from Stage 1 alone, meaning that outside the Ryder Cup, it's allegedly their biggest source of income.

But really when you look at some of the scores from Stage 1, a fair percentage of entrants shouldn't actually be allowed to part with their hard-earned, or more likely donated, cash in the first place. It's not far off robbing the blind. And despite the often-used line that it's all aspirational and no one should take that, or people's dream, away, Stage 1 is frankly a colossal waste of everyone's time and money. Surely there has to be a better way of filtering out the wheat from the golfing chaff?

The other thing I've also always found strange about Final Stage is why it's played over six rounds, when every other tournament on the DP World Tour schedule is played over four rounds. Ostensibly it's so that a bad round early on doesn't mean you're dead and buried, which might be a decent argument if that also applied to regular tour events. Which obviously it doesn't.

But like a lot of things on the DP World Tour, I actually suspect it's like that because it's always been like that. And different thinking is dangerous thinking, because that might rock the boat. And a boat staffed by a lot of ex-professional golfers doesn't like rocking, never mind change. Mainly because that change might include them. And so until it does change, anyone caddying in Final Stage can look forward to eight rounds in eight days for the foreseeable future. Because the more things change, the more things stay the same.

And that is precisely the charge I, and many of my colleagues, level at the Challenge Tour: effectively the second division of European golf, and where you basically end up if you make the 72-hole cut but don't get a card at Final Stage where you will have full playing rights.

The point of the Challenge Tour is that at the end of the season the top 20 guys get their cards to play on the DP World Tour. And although they slot into Category 14, just like guys who get their cards from Tour School, that doesn't get them into every event. Like this season for example, when a high finish on the Challenge Tour rankings in 2022 might have earned you around 30 starts on the DP World Tour in 2023, but none of these would have necessarily been in the Rolex Series events. And then of course there's the question of whether the Challenge Tour really prepares these guys for life on the DP World Tour in the first place. This isn't just about the huge step up in terms of course difficulty and set-up; for me it's more about how the Challenge Tour is seen, if not as the black sheep of the family, then certainly the one that's not really worth putting too much effort into.

For a start the prize money is paltry: some of THE best golfers in Europe play for less than €300,000 each week, yet on the Korn Ferry Tour in the US (the equivalent of the Challenge Tour over here) they play for $1m every week. Why on earth players tolerate this has always been beyond me. And while there is the argument that that is what the sponsors will pay, I'd say it is, but only if that's the value you actually put on your product.

If you believe that your product has a greater value, you sell it at that value – by going out and marketing at that value. Like they do on the Korn Ferry Tour. And you also have a title sponsor for the Tour itself. Because that's the headline name: it's important.

Something which, if rumours are to be believed, was on the table a good few years ago now. But was rejected by the-then European Tour hierarchy as they effectively wanted players to struggle like 'they' had early in their careers, which is as unbelievable now as it must have been then. And another reason why having your organisation staffed, certainly at that time, primarily by ex-players was a poor idea.

And so it's no real surprise that the Challenge Tour comes nowhere near what they do on the Korn Ferry about generating drama and placing importance on being in one of the top places on the Road to Mallorca, their equivalent of the Race to Dubai. Over there they have 'The Twenty Five'. Twenty-five being the number of PGA Tour cards given out at the end of the season. Just having a name for these guys makes it 'a thing'. And an important one at that. Something which the Korn Ferry Tour really push on their socials throughout the year, generating that all-important interest. Especially towards the end of the season. Whereas the Challenge Tour feels like a collection of random tournaments, with an end-of-season event that is important to those involved, but fairly invisible outside that. So that could do with changing too.

But however you do any of this, bringing together all the various tournaments and sponsors under a meaningful umbrella name (the 'Challenge Tour' just doesn't cut it) would give the whole thing more solidity, structure, visibility and value. And make the Challenge Tour a place where, in addition to getting a proper taste of what life on the DP World Tour will be like, some of the best players in Europe can make a proper living.

And while better courses and better set-up might not benefit caddies directly, playing for decent prize money with an overall title sponsor would, because more guys might take a full-time caddy. Offering more opportunities for tour caddies to work. And more opportunities for them to earn decent money.

But as a player, wherever you play your golf next season, if you don't play well enough then all roads will, once again, lead back to where we are today. Apart from, it has to be said, the guys for whom getting slung out of the last chance saloon last week just confirmed what they'd already known in their heart of hearts for a long time now. And that was that their game is no longer at the level it needs to be to compete at the highest level of European golf. Nor will it ever be again.

And so for them Qatar wasn't just the last chance saloon. It was the end of the line.

Chapter 12

Free Money Anyone?

The Story of the Week of the Nedbank Golf Challenge 9–12 November 2023

They really ought to have a sign at the entrance to Sun City saying 'Welcome to the Caddy Graveyard'. Because that's what every tour caddy who has ever been here calls it. And if you thought a lot could go wrong round Paris National, then believe me, that is multiplied ten times over round here.

For a start it's 1,070m up on the Bush Veld so altitude comes into play. Then there's the heat which also affects how far the ball goes. And also obviously there's the rough, which might look nice and fluffy on TV but in fact it's like strands of wire and the ball always drops down to the roots, requiring even the strongest to pull out the wedge and simply hack the ball down the fairway. And if it's not sitting down off the fairway, then you'll need to factor in whether the ball is going to fly. Or not. And if you play for a flier, but the ball comes out soft, then where's it likely to finish?

But none of this is actually why it's known as the Caddy Graveyard. That is all to do with the wind. Because it is, to be charitable, 'unpredictable', and not that it is much consolation to any tour caddy with the good fortune to be here, but this is entirely due to where the golf course itself sits: basically in a circular volcanic plug with side valleys running to the north, south, east and west. And as the wind funnels through these side valleys and across the golf course, its direction seems to constantly change throughout the round, and even just on a tee box.

In fact a few years ago now one caddy famously pointed both left and right when his man asked him where the wind was on the par-three 4th hole, while there's been many a ball nosedive out of the sky at holes like 9 and 17 when the wind suddenly switches mid-shot. Where, rather inconveniently, there's water short of the green when it does. All of which makes club selection at times 'tricky' and at others complete guesswork.

So coming into the week you know you're going to have to make a few tricky calls across the four rounds, and that if you get enough of them wrong, then even the most solid of player–caddy relationships can be put under strain, and possibly then snap completely. And so you really hope it won't be one of those weeks when the harder you try to be right, the more often you end up being wrong. No, not this week of all weeks.

In fact, I'd go so far as to say that I think every tour caddy who survives the week here breathes a quiet sigh of relief on Sunday night. I certainly do. But whether or not I'll be doing so this year I can't say, as with only 66 players and 66 caddies at Sun City, then that would open the door to someone sad enough to create a list of 'probables', 'possibles' and 'no way, they can hardly speak let alone write' in an effort to unearth my identity. And we can't be having that.

But never mind about us caddies. Because if you have ever fancied getting away from the onset of winter in Europe to somewhere hot where you can go on safari, watch professional golf and gorge yourself on some of the best steak in the world, all on the same day, then this is the place to come in early November.

And you don't even necessarily have to specifically go on safari to see some of the Big Five here as the bush starts at the edge of the golf course, albeit thankfully the other side of very big fences, meaning you often see elephants trudging along with seemingly zero interest in the world-class field that has assembled to their right-hand side. Because if they just simply looked over once, just once, they'd see the likes of Max Homa, Justin Thomas, Tommy Fleetwood, and a few other Ryder Cup players plying their trade. No wonder they call this 'Africa's Major'. It really is one hell of a tournament.

And while for me the likes of Joburg always start to grate after a few days, this place delights. Mainly because it's essentially a huge compound, where that fine steak washed down with a fine glass of red still doesn't cost more than £15, but where you can take that leisurely walk back to the hotel after dinner, without worrying about whether you'll make it back safely. Or at all for that matter.

Also at this event there's never any of the underlying stress and tension that's been heavy in the air at the last few tournaments of the regular season just finished. Because by definition, if you're here, as a player you've had a pretty decent year, and it's now just a question of how much free money you can take home before the break you're about to have over Christmas. And the same goes for every single caddy who's here. All of which would give the week a relaxed feel if this wasn't the Caddy Graveyard.

The tournament also ensures we don't end up in a real graveyard either. Specifically by cordoning off areas of the course where things like cobras and black mambas have been seen lurking; after all, the bush is literally just off the fairways in some places on the course. And while it's quite unnerving the first time they tell you that the back tee is roped off today because there's one of these things in the shade at the back of the tee and that these things are fast, nervous, venomous and, when threatened, highly aggressive, I'm sure I wasn't the only one whose first thought was, 'Hold on, I'm sure I've caddied for him.'

And speaking of the fairways, these are fairways that really ought to get the bulldozer treatment sometime soon, as although they're okay if your preferred shape is a raking draw against the camber; if it's not, then everything seems to kick right into the rough or trees on the right. Like on the 5th hole for example, which is maybe why the elephants walking up the hill to the left always appear to be shaking their head as if they're saying, 'I know ....' Maybe they're waiting until the architect passes away before they do so; but do so they should.

That said, the course certainly gives you enough chances if you're playing well, and your caddy is on top form. But even then, the final two holes can take away all that hard work in a heartbeat. Because they are two of the toughest we play on tour each year, one over 500 yards, the other just under, but with water in play on both. Holes that may yet book your place in the Caddy Graveyard.

Negotiate them well though, and all will be well, and so it was for Max Homa, easing to his first title outside the US in front of record crowds for this tournament across the weekend: there were 22,000 spectators on Saturday alone, and more on Sunday. And with the other star invite Justin Thomas also finishing in the top five, all was also well for Nedbank: fully justifying both their choice of invites, and their intention to do pretty much the same in future years.

And that could be very good news for JT's last-minute stand-in caddy from the Sunshine Tour because he'll hopefully get the call this time next year to do the same again. But who in the meantime can have a very nice Christmas on the back of the bonus he'll have got. And being such a fine caddy, and an even finer human being, no one is begrudging him that.

Nor would anyone begrudge Nedbank giving an invite in 2024 to someone from this week's main sub-plot, which was the second-to-last week of the season-long race to get one of the ten PGA Tour cards up for grabs for their 2024 season. And in that one, the big winner was the Højgaard household, as with Nicolai having already secured his PGA Tour card over there anyway, Rasmus's top-six finish meant that he will go into the last week in the tenth and last spot, meaning both brothers could yet end up playing across the pond next year. But with a few guys still only a good week away from pipping him at the post, then this race, just like the race to keep your card the other week in Qatar, will also go to the last tournament of the year, where the real prize might just be that final spot rather than either of the two big trophies on offer.

And actually never mind 'might', because with McIlroy having already sealed the Race to Dubai title, this *will* actually be where the drama is in Dubai. Because without it you could argue that the tournament is little more than a four-day exhibition event with a huge first prize. Certainly every time I've been there, a bit like the old WGC events, unless you're at the business end of the tournament on Sunday, everyone is pretty relaxed, giving the whole thing a real 'end of term' feel, which for a good few it is, given that the next time they'll tee it up in anger will be next January. And while for whoever does win, winning will obviously be nice, it won't necessarily change their life, but for the winning caddy, their $300,000 bonus may well do just that. But unless that caddy is a mate, I for one won't give a toss. And it's the same for every other tour caddy out here: because like I said at the start of this book, unless it's a mate, we really don't care who wins.

But that's next week. And so even if the week did finish with another grave in the Caddy Graveyard, this time with your name on it, you'll have left Sun City knowing that it's two years before we're back here again, because in 2024 the Nedbank is going back to its original format of being an end-of-season invitational for the very best players from the DP World Tour and the PGA Tour. And who's to say that the entry criteria won't stay pretty much the same when it returns to the DP World Tour schedule the year after? Because Branden Grace getting an invite, despite him playing on LIV Golf, to me very much suggests that it will.

Either way that gives you until 2025 at the earliest to find a player who'll bring you back to pit your caddy wits against this place once again, which admittedly might be scant consolation as you make your way home clutching your P45.

But for the fortunate few, there's one last trip of the season to make. And even if you had a stressful week or even one where you became part of Caddy Graveyard folklore, as you pass through the townships on the outskirts of Joburg on your air-conditioned private charter bus before your business class flight up to Dubai for the DP World Tour Championship, it really ought to remind you that in the great scheme of things that things aren't so bad after all.

Especially as more free money is waiting in Dubai.

LIV and Let Die

Next week is the final tournament of the 2023 season: arguably the most tumultuous in the history of professional golf. So it would be rude not to give you what I think is the general view of it all from the Caddy Lounge. And that is that the disruptor has disrupted. And rather well if you ask me or a lot of my colleagues out here.

But perhaps not exactly in the way it might seem from 'the outside': it's more subtle than that. Or certainly more subtle than the main headlines of LIV playing for massive, massive money, the other tours giving LIV players bans and exorbitant fines, or even just the three main golf tours eventually doing a wee bit of back-pedalling and seemingly on the brink of all merging under the PIF of Saudi Arabia.

Instead what I think we all take from this is that the balance of power has started to move away from the world's tours, and more towards the players. Because when, in our case, the European Tour was set up, arguably the players then needed the Tour more than the Tour needed them. It was the Tour that provided the best professional golfers in Europe with a series of tournaments to play in, from which spawned the tour pro; and without this, being a professional golfer would have remained giving a few lessons supplemented by however many Mars bars you could sell in the shop. Like I say, tour pros needed the Tour more than it needed them.

But times have changed, and in the modern era the tour pro is a highly visible, highly marketable and highly valuable commodity, mainly thanks to TV coverage and social media. And that gives them leverage. Or at least it ought to. Their talent should unlock doors, give them choices, and certainly make the Tours work harder for them.

It's just that they seem, certainly as a group, to only just be waking up to this in Europe. Slower than the PGA Tour's hierarchy did. And much, much slower than LIV Golf did. Because what LIV Golf did was to give some of the world's best, or certainly most recognisable, players a choice, which was no more complicated than either stay where you are and continue doing what you do, how you do it and get paid about the same; or come with us, play the same game less often for more money (which by the way is actually about what your talent is worth on the open market), and we'll royally look after you as you'd expect given your talent and status in the game of golf.

It was a choice none of them had ever had before. And really not a surprise, certainly not to those of us who actually know some of the guys involved, that they didn't choose the status quo. Nor was it a surprise that the tours then immediately went into vitriolic brand protection mode, using the involvement of Saudi money as a convenient justification for it, backed up by a significant section of the world's golf media. After all, Khashoggi was a journalist, so one of their own.

But if truth be told, any imposter to the PGA Tour throne would have received similar treatment. Just like the original imposter to the throne, Premier Golf League, did. Some excuse, some justification, some reason why not would have been found which, you could be forgiven for thinking, was because a lot of people have a lot of vested interests in what is effectively a golf monopoly. None of whom actually play professional golf.

In our ranks though, yes there were the usual suspects who jumped to the defence of the DP World Tour, trotted out the 'got to support the tour' lines fed to them, and railed against the players who jumped ship; but overall I think everyone wished those caddies who went over to LIV all the best. Casting slightly envious glances as they did. And very envious ones after we started hearing how they get looked after over there.

Yes, it might have been slightly different and slightly less generous in this second year, but each caddy on LIV Golf, on top of their wages, still gets a pretty substantial travel allowance each month; their accommodation is high end every week, and paid for by LIV every week; players and caddies eat together in the same lounge; they all receive full team apparel for free, and some even get to fly private between venues with the team. That and obviously with last place paying around $120,000 each week, their annual bonus is a minimum $84,000. With no expenses. For only 14 weeks' work on that tour.

And as an extra bonus they are free to work on any other tour in the world when they're not at a LIV Golf event; unlike their employer. And when they do come back to caddy in Europe, there is zero aggro towards them from us. Which, as we've said before in these pages, makes us look like the adults in the room for once.

Now being treated like this might be a pipe dream for those of us who continue to work on the DP World Tour with occasional forays on to the PGA Tour. But it does show what can be done if the vision, and obviously the money, is there. And this is perhaps my other personal take on this season: where the power of the players ought to drive the world of professional golf in the next five to ten years.

The tours will end up, albeit they might be dragged there kicking and screaming, being driven by the necessity of making their 'shop' the one individual players want to shop in. Tour pros will dictate the agenda. Because their individual talent, reach and name allows them to. After all, they are the most talented at what they do in (in our case) Europe and, collectively, the world.

It's like the players collectively saying to the world's tours, 'Look, here's what is going to happen. You put on a tournament that I want to play in (which might be because of the way I'm going to be treated when I get there, the course the tournament is being played on, etc., and not just the money) and I'll be there. I'll play. Because I want to. Because I want to shop in your shop this week. Next week might be different, of course.

'Next week's shop might be halfway across the world on another continent, but I'll be playing there for the same reason as I played here this week. And that's because I wanted to. Oh, and yes, that could be on any tour in the world: the PGA Tour, LIV Golf, the DP World Tour or the Asian Tour. Make me want to come to your tournament. Because no one dictates where I can and cannot play any longer. These days it's me that chooses where I play. No one else. You certainly don't.'

This is effectively why, if the rumours are true, next year's Nedbank is off the DP World Tour schedule. And that's because it's going to revert to its original format of inviting however many it ends up being of the world's best down to Sun City in November or December, treating them like kings, and putting up a hefty amount of money for them to play for. Not being able to have a few of the big names of South African golf in 'Africa's Major' this year might have been the final straw that broke the camel's back of frustration for Nedbank.

Because for years now, as Africa's biggest bank, they have been pouring millions into this event, without necessarily getting the really big names that would deliver them and their customers the value they're after. And these aren't necessarily the guys who may have been 'financially encouraged' by the DP World Tour, with Nedbank's money, to come and play, when arguably they would have come anyway. Instead Nedbank want a truly stellar field chosen by themselves, irrespective of what tour anyone in that field plays on. Because it's that that will deliver them true value.

And then that makes me think that Nedbank know that by 2025 when the tournament returns to the DP World Tour schedule (this was confirmed a month or so ago in a pretty low-key announcement), it will return with them having, if not total freedom as to who plays like they will in 2024, then rather more than they do in 2023. Nothing else really makes commercial sense when you think about it long enough.

And I think we'll see more of this, if not in 2024, then certainly from 2025 onwards. The best tournaments in the world, whether they are on the PGA Tour, the DP World Tour, the Asian Tour or LIV, will be able to have absolutely stellar fields, free of any restrictions.

And being parochial for a moment, five years from now, if you're a tour caddy caddying for anyone who gets into these events, then you'll be doing very nicely. If you're not though, barring a significant trickle down of money and sponsorship to the other events on the various tours' schedules, you might not be doing quite so well. Or even doing so at all.

But by that stage I'll likely be past my sell-by date out here and out to grass in the afterlife that is the EU Legends Tour – which, thinking about it, might not be a bad thing.

The Story of the Week of the DP World Tour Championship 16–19 November 2023

This time last year I was sat on my settee at home watching Jon Rahm holing the winning putt on Sunday afternoon. This coming Sunday, a mere 364 days later, I suspect he might be doing the same thing. But as to whether I'm sat outside the amazing Caddy Lounge 200m away or 7,220km away on my settee again is another matter. And again, fairly obviously something I'm not divulging.

Safe to say though that a year on in Dubai, it will probably be the usual suspects fighting it out for both the tournament and the Race to Dubai title itself. Rarely, if ever, has there been a surprise winner here, which kind of goes for this week in general.

Every year the route here is always the same. First, be in the top 50 of the Race to Dubai rankings after the Nedbank. Then either get yourself here from wherever you've been practising last week, or via the overnight or Monday morning flight up from Joburg. Every year everyone always stays in pretty much the same place: the players at one of the hotels on The Palm; everyone else in Al Barsha. Every year it really is a pretty stress-free week caddying-wise: there's none of the swirling winds of last week up on the veldt that can cause havoc. And every year the tournament is played on the Earth Course at Jumeirah Estates.

So pretty much everyone knows the routine and knows the course. Even those players who have qualified here for the first time have likely played the course a good few times when over here practising in the European winter months. And with many players and caddies bringing their families over on the back of what they've earned last week and will earn this week, all in all it's a pretty relaxed week.

Well, it is unless you're still in with a chance of securing one of the ten PGA Tour cards that will be handed out to the top ten non-exempt players on Sunday night, which might actually be as many as half the field as the points on offer this week are huge, and very much frontloaded. Meaning that missing a shot down the last few holes could make the difference between having a schedule in 2024 that includes not a single tournament with less than a $6,000,000 prize fund all year, or having a schedule that routinely includes tournaments with a prize fund of $2,000,000. Probably not quite as much pressure as needing to par the last in Qatar (or even Tour School) to have playing rights for 2024, but it's still pressure. And funny things can happen when that rears its ugly head.

And having said that a lot of things here are the same every year, this is where the differences this year start. Because it's the first year that these PGA Tour cards have been on the line at the DP World Tour Championship. And that's actually where the story will be this week, rather than it being about who wins the tournament and who wins the overall Race to Dubai.

But if it's the first year for PGA Tour cards being handed out, it's the last year we'll be using the DSI yardage book round here. Because having been providing them for around 15 years now, suddenly it appears that our yardage books will be supplied by Clere Golf next year, and not Dion Stevens, which was a bit of a shock when news emerged of the change, which first surfaced the week of Qatar. Although quite how a decision that affects predominantly ourselves can be taken without consulting ourselves is 'surprising'.

And while it subsequently emerged that this is part of a much wider package of logistical support and cost savings being offered by the new supplier, certainly as a courtesy the rationale behind the decision ought to have been communicated to the ETCA. Although whether it actually was or not still isn't exactly 'clear', but if in fact it had been, then certainly there are some questions to be answered around why we found out via the grapevine.

All of which I think is a shame, because the quality of his yardage book is unsurpassed anywhere in the world; in fact no one else gets close to it in my opinion. However, what's not a shame is that the guy whose payment engine sits behind DSI's online presence will no longer take his little cut of every £ or € we spend on these books every year. And that guy happens to be the ETCA chairman. Or used to be, as there are whispers that he's now resigned from that role.

Now whether that's just a coincidence time-wise, or as a direct result of his payment engine no longer being required, I'll leave to my more cynical and vocal colleagues. I'm too old to really care. But it might actually be just as well he hopped it to LIV Golf (to caddy for a reserve by the way) earlier in the year. Never, if we're lucky, to be seen again.

While only time will tell whether the DP World Tour have crossed all their Ts and dotted all their Is in dispensing with DSI's services in such a seemingly hasty way, I do actually see this change as part of the ongoing shift towards business acumen on your CV being a bit more important than whether you played on tour at some stage in the dim and distant past. Something that can only be good for the Tour, and ultimately ourselves as tour caddies. Even the recent announcement of the changes to the 2024 DP World Tour membership criteria is another that arguably falls into the same category. And while all of this might be invisible outside the DP World Tour bubble, they're changes for the better if you ask me. As well as being a sign of things to come.

And in another sign of things to come Nicolai Højgaard holds off the likes of Fleetwood, Hovland, Hatton and Rahm to win on Sunday afternoon. These four, along with McIlroy obviously, are basically going to fight it out between themselves for the mantel of being the best player in Europe for a good few years to come. They are that much better than anyone else at the moment. Especially when it really matters.

Likewise the fight for the last PGA Tour card on offer also went down to the wire. And despite being pretty much outside the top ten all year, a top five here for Matthieu Pavon and the huge number of points that came with it meant he will be plying his trade on the PGA Tour next year. And Rasmus Højgaard, who dropped one spot to 11th, will not. None of which, the more you think about it, feels quite right.

On an individual level, a bit like Meronk not getting a Ryder Cup pick, you look at guys like Yannik Paul, Marcel Siem and Joost Luiten, who've pretty much been inside the top ten all year and end up out of it; when others arguably get in but on the back of one decent finish all year: they just had it in the right event. Consistency across the year, which is what will help you retain your PGA Tour card, counts for nothing under the current system. And that is a serious weakness in it, which (a) really ought to have been spotted when the Tour thought this up, and (b) really needs rectifying before this time next year – or the same thing will happen again.

But the other thing that doesn't feel quite right, in fact it just feels totally wrong, is that the DP World Tour is giving away ten PGA Tour cards in the first place. Yes, it might be good for guys who got their cards through the Challenge Tour this year, because ten less guys means certainly a couple more spots open up in some of the bigger events earlier in the season.

It might also be good for guys who got their cards at the Tour School which ended last Tuesday, because again, theoretically, it might open up more spots to them towards the middle and end of next season. And arguably it might even be good for the PGA Tour as a couple of the guys getting one of the ten cards on offer are definitely 'box office' material. Although others most certainly aren't.

But what it cannot be good for, no matter how it's dressed up, is the DP World Tour as a business. Because, and admittedly I've never worked for one, what company lets, in fact actively encourages, its ten best-performing employees leave the company every year? For a competitor? It just doesn't make sense. Unless of course you're one of the ten guys in question. When in fact it makes perfect sense.

But right now that is all in the future. And instead what strikes me the most is that if the scenes on the 18th green just now were pretty much the same as this time last year, and may well be the same as we see next year, then so those at DXB tonight will be too. Because in amongst all the transit passengers heading somewhere nice, and the tourists heading home from somewhere nice, a keen-eyed golf fan would be able to see a whole host of recognisable tour caddies. Also all going somewhere.

Some would have been heading south to Joburg, the slate wiped clean, for the Joburg Open; some would have been heading a good bit further east to Queensland for the Aussie PGA Championship, also with the slate rubbed clean; while others would have been heading east, west, north and south as they were just simply heading home at the end of another long, hard season. Because, almost before the curtain has actually come down on the 2023 one, the 2024 DP World Tour season will start next Thursday.

And start with a good few LIV Golf guys in the field at both venues, which probably tells you that somewhere in the not-too-distant future, choosing to play on one particular tour isn't going to stop you playing on a different one. And that is good news for sponsors; for spectators; for TV. And especially for the DP World Tour. Because whatever they might be saying publicly, they know this is the right answer for their business.

But whether I was in England, or DXB, or in fact somewhere else, Sunday night had me at something of a crossroads in my life as a tour caddy. Which fork in that road I decide to take, though, remains to be seen.

Chapter 13

That Was the Season That Was

Journey's End

And just like that the 2023 DP World Tour season was over. And as it ends, so does this book.

If you weren't a golf fan at the start, then hopefully you're now interested in the game we all love. If you were already a golf fan, then hopefully you now know what life inside the ropes is actually like, as well as having a better understanding of what we do, and how it all works. But whichever you are, more important is that you've enjoyed reading about my twenty-something-plus-one season out here: it was certainly one of the more eventful ones.

As for my twenty-something-plus-another-one season, well that's starting in unfamiliar territory. Because normally at this time of year I know what I'm doing, where I'm going next and when, how I'm getting there, and am just waiting for the optimism of a new season starting to envelop me. But this year it's a bit different.

Because unbeknown to my man I'm sitting on an offer to go caddy for someone who has just secured their PGA Tour card for 2024, which he didn't. To be fair the offer came completely out of the blue. I was walking through the airport the other week when I bumped into one of the player managers. We exchanged pleasantries like we always do, only he finished up with a hushed 'ring me'. Which I immediately knew meant I was going to be offered something. Although to be fair, up until I did actually ring him, I thought this might just be him asking me to work the Tour School for one of their up-and-coming guys.

Except it wasn't. It was an offer to work for one of their other clients who will be playing on the PGA Tour next year. Because it appears he, and presumably his management too, feel that a new face is needed for a new season on a new tour. And that face is mine. Albeit very possibly because the guys whose names were before mine on the original list of possible new caddies either didn't fancy the prospect of working for this guy, or were settled with their current player. Either way I didn't like to ask, and said obviously I'd be interested, but would need 'a few days'.

Inside, my immediate reaction was 'yes', but I've been in this game long enough to know a few hours thinking about job offers is often a very wise move. And definitely when it comes to jumping ship. But when that ship has PGA Tour on it, on the face of it I'd be mad not to. Because even a half-decent year out there would mean things like the mortgage gets paid off, or even the kids getting sent to private school next year.

While, with all the rumours circulating about the PGA Tour and LIV Golf properly merging in 2025 to create a schedule of 18 mega-money events, a good year out there could be the gateway to all that, and with it would come 100 per cent financial security for me and the family for the rest of our lives.

But more importantly, a chance to hang up my latest pair of Mizuno trainers for good.

Decisions. Decisions.

A Word about Rahm …

Not long before this book went to print, Jon Rahm signed for LIV Golf, so here's my take on it.

There might not have been any seismic activity recorded from the volcanoes around Sun City the other week, but about 12,800km away in Miami this week there most certainly was. Because the news that Jon Rahm is going to play on LIV Golf next year was just that. Seismic.

Well, it was seismic if, unlike every tour caddy I know, you'd not seen this coming. Especially after he dropped out of the cast list for TGL, which was meant to start in January 2024 but is now postponed until 2025 – which the cynics, whose messages I've been reading recently, believe has some of the gimmicky hallmarks of the DP World Tour's cringeworthy set piece Hero Challenges from 2020. And might very well be as short-lived as they were. If it now happens at all.

And now that everything's been officially confirmed, I think it's fair to say that the unanimous opinion from inside the ropes is that it 'stops the bullshit'. At a stroke. Which is great for the future of professional golf.

The detractors are no longer able to say that LIV Golf has no credibility when patently five of the best ten players on the planet (Rahm, Koepka, Cam Smith, DeChambeau and Taylor Gooch) play their golf on it. There is no justification for a World Ranking system that doesn't find a way to include these guys, because fairly obviously they could if they wanted to: I think I'm right in saying that the Sunshine Tour attracts World Ranking points and they have three-round tournaments too. And the PGA Tour sycophants fronting up some of the golf programmes on TV, especially in the States, complete with their curled-up noses at the very mention of LIV Golf, won't be having a go at someone of Rahm's stature and integrity.

But the thing is for those who didn't see this coming, or were hoping the rumours were just that, the signs have always been there. It's just that the detractors chose never to look for them. Let alone see them. Signs like, if you look back over the last year or so, Rahm's has been one of the more considered voices about all things LIV Golf. He's never had a go at individuals' choices: he's always said he respects them. There's been no toeing of the party line, presumably much to the disappointment of the PGA Tour: instead his comments have all been measured, making clear it wasn't the right place for him at that time, but never closing the door on it either.

A door he's now chosen to walk through, which in itself is probably indicative of what seems to be a growing sense of dissatisfaction amongst the players that the tours have got very complacent, make a lot of fairly transformational decisions without proper, or in some cases any, consultation with them, and generally forget that they work for the players, not the other way round – which explains the letter signed by a number of PGA Tour players that was apparently sent to Jay Monahan last week, and maybe was in fact that straw that broke Rahm's back.

But irrespective of all that, more importantly, what it definitely tells me is that at some stage in the not-too-distant future all the inter-tour furore will be resolved under whatever golf's new structure looks like, and Rahm will be back playing in some form of 'the best playing against the best more often' golf. And that includes the Ryder Cup.

Something that even McIlroy alludes to if you read between the lines of what he's been saying publicly over the last 24 hours in what looks like the first proper green shoots of proper player power in a world where the world's golf tours have held the upper hand for far too long. Like Jon Rahm will be on the 2025 Ryder Cup team at Bethpage (meaning the DP World Tour HAVE to now change their rules: there is no scenario on earth where they will ignore their number one asset); and definitely when he says the other interesting bit about letting 'bygones be bygones' (which means that all the best players in the world WILL be playing against each other more than four times a year sometime in the near future).

In fact, it just makes the whole thing even more inevitable. Assuming you can see past the end of your curled-up nose, that is.

The 18th Green
And finally …

There's been many a time, especially this last year, when I've found myself standing on an 18th green thinking how lucky we as tour caddies are, not only to be this close to the action and some of the best players on the planet, but also to be this close to what goes on behind the scenes in the crazy world of professional golf.

Lucky because, if nothing else, that makes my, and every other tour caddy on the planet's, opinions about professional golf 'opinions from inside the ropes'. And that means they carry a unique perspective; are unbound by the restrictions placed on members of the world's golf tours by those tours; or worse, the unspoken player omerta. There are no sponsors to upset. Or outside influences to pander to. They're just genuine opinions from genuine people. They ought to be sought out more often. And they definitely deserve to be heard.

But I'm going to leave it to my younger, and dare I say more intelligent, colleagues to bring these to you using the platform that this book gives them.

And while they do that, I'm going back to my day job. So from now on the only writing I'll be doing will be numbers in a yardage book.

Which only leaves me to say that for those of you who haven't enjoyed this book and are pleased to hear this, then I'm afraid a lifetime of the shanks awaits.

TSTC